© *Decoopman*

I.S.B.N. : 978-2-36965-160-4

Dépôt légal : 1ᵉʳ trimestre 2023

© La loi du 11 mars 1957 interdit les copies ou reproductions destinées à une utilisation collective. Toute représentation ou reproduction intégrale ou partielle faite par quelque procédé que ce soit sans le consentement de l'auteur ou de ses ayants droit ou ayants cause, est illicite et constitue une contrefaçon sanctionnée par les articles 425 et suivants du Code Pénal.

Book cover : Antoine Pintard - 1658 - 1732

1975.9 by Gerardus Duyckinck ; oil on linen ; Dimensions : 31 x 25 x 1 in. (78.7 x 63.5 x 2.5 cm) ; © New-York Historical Society.

Antoine Pintard
1658 - 1732

1975.9 by Gerardus Duyckinck ; oil on linen ; Dimensions : 31 x 25 x 1 in. (78.7 x 63.5 x 2.5 cm) ; © New-York Historical Society.

Books by Philippe ROUEN

– in French –

- *Le géographe de l'Amérique* - Ed. Decoopman - 2021
- *L'angélus des Appalaches* - Ed. Decoopman - 2018
- *La croisière du ginseng* - Ed. Decoopman - 2016
- *Les laboureurs d'Amérique* - Ed. Decoopman - 2015

Éditions Decoopman
30440 Saint-Laurent-le-Minier - FRANCE
Tel : +33 (0)4.67.73.90.95
web : www.decoopman.com
e.mail : livres@decoopman.com

THE PLOWMEN OF AMERICA

From the Corniche of the Cévennes to Wall Street. The extraordinary destiny of Antoine PINTARD

Philippe ROUEN

Translation of

Les Laboureurs d'Amérique

by

Alfredo Searle and Valeria Ferrari
Santiago de Chile – 2022

Translator's notes

It is not often that the translator of a work has a "personal" and not only a professional interest in the work. However, this is the case here. A few years ago, while researching the history of my family, I came across the work of Philippe ROUEN which deals, among other very interesting aspects, with the motivations that led Antoine Pintard, who is one of my direct ancestors, to leave France, his native land, and continue his life in America, founding a large family.

Together with Valeria, my wife, a translator by profession, we think that ROUEN's work deserves dissemination that goes beyond the French-speaking world and we have tried to do something about it, translating his books into English, which we hope will be of the reader's liking.

ROUEN makes a historical account, showing from a perspective focused on people of flesh and blood, how circumstances lead them to make decisions and to be involved in activities that over time have great consequences for themselves, for their communities and for the world in general. When we talk about flesh and blood people, we want to draw attention to the fact that often the reasons that lead to making certain decisions are much more mundane than might appear when judging them from a historical perspective, when one has the advantage of being able to appraise the long-term consequences they have had. It is a phenomenon similar to what is often observed today when attempts are made to rewrite history in order to *sanitize* it or explain it with our present mentality, and even assign blame or bad intentions to those who took perfectly acceptable actions according to the canons of their time, but which had consequences that today we would prefer not to face.

With a strict adherence to historical facts, and leaving no room for speculation, ROUEN builds up a plot that shows in a very interesting way the events that mark the development of a family that begins its journey in the Languedoc in the south of France at the end of the 17th century and that by the beginning of the 19th century has already spread to a dozen places in various countries, among which is our own in the tip of South America, and whose members have been historically relevant in many ways.

This translation must necessarily have additional support to the original text, which presupposes an advanced knowledge of the history of France. We have tried to provide this through the use of additional footnotes, and by adapting some texts to make them accessible to a more universal reader.

As for more technical details, we would like to state that we have taken the liberty of retaining many names in their original language, although English equivalents exist, which we do not believe will be distracting, but rather help the reader to remain in context.

This work of historical prosopography begins with this volume, which is part of a set of four, which cover from the settlement of the Pintard family in colonial New York, passing through the process of independence of the United States, to continue with the expansion of its international trade in the Atlantic and with China, to continue with the development of the lands beyond the Appalachians, to end with what is now known as the Conquest of the US West.

The Plowmen of America is the first volume translated into English while the others remain only in their original language : *La Croisière du Ginseng, L'Angélus des Appalaches* and *Le Géographe de l'Amérique*. We hope to make these volumes also available in English in the future.

Alfredo Searle and Valeria Ferrari
Santiago de Chile, 2022.

Particular thanks for proof-reading go to Stephen Ward, editor/publisher Friends'Gazette, London, England, and to Sudeshna André, Paris, France.

Introduction

Between 1540 and 1550, the population of the Republic of Geneva increased from ten thousand to twenty thousand souls. This increase was largely due to the arrival of French and Italians Protestants who came to seek religious refuge.

The positive economic consequences of integrating an educated and hard-working people were not long in coming ; so much so that Jean Calvin himself saw it as a divine sign. The establishment of laws intended for all soon followed. Indeed, Calvin believed that faith could only flourish under a legal system that must prevent evil from being the victor. The ecclesiastical ordinances of which he is the author would also, paradoxically, avoid the intrusions of the Geneva civil authority in religious affairs as was then customary.

Not intending to establish a theocracy, Calvin nevertheless strove to regain control of the church and its faithful who, in protestant Geneva, were subject to the civil authority of the Magistrate, the Geneva executive : an attempt to separate Church and State which received no better reception in Geneva than in Paris.

The Grand Council of Geneva would integrate finally the ecclesiastical ordinances while leaving the last word to the Magistrate in the event of a conflict between pastors who placed themselves under the government of the Republic of Geneva. [1]

This framework was to inspire the Reformed Churches of France and the Netherlands, which influenced the Huguenots in their emigration to New Amsterdam founded by the Walloon and Dutch Calvinists in 1624. Subsequent waves no doubt had this pattern in mind when the Revocation of the Edict of Nantes of 1685 proscribed the Protestant

---

(1) An independent state between 1534 and 1798 when it was annexed by France before it joined the Swiss Confederation in 1815.

separatism from the state which France had, according to King Louis XIV, unwisely supported since 1598. Prohibited from protestant worship in Catholic France, they believed they could thrive in the city whose rulers were Calvin's children. To one of Calvin's detractors, condemning his doctrine on grounds that his lack of offspring after the death of his son was the judgment of God, Calvin simply replied that he had thousands of children. Many of them ended up in New York in compliance with Jeremiah's comment : "Where we know God, humanity is well taken care of". [2]

These thoughts undoubtedly aroused the joy and hope of the first arrivals. The evolution of the colony toward serving mammon did not allow keeping intact the orthodoxy of Calvinist thought and the city had to abandon the project initiated in Geneva. A state of mind remained that was to contribute to the willingness to trade and create businesses, a rights-based approach which implied respect for the individual, and the assumption of responsibility.

Failing to become the city of God to which the Calvinists had aspired, New York nowadays has turned into the city of hopes ; in any case of liberation, allowing everyone to flourish while abiding by the law whose penalties for violations are always surprising for a stranger to this way of thinking. It is the consequence of freedom and undoubtedly a question of moral legacy.

It is about this journey of a modern man that we will be talking about here.

---

[2] Jeremiah (650-570 BC) is one of the major prophets of the Hebrew Bible.

Prologue

New York. The city and the port are white with snow and ice. It is December 6, 1843. John Pintard is bedridden. His health is still not improving. Tonight, he will be absent from the Saint Nicholas dinner hosted annually by the New York Historical Society since December 6, 1809.

John Pintard is 85 years old. He is blind and nearly deaf after his eardrums were damaged by a blast from an explosion during a 4th of July celebration.

He knows he is facing the end of a busy life, but he wants to witness once more the unique birthday celebration he helped create. The man who reputedly invented Santa Claus doesn't want to die. He is sleepy.

He keeps close at hand the book that has guided his behavior during his life. He never names it but he often refers to it. He knows by heart many pages of Scott's Bible. [3] So, when he browses it, it is not to grasp a thought or an interpretation in the light of the experience of his age but rather to taste the charm and the music of the words that compose it. He is indeed convinced, like many of his fellow citizens, that the words of Jeremiah or Ezekiel are just simply beautiful. Saint Louis, king of France, had chosen to include the two prophets in the stained-glass windows of the *Sainte Chapelle*, a marvel at the heart of the City Palace in Paris, sheltering the relics of Christ's crown of thorns.

The quest for beauty is still in him a few months before his death ; the quest to recognize our unique place in the universal order.

In New York, as in all of America, reading the Bible has supplanted the interpretation of the glory of stained-glass with a return to pure text. Medieval visual art has given way to the quest for a practical

---

(3) Thomas Scott (1747–1821) was an influential English preacher and author. He is principally known for his widespread work *A Commentary on The Whole Bible*.

and individual model to serve as a guideline. The Holy scriptures have inspired John Pintard throughout his life. He is convinced that the vocabulary used also corresponds to the meaning to be given to his life. He knows, and still tries to convince those around him, that the significance of simple sentences, understandable by all, cannot remain unheard. He readily admits that the pleasure of reading can be combined with the passage on earth of a Christian on the condition that words flourish in action and utility as testified by his whole life.

Let him doze off in Manhattan, the Bible resting beside him, deep in his thoughts, his memories, or perhaps his latest projects. Manhattan is arguably his family's last destination. It is the culmination of a long trip filled with tumultuous events which gave birth to consequences that finally combined harmoniously. The history of the Pintards covers a long journey westward, thus underscoring a quest for freedom peculiar to the Calvinists. It marks each epoch of their journey begun two centuries earlier. John is just a link like those in the chain, stretched between its towers, which at night closed the port of La Rochelle on the French Atlantic coast, from where, family tradition has it, his great-grandfather Antoine had left.

The dozing old man cannot see the ships come alive any more on the Hudson, a spectacle that had cheered him up during his life. He cannot participate in the moments of collective enthusiasm when the boats that had been stationary for days set sail again as the favorable winds return. These minutes of rebirth have always appeared to him as unique moments, bringing great satisfaction. The brevity and precision with which they are described in the correspondence to his daughter Eliza Noel [4] reveal the restrained sensitivity of the former New York dock owner.

Just as the rising breeze disperses the boats in the bay, filling with joy the merchants of the nascent metropolis, who finally see a whole fleet of sailboats that were immobilized for ten days, taking to the sea, the wind of the Reformation has scattered men across the oceans. Today the sails of the Niagara and the Phoebe Ann are hoisted by sailors who load their cargo destined for Le Havre and New Orleans just as words and ideas once carried men across the Atlantic Ocean. The Huguenots of France actively contributed to the birth of the United States of America. John Pintard may have been the last of them.

---

(4) "Noel" means Christmas in French.

Book I

STEP INTO EXILE

1

There are days like this when the King of France should regret having forced certain men to leave his Kingdom, because they were often the best of his subjects.

It is April 4, 1688.

Goodbye Pintard and good luck !

The citadel of *Saint-Martin-de-Ré* has recently been completed. Limestone rubble piles, which time has not yet stained, sparkle in the light of spring. The huge gate of the military structure crowned with the *Soleil* of Louis XIV faces east and the old continent as if for a last farewell. A wide esplanade leads the way to the entrances and exits of the military compound. It also gives access to a tiny harbor surrounded by low walls, which connects the construction with the ocean like a lock, made to allow passage to both incoming prisoners and outgoing deportees. It looks like a tank with its lid removed. On the west wall, a stone staircase reminds us of the maritime function of the structure : the harbor is emptied or filled according to the tides that mark the arrivals and departures of men.

The strong undertow between the *Ile de Ré* and the mainland generates a swell that hits with a great crash and resonates with force in the narrow corridor that leads to the ocean.

The boat destined to reach the ship anchored beyond shakes like an empty box dropped into the open sea.

The men are silent ; Antoine Pintard is alert and thoughtful. He no longer thinks about what he is leaving behind. It is nice that the departure procedures make any introspection, even momentary, impossible.

Over the last weeks, Antoine Pintard could not avoid ask himself loads of questions about the advisability of his permanent departure, the consequences of his absence for his family, and the long-awaited discovery of the unknown.

Antoine greets Michel, the jailer, for the last time. The latter had confessed that he had previously been in the galley corps of Marseilles. A detachment of some war galleys on the Atlantic flank of the kingdom had taken him to the naval dockyard of Rochefort.

The proximity of La Rochelle and the start of prison activities before the departure of religious exiles to America had led Michel, the jailer, to be transferred to the citadel of Saint-Martin where his experience as a sailor could be useful to his King, or so he said. The last days that Antoine spent waiting for transport to the colonies had allowed the jailer to express all his compassion for the Reformed Christians, regretting at the same time, and probably to try to soften his words, the mistreatment inflicted on the rowers of the galleys of France.

Antoine knew all this by heart. He had previously heard the worrying information transmitted by travelers and merchants from the *Cévennes* [5] returning from the Beaucaire fair. He had heard the gossip that came from the city, highlighting the strictness of the prison regime applied in the naval dockyard of the Plan Fourmiguier, built at right angles to the rear of the port of Marseilles. He also could not ignore that the criminal convictions to the galleys had been extended by Article X of the Edict of Fontainebleau, to those of the so-called reformed religion who were fleeing their home country. [6] He was

---

(5) The Cévennes are a range of medium mountains extending from east to west in the South of France. Robert Louis Stevenson made them well-known in the English-speaking world after he published his first novel in 1879. Travel with a Donkey in the Cévennes is considered nowadays a pioneering classic of outdoor literature. Stevenson wrote many pages about the protestant uprising called The Camisard Revolt which took place there between 1702 and 1704. This narrative also influenced authors like John Steinbeck. The Stevenson Trail is well known to hikers today.

(6) N of T : Scope of the regulations established in the Edict of Fontainebleau were :
    1 : The Revocation of the Edict of Nantes (1598), signed by Henri IV, and the Edict of Nimes (1629), signed by Louis XIII. It ordered the demolition of all the churches that were still standing.
    2 and 3 : Worship of the alleged Reformed Church was banned, also applicable to the Lords.
    4 : The banishment, within two weeks of pastors who did not want to convert – on pain of the galleys.
    5 and 6 : Inducements to get pastors to convert : life pensions and vocational retraining in the legal profession.
    7 : Ban on Protestant schools.
    8 : Obligation on members of the Reformed Church to have their children baptized and educated in the Catholic faith.

also familiar with article XII, the last article of the Revocation edict. It granted freedom of conscience to the Protestants provided they did not meet for worship or prayer, under penalty of deprivation of liberty and property ; better to pray at home.

On the way to La Rochelle, Antoine had met the Guyenne [7] chain gang which included deserters and murderers, thieves, swindlers and poor people, who had all been forced to leave for the Phocaean [8] city. For them, it was like a foreign country, like all the provinces of a kingdom with various dialects. Only the courts and tribunals of the kingdom united men with a chain that bound their feet when they offended or committed a crime. Judges applied a simple criminal policy that included whipping, the death penalty, exile. The galleys of France were an exception in the repressive arsenal of the monarchy since it combined the whip with the deprivation of liberty. To be condemned to a position as an oarsman in a galley corresponded to the desired criminal punishment since the refusal to recant was a permanent offence, unbearable in the eyes of an absolute monarch ruling over a kingdom in the process of centralization.

Antoine was far from such analysis when he met the harsh stares of the chained prisoners, but he knew that he was facing the judicial institution whose decisions made in Bordeaux, Toulouse, or Angoulême, led to this gloomy parade. He knew his King well and suffered today the consequences of the Revocation of the Edict of Nantes ; the end of the freedoms granted to his ancestors, which was to lead to the misfortunes of his province. He also knew from experience the risks involved in breaking the prohibitions. Perhaps he was imagining the presence of Protestants among these men with a swinging gait weighted by irons. The pleasant spectacle of the surroundings completely disappeared in the long silent procession that absorbed the hum of human activities and the sound of the birds gathering for their annual migration to more welcoming places.

---

9 : Confiscation of possessions of Reformed Church members who had gone abroad, unless they return within 4 months.
10 : Ban on members of the Reformed Church emigrating – on pain of the galleys for men and prison for women.
11 : Punishment of "new converts" who went back to Protestantism.
12 : Permission for those who had not yet converted to reside in France, so long as they complied with the rules previously mentioned.

(7) Guyenne is an old province of France whose main city was Bordeaux.
(8) N of T : Phocaea refers to the city of Marseilles.

The sight of the galley slaves leaving for Marseilles had comforted him in this wise decision to leave the kingdom of France. His voluntary departure for America, and its unknown lands, seemed to him now more appropriate to the life he intended to live than the gloomy moral solitude which he could surmise from the sight of the chain of emaciated humans who swayed from one side and then the other, feet chained in shackles, staring at the horizon. The song of the birds once again drowned out the sound of irons that had disturbed their path, and then he fully understood that he had made the right decision. However, Antoine could not forget the ones he left behind, with no hope of ever seeing them again. But his decision had been the result of long reflections and he was not a man to easily change his mind. Therefore, he continued on his way but staring at the ground, avoiding disturbing the Reformed Christian convicts who, upon meeting his gaze, might have believed him to be complicit in their fate.

In the seventeenth century, Petrarch's humanism [9] had already entered the debate. It was gaining strength as the old institutions became obsolete and feudal ties between men were no longer necessary. Individualism also made its appearance ; it had taken in the *Cévennes* mountains the shape of the black hat that the Protestant faithful wore fitted on their heads when they entered the church. Catholics did not. God's good friends would have liked to instruct their lords of the manor and their king. But the beautiful ornaments of the monarchy were strong enough not to fall apart at the first hitch. The only thing left for the recalcitrant was to leave. As for the others, they could always hold their neck or knee more stiffly when bowing to His Majesty or his representatives.

The less docile ended up in the war galleys, their backs to the royal figurehead churning the waters by the force of their oars, giving the crew one last satisfaction, that of serving the king, but backwards.

---

(9) N of T : Francesco Petrarca or Petrarch was a scholar who laid the foundations for Renaissance humanism, which emphasized the study of Classical authors from antiquity over the Scholastic thinkers of the Middle Ages. He defended this idea to his more conservative contemporaries. He lived about 48 years of his life in Avignon or in the South of France where the Papal Court settled during the 14th century.

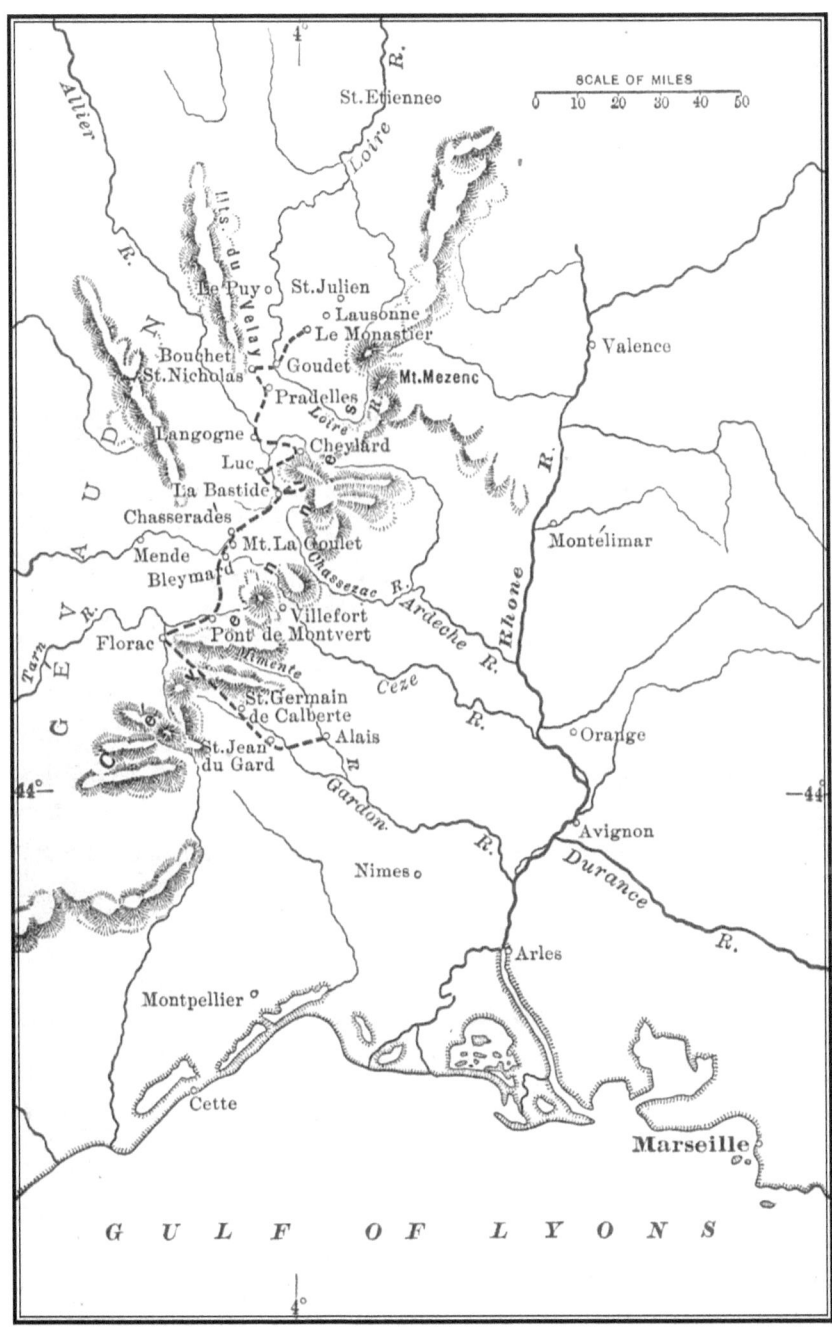

Travel with a Donkey in the Cévennes (dotted line) by Robert Louis Stevenson

2

In the year of Our Lord 1686 of the Old Regime, in Saint-Roman-de-Tousque as in all the *Cévennes*, daily life was difficult for "those of the reformed religion". The previous year, Louis XIV had revoked the Edict of Nantes that had guaranteed freedom of worship to Protestants in France since 1598. Catholic baptism was now mandatory for newborns and Sunday Mass was a general imperative.

The first consequence was massive recanting. By entire families, by the dozens, by the hundreds, Protestants simply abjured their faith in order to continue living without fear of occupation of their home by the king's dragoons and the demands they would inevitably bring down on their families and their property. The cornerstone of absolute monarchy lay henceforth in the unity of the religion of the kingdom. The union of Church and State did not allow for freedom of conscience.

Antoine Pintard is twenty-eight years old.

Lately, discussions have been lively within families and in the Reformed community. Antoine actively participates in them, to collectively develop a coherent strategy to address the challenges posed by the Revocation. Three different groups emerge, corresponding to three different attitudes to the repression that looms.

The most numerous, concerned about the future of their children, recant, even if that means practicing their worship clandestinely and making sure to destroy at night the "papist lies" the priest has transmitted during the day. These people want peace. The wars of religion that blood stained the kingdom before the Edict of Nantes are present in everyone's minds, and also the cruelty exercised by the two communities towards each other, particularly in the province of Languedoc.

The ban on Protestants accessing certain functions, mainly in the judicial hierarchy, condemned them to subordinate jobs that did not befit their qualification. While all social categories of the population adhered to Calvinism, many Reformed Protestants came from the nobility, lawyers, merchants, and craftsmen. The impossibility of exercising their professions, their noble or judicial prerogatives, mainly due to the Royal Decree of July 8, 1686, was now coupled with the ban on passing on their heritage to their children who were not baptized Catholic. They simply had to accept their exclusion from all institutions. It is understandable that for one category of the population, the best option would be recanting. The second choice would be exile ; the third disobedience.

Louis Pintard and Marguerite Roux had five children.

In this year of 1686, we can assume that the discussions were long and difficult among the three brothers and the three sisters at Mas de *La Cabanarié*, the farmhouse where they lived with their mother. Indeed, what attitude would they adopt on the prohibition that applied to them ? Lower their heads ? No way ! This will not be the choice for any of the children of the late Louis Pintard nor the prevailing attitude among the Pintards !

In this family of locksmiths that have achieved a certain degree of renown, Antoine will emerge, amid the political events of the turn of the century and give birth to a remarkable North American lineage. Probably installed in the *Cévennes* mountains for centuries, [10] they have transmitted iron crafts from father to son : locksmith, blacksmith, barrel maker. Over the generations, they have evolved into lawyers. Jean, the grandfather, was "jurisdictional prosecutor of the barony of Moissac". The godfather of his first grandson is Jean de Ginestou, the present holder of the barony.

The Ginestou family, a branch of Montolieu, has its feudal stronghold at the Château de Galon in Sumène and represents one of the oldest noble families in Languedoc. The exercise of religion, through baptism and sponsorship, is for the Pintards a sign of an

---

(10) As far as we can go back in time, we generally find this surname in a triangle between Saint-Jean-du-Gard and Saint-Marcel-de-Fonfouilhouse to the north and Sumène to the south. A generally accepted hypothesis places the cradle of all the Pintards in Saint-Marcel because the notarial acts here are the oldest. Furthermore, if it is difficult to trace Antoine's ancestry beyond the 16th century, we know that his grandfather, Jean, who gave *de jure* recognition to the nobleman Jacques Sabatier, Lord de la Roquette on June 10, 1615, is qualified in the said act as "jurisdictional prosecutor of the barony of Moissac".

undeniable social integration and the fulcrum of their future ascent, and destiny.

Equally evident is the determination of Jean Pintard, Antoine's grandfather, to educate his descendants to the point of noting in the will that he dictates on June 8, 1629, his desire to have his son Louis "educated in schools and given a job that will be well-appreciated by his friends." He will become the *viguier* [11] and the regent of the barony, as found in the records of the Saint-Roman consistory of September 2, 1665.

The son, Antoine's father, in addition to his duties as a judge, had an important religious activity since he regularly participated as an elder in regional synods. The spirit of Calvinism shines in the Pintard family through the interest shown in the two pillars of Protestant doctrine, law and religion, and through their concrete implementation within the community of the village. Unfortunately, the Revocation and the conditions of the ban no longer allowed the family members to thrive because they were now deprived of the freedom to exercise their talents within the judicial or religious institutions of their time.

Undoubtedly, long discussions took place in *La Cabanarié*, their home, on the attitude to adopt in the face of the civil and religious annihilation that would be suffered by the devotees who persisted in practicing their faith. The ban on access to judicial functions and the impossibility for the Protestant lords to impart justice effectively deprived them, their *bayles*,[12] their *viguiers*, and their regents of any possibility of social advancement and subjected them to radical demotion.

Seizure of their property made them irremediably dependent on charities, known under different names of saints, that were in charge of distributing alms. Hence, the fate that awaited them was resolved only by total submission to the Catholic institution that had taken over these charities which had been administered for more than a century by the Protestants of the *Cévennes*.

Such a solution was out of the question, for both Antoine and his brother Jean.

"And what will you do if they come looking for you ?" said Jean, the older brother.

---

(11) N of T : *Viguier* : Judge that as the royal *Prevost* in the other provinces of France, administered justice in the South (Languedoc, Roussillon) in the name of the king.

(12) N of T : *Bayle* : In the Middle Ages, in Languedoc, the prosecutor of the lord of the manor.

"Why would they come looking for us ?" Answered Samuel, the youngest of the three sons.

"Because prayer and worship are prohibited".

"But we can meet in secret", Samuel replied.

"Yes, but for how long ? The bans have been in effect for six months. Are we going to live in hiding for years, waiting for the unlikely support from foreign Protestant kingdoms and princes ?"

"They say that..."

"Let's speak and consider the events with less emotion". Samuel allowed Jean, thirteen years older than him, to speak.

"Our condition is inexorably deteriorating. Our mother is there to testify to it and our father has confirmed it to us too often for us to ignore. The King wishes to question the privileges granted to the Protestants. He wants to ensure the unity of his kingdom. He has not forgotten that the provincial parliaments opposed the application of the Edict of Nantes a hundred years ago. Hence, he knows that he will have reliable allies who will ensure that his commands in this area are enforced in the future."

"But, some of them are Protestants !" Samuel exclaimed.

"It's true," Jean continued, "but a large number have already recanted. What are we worth in hiding ? We will be more useful to our faith and worship if we retain our functions and our property. What will we be when they have relegated us here to *La Cabanarié* to live with reduced resources, praying in secret and leaving our functions to nobles of Nimes or Ales[13] appointed by the bishop or the court of justice to occupy our positions ? Our influence will end and our teaching, for which our ancestors fought, will be over. Because without independence, to put it bluntly, without fortune and words, it is difficult to maintain what one believes".

"And do you think that by retracting you transmit the teachings of the elders ?"

Jean ignored him.

He continued in the same tone that he had used until then and that only made it possible to prevent the discussion from sinking into the twists and turns of passion where reason goes astray. He liked to point out that you could exercise faith through behavior. He added that today's challenges not only served to test one's faith but also one's faculties and their solidity in the face of adversity. He took the opportunity given

---
(13) Cities in Languedoc

him to recall Calvin's views on predestination according to which God destines some to salvation and others to damnation by the sheer force of his grace.

This way of presenting things, excluding free will, so to speak, allowed him to accept the disastrous consequences of the Revocation, by submitting himself reasonably to the afflictions he would face. Success or failure in this endeavor would teach him so much about himself that he was ready to face adversity. In the future, his discreet but effective attitude would allow him to be of service to his brothers of religion, probably less equipped than he was himself.

After this long presentation, there was silence. Everyone understood the position of their older brother.

Jean Pintard recanted in February 1686. Strangely, the fact was not recorded until September 17 of the same year.

Antoine and his mother had been silent during the exchange. Marguerite Roux appreciated the rigor of her eldest son's reasoning. He, alone, was capable of providing a reasonable foundation for recanting. She found in him the confidence of Louis Pintard, her husband, now deceased. Louis's schooling, legal books, and the Bible, in addition to conversations with high-standing Huguenots, had allowed him later in his life, to understand complicated situations. Thus, he had carried out juridical work even in the Protestant churches and regional synods charged with passing judgments on the behavior of fellow worshippers. The close relationship which then linked the sanctions imposed by the religious authorities to the application of civil justice magnified the conclusions of both.

The position of his eldest son was part of this duality of judgment. Indeed, how to escape the edict of Fontainebleau, the edict of the Revocation, and the ordinances which were their consequences ? On the basis of religious precepts ? The Pintards were educated people and they knew that Calvin was a Doctor of Law. The city of Nimes, whose influence on the Protestantism of the *Cévennes* is undeniable, soon became the eldest daughter of Geneva. The two pillars of society, according to Calvin, could not be confounded or exclude each other. One had to stand in front of the other as two pillars of the same temple. Therefore, it was better to exercise the virtue of patience rather than to plunge into a confrontation in the heart of an unequal battle. It was desirable to exert influence within the institutions in which the right of entry was preserved. This was Jean's position.

Antoine contemplated some religious works that were familiar to him : the small library of the notables of the time, so important was the market value of books. He placed his hand on the *Treasure of human and divine comforts* [14] and remembered the words of his elder brother. His position was different. While he also had an undeniable taste for the law, and legality, he had at the same time inherited the younger son's destiny. The meager inheritance allocated to younger sons made the purchase of profitable land impossible.

Calvin's teaching on the independence that is desirable to seek to reach God seemed applicable to everything. But the order of things was enshrined in law. Therefore, he abandoned his reflections with no other idea in mind than the search for a solution. The subheading of the *Treasure of Comforts*, which he had read many times, caught his attention : yes, the Christian must learn to overcome the afflictions and miseries of this life.

This book had been part of *La Cabanarié* for a long time. Each of them absorbed its teachings through solitary readings sometimes supplemented when they were children with collective explanations led by their father. The obligation imposed on Protestant children to learn to read applied particularly to the Pintards, including the girls, who drew from it the powers of understanding and synthesis necessary for any decision-making as adults.

Antoine put down the book and left. The undulating terrain that surrounded *La Cabanarié* extended to the mountains of Gévaudan.[15] Antoine suddenly felt the weight of dependence completely penetrate him just as the autumn mist widely invaded the horizon - dependence on the law that mistreated him ; dependence on the family that restricted him ; dependence on the Catholic religion that oppressed him. The open landscape seemed to shrink and the gains made under Henry IV[16] completely disappeared in the depths of the enclosed valleys where life was no longer good.

---

(14) *Trésor des consolation humaines et divines, ou, Traité dans lequel le Chrétien peut apprendre à vaincre et à surmonter les afflictions et les misères de cette vie.* Treasure of human and divine consolations, or a treaty from which a Christian can learn how to conquer or to surmount the afflictions and the miseries of this life. Translated from Latin into French by Jan Bourlier, Antverp (Belgium) 1566, Jan Waesberghe.

(15) Gévaudan is an old province of France whose main city was Mende

(16) Henry the 4th is the signer of the Edict of Nantes which gave freedom of worship to protestants of France as of 1598. He recanted his Reformed faith in order to become the Catholic King of France. The following statement made him famous : " Paris is worth a mass ".

Antoine would never separate from the *Treasure of Consolations* and would take it in his bag to the New World, just as Petrarch, the father of humanism, made his ascent to Mont Ventoux [17] without detaching himself from the *Confessions of Saint Augustine*.

The youngest of the Pintard children had also left the house. The girls had gathered outside to continue a conversation that Samuel did not join. For Françoise, Suzanne and Isabeau, it could not be a question of law or patience. The endless discussions about the preponderance of law over moral principles did not tempt them at all. Their elder brother's contact with educated people, particularly the Ginestou family, had accustomed them to these arguments. The need to ensure the coexistence of the law of men and of religious principles, the two pillars of Calvinism, was familiar to them, especially during the visits of Pastor Alméras, one of their relatives. The girls' opinion was summed up in their secret plans for a departure to the Principality of Orange. The Protestant Way that cut through the low mountains of the Uzès region was said to be increasingly traveled by Reformed people seeking protection in the lands of the Nassau family. [18] The girls intended to quit the game instead of continuing to argue its rules forever.

Samuel was only sixteen at the time. He saw in the restrictions imposed on him only a series of humiliations and questions. His desire not to intervene in the discussions or give his point of view was not only related to his age and its consequent family prohibition. He had his own ideas on the matter and secretly refused to accept, negotiate, moderate, and finally submit.

Each individual thus sought the solution to the equation proposed by their King. In any case, the possible conclusions could only lead to profound questions about their being, their existence, their way of life that had to change ; issues of such magnitude that today they seem to be the foundations of individualism. Such a quest, such reflections on one's future could only steer individuals away from a fatalistic analysis of their existence.

The answer was in themselves and they guessed at it that day. They were at the crossroads where the discovery of the rest of the world, the development of knowledge, the nascent appreciation of humanism,

---

(17) Mont Ventoux is well-known today as a summit (6260 feet high) in the South of France on a stage of the *Tour de France*, the most important cycling event in the world.

(18) The Nassau family headed at that time by the Prince of Orange, controlled a tiny principality it had inherited in the South of France. Its main city was Orange (see map p. 19). The Mont Ventoux is only 20 miles away.

the progress of techniques gave them a glimmer of freedom. They understood that the solution was in their hands ; each one could choose, alone, the impetus he was going to give to his own destiny. Their father had died in 1672 and their mother would have liked to have them all with her.

The pastors of the surrounding towns had been forced to leave the kingdom at the time of the Revocation. Their religious brothers had recanted *en-masse* since November 1685. Threats were placed by royal ordinance on the doors of churches, and public houses. There was no longer any link between them, except the certitude that the behavior of some put the existence of others at risk.

They were thus alone.

3

Antoine understands during the year 1686 that he is finally the master of the game in which he is immersed against his will. He often goes through the *Treasury of Consolations* in search of answers to the questions he asks himself, and the difficulties he encounters. If he must find himself alone, at least he will have this book. It will give him the necessary elements for his reflection. But Antoine is not a man given to improvisation. He is not an adventurer. He must make his decisions as a Protestant free in his actions. Therefore, he does not wander aimlessly but maintains the course that will allow him to achieve his objectives.

Antoine does not dream ; neither does he deceive himself. He will not encourage or exhaust himself in any revolt. The feeling of freedom that he discovers will lead him to integrate himself into events in order to build and strengthen himself.

He now understands the position of his elder brother. Beyond the first impression he felt at the recanting of his brother, he realizes that Jean's decision corresponded to a break with the past. At present they are all drawn into events that transcend them. It is important not to fight, but to adapt. The king is the head of a kingdom that is being born, right there before their very eyes. Antoine feels this rupture with the old society based on loyalty to the lord of the manor, with whom it was possible to reach an understanding. He also knows the financial fragility of the Baron de Moissac and his neighbors, who are too busy enforcing their manorial rights eroded little by little each year by the depreciation of the currency.

What amazes him is the implementation of important military posts and the installation of a multi-level administration aimed at eradicating from the mountain peasants in prayer without hierarchy or cumbersome liturgy, among their goats, and their inaccessible chestnut groves. And he understands, through the royal ordinances, that the Reformation was more of a regrettable emancipation than a new religion. Understanding now all the significance that should be given to a struggle that dates back more than a century, he realizes that the end of freedom is not a defeat, but just the sign of a dying society.

Already weakened local powers will eventually die out. Unequal conditions and the power of King Louis at the head of his kingdom make the combat unequal and submission is not dishonorable. The balance of power has changed.

The feudal bonds that united men are declining. From now on, honest men will exercise their talents with a close relationship with their distant sovereign through his administration. Uniformity is gaining ground.

The complexity of the new relationship is not obvious. Ancient society, formed partly by an accumulation of rights, was understood and known by all. Now each person will have to exercise his or her skills in a different society. The major elements of its composition will be established within the framework of a central and powerful state, where the difficulties of the objectives to be achieved will inevitably lead to the flourishing of an endless number of local administrative authorities for the implementation of policies applicable to the entire kingdom.

Understanding the nature of the power that has been brutally exercised in the *Cévennes* for over twenty years is, for Antoine, the everyday example of the ongoing reconstruction. The Revocation is only the final stage of this evolution.

All-in-all, adaptation is possible. This feeling reassures him. Accepting restrictions and afflictions can only strengthen one's level of morality because enduring them requires the implementation of a virtue such as patience. He assumes that he will come out stronger from these tests.

Furthermore, he will have respected the precepts of his parents and his Church without violating the law. This triple fidelity fills him with joy and hope because it brings change and cannot end in chaos or death. By accepting the limitations imposed on him and submitting to the law, Antoine does not follow sudden and immediate reactions that bring instant satisfaction but solve nothing in the long term.

Antoine discovers the uniqueness of his existence and glimpses the meaning of predestination according to Calvin. The peace that seizes him leads him to believe that he has found the truth. He will work from now on to fulfill his hopes. It remains for him to find the right solution.

4

During the months that followed these happy moments, Antoine made sure not to reveal any of his plans, especially since he didn't know exactly how to erect the structure that he envisioned. He was cautious enough to avoid reasoning with his younger sisters and Samuel, who had not yet taken stock of the events they were facing. Daily life kept pace with housework and bad news.

Each day brought its share of unsettling information and also underscored the unpleasant nature of the men in charge of enforcing the royal ordinances and the violence of their implementation by the king's dragoons.

In the midst of the uproar, the secret meetings increasingly broadcasted their message of resistance and disobedience. Antoine saw in it the fierce manifestation of wounded souls and betrayed subjects. He felt close to his religious fellows, at times, willing to join them.

This situation could not last forever. He had to act. The newly acquired freedom had to be implemented. He had to choose.

Antoine recanted.

5

He finally felt free to come and go. The decision made earlier by his older brother saved him from too acute a sense of guilt. He thus joined the mass of anonymous people. The strength of the family ties also softened the reproachful looks that he felt weighing in on him.

His attitude elicited neither approval nor consolation within the Reformed community, which was now in tatters. Many of his neighbors had already taken the step. There was no question of encouragement or invective.

No one had the right to distribute laurels or surround the forehead with crowns of thorns.

Humiliation, helplessness, and reason combined into a bitter-tasting mixture that everyone drank in small sips every day. An entire community had been devastated and some of its members secretly envied the few families who remained Catholic and who had not needed to recant.

Antoine at present understood the importance of the decision his ancestors had made more than a century earlier and the consequences they had had on his life. He now thought about the meaning of predestination as formulated by the Calvinists.

The limitation of his free will reminded him how dependent we are on past events that sooner or later will resonate with us. He wanted to stay true to that legacy, but he also wanted to tame the freedom newly acquired during his reflections a few months ago.

He didn't want to give that up in any way. He was convinced of it.

The following weeks were rich in events. News, seldom verifiable, came of the departure of notables from the Gardon valley or of prominent people who were related to them. It was rumored that some members of the Vignolles family had left the kingdom for Geneva or Brandenburg, without the news being confirmed.

Indeed, the penalties for having emigrated became so severe, in particular the confiscation of property, that the exiles did everything possible to keep their departure secret. Therefore, they reserved their right to return without judicial conviction if, by chance, the situation changed one day.

Since the creation of the court following the edict of Castres, [19] charged with rendering justice to the Protestants, the Vignolles had secured the presidency or acted as court counselor and thus enjoyed great renown.

The departure of some of them influenced the analysis carried out by the devotees of the *Cévennes*. Antoine had met them in the presence of his father or his brother and regarded their choice as a worthy example. Furthermore, the son-in-law of the Baron de Moissac, also a member of the Ginestou family, was considered a fugitive bound for Lausanne. The information was safe, given the ties that united the two families through Jean, his older brother, and all this necessarily had an impact on Antoine's reflection on what attitude to adopt.

Antoine also witnessed daily the efforts made by Samuel and his sisters to maintain in *La Cabanarié* a resistance to the royal ordinances, through the organization of meetings and prayers around the Protestant cult. Jean did not try to dissuade them. The farm was far from Saint-Roman and Moissac in a particularly isolated valley. Furthermore, the example of his aunt Madeleine Pintard and her husband David Vieilles, living at the Mas de la Baume in Peyrolles,[20] a few kilometers away, could only reinforce their desire not to compromise, by participating in or even organizing assemblies.

Antoine sometimes compared the attitude of Samuel and his sisters, and the risks they took, with the departure of members of the community to countries of refuge such as the republic of Geneva, Holland or Lower-Saxony. [21] He couldn't help but notice the desperate nature of their resistance. Antoine saw no way out of such moves since they would not influence the king who had had this plan in mind for

---

(19) Castres is a town in west Languedoc. John Locke makes reference to it when he crosses Castres. The Court had been transferred to Castelnaudary, a Catholic stronghold, in 1670.

(20) During the Middle Ages a "mas" was the smallest agricultural production unit in the South of France. Then, it meant a farm.

(21) Later England or the American colonies.

a long time. The abolition of the Castres court ten years earlier, when all Protestants had witnessed the referral of their cases on appeal to the ordinary courts, had not gone unnoticed in the particularly procedural society of the Old Regime. Antoine had understood perfectly, through his exchanges with Jean, that this judicial exception, issued as a reaction to the edict of tolerance of 1598, could not last. He today understood all its meaning. The unification of royal justice without distinction between Catholic and Protestant courts sounded like the death sentence for the recognition of the Reformed community.

The king, relying on public opinion that considered the court of Castres a particularly lenient court towards its litigants, had soon taken the decision to suspend it intending to improve justice. The rediscovered judicial unit could only lead to other harmonization, to other questionings of the articles of the tolerance treaty until its total revocation. The desire to unify the kingdom received a favorable echo in the Catholic population, who saw in this only a just return to equilibrium, to equal treatment for everyone through the elimination of particularisms and exceptions.

What was conceivable at the end of the 16th century, culturally linked to the Middle Ages, no longer had a reason to exist in a society in search of uniformity, moving towards a nascent rationalization.

6

The Pintards, *Viguiers* and *Bayles de Seigneurs* understand these developments. They deal with legal matters on a daily basis and are familiar with the *Villers-Cotterêts* ordinance that made the French language mandatory in 1539. Antoine carries out his analysis in French. He understands the importance on the population of such a decision. He also realizes that the use of French instead of Occitan within his family was only the consequence of the judicial functions carried out by his ancestors. The mastery of a new language by the Reformed community is thus a sign of its social standing. This also leads him to see the complete fragility of the fabric of society and its dependence on royal power.

Their social ascent is only the result of feudal complexity, and their material comfort is in part linked to the mastery of French, imposed with the aim of suppressing both Latin and provincial languages. Breaking the rules goes against a harmonization that began more than a century ago and to which they are now the heirs. His exclusion from a legal position would come as a greater financial disaster because he was considering taking the position of a judge. He would have to obey or leave. The example of the Vignolles family appears to him to be all the more significant.

However, he reacts to the choice posed by his King and in those moments, he would like to participate in actions that would restore the effects of the Edict of Nantes. When in doubt, Antoine acts and also takes risks, to no avail. He is aware of the fate of those who do.

Death does not tempt him, nor do the heroic acts that can lead to it, and do not necessarily change the order of things. Antoine measures the weakness of individual actions just as he refuses the principle of an inventory of fugitives drawn up on January 18, 1687, by the priest

Monbel of Notre-Dame de Valfrancesque, a neighboring parish ; but he later submits to it. He would like to blend in with an organized and powerful resistance, but he knows that he has in front of him, according to the Baron de Moissac, "the greatest king in the world." He is aware of his impotence. A century earlier, Catholics and Protestants had killed each other both in the provinces and in Paris because of their religious affiliations, but also because of issues of domination between factions. Today, power is in the hands of an absolute monarch, and the Catholics who once faced the protestants have turned into regiments of dragoons.

He feels shamed and degraded, in front of the stubborn people of the community who have gone against the priest Monbel, the servant of God. They do not cease to emphasize quietly their solitary behavior at a time when, courage being reduced to impudence, they would have liked not to have been alone in their action.

That day, the day of his recantation, Antoine also understood that the ties of family affection could be destroyed if, combining his words and his thoughts, he disclosed his analysis of the attitude to be adopted in the face of the events and turbulence of the moment. He preferred to remain silent because words are sometimes just a source of infinite emotions. Thus, one must keep the course set for oneself a secret and refuse to blend in with the goals of others.

Reasoning thus, Antoine realizes that he is abandoning his family and religious community and that he will have to bear all the consequences. Ancestral society is changing. The end of the freedoms granted to the Reformed, supported by growing public opinion, will only facilitate its breakup by highlighting differences of opinion and the loss of common goals.

The rigor of legal reasoning that had been the strength of his family philosophy will soon have to disappear in a torrent of emotions and will have to resolve itself on an individual basis. The Protestant faith, made up of individual readings and collective investigations, which fostered dialogue and intelligence through the implementation of a discipline that its members imposed on themselves, will now be corrupted by resentment and invective.

This nascent democracy, definitely moving in the care given to shared family readings, in the form of explanations of texts by candlelight, in the middle of distant hamlets on the edge of dark forests of chestnut trees, is threatened like the family unit which is its vehicle. In ancient

Map of the Cévennes

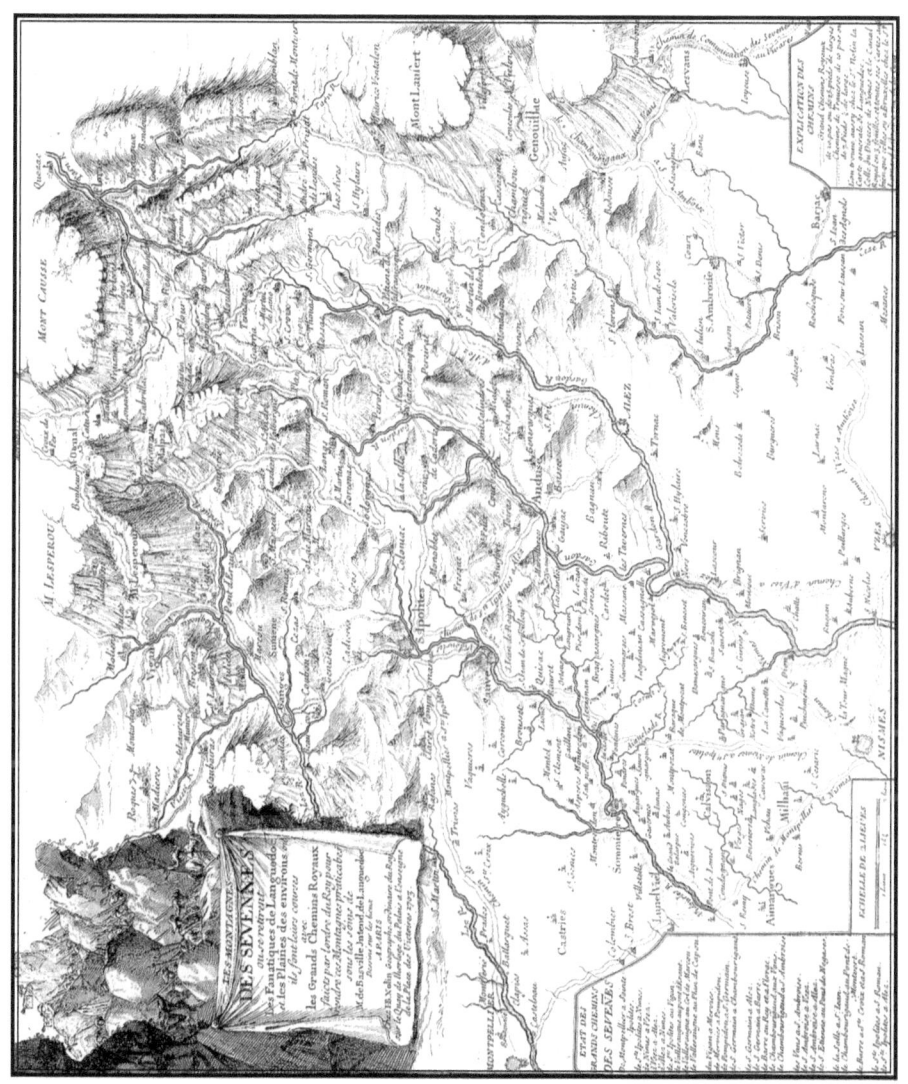

times, the little priors had piously preserved a conscience, a light, even when it was flickering in times of Barbarian invasions. In this way, they had enabled the Christian world to conserve the strength to revitalize men when the time came.

The Reformed of the *Cévennes* also made it possible, due to the geography of the place and the fragile light that spread from valley to valley and from farmhouse to farmhouse, to cement the sense of belonging to a community. Antoine knows it like all the men of his generation, and the disappearance of this bond heralds the end of a world imbued with dignity where all communicated together each evening, around the table, making words resound as if overcoming this poor earthly condition. Every day, at the same time, hundreds of peasants left their state to access another ; and so, they were all together, beautiful and good like the traditional figures adorning the Christmas *crèches* of Provence holy men, who saw when night fell, the slowly fading lights in the homes of neighbors at the end of their universal prayer.

Antoine understands that the uniqueness of the valleys and the society they have forged limit his knowledge of the world. This world will not return. He cannot leave this community to go underground. He cannot join the countries of refuge because belonging to the Reformed religion is not just the application of religious rites. Their religiosity existed in the barns and ravines, in the trunks of the now felled trees. Furthermore, he knows that, as the oaks that still grow on the slopes of *La Cabanarié* do not mix with the chestnut trees, he will have great difficulty fitting into an environment that is imposed on him. He must emigrate to a new world.

Antoine will leave.

7

His brother gave him regular reports on his conversations with the Ginestou family and the possibilities the New World offered. Furthermore, the memory of the Maréchal de Toiras, of Reformed religion, who had successfully defended against England the island of Ré for his very Catholic king, was still alive in the valleys where he was born. All the information from La Rochelle therefore took on a particular, almost sacred, turn among the mountaineers, such as the confession of faith of 1571 ratified in this city by the Reformed churches of Bearn [22] and Geneva when all was still going well.

"La Rochelle is the great port on the Atlantic coast. The Baron de Moissac told me that some of our brothers are going there," Jean told his younger brother.

"For what destination ?" asked Antoine.

"The Windward Islands."

"But do these people go there of their own free will ? I heard that some were deported there ..."

"Many deportees joined New France and settled in the banks of the Saint-Laurent. The islands of the Antilles grant a favorable reception to the Reformed because we are recognized for our skills and our morals there ; and in addition, you would be free."

"Free but to do what, so far away ?" Antoine asked.

"I learned from the Baron de Moissac that it is possible to put oneself at the service of the *Compagnie de Saint-Christophe*. Saint-Christophe is an island in the Caribbean Sea where tobacco cultivation is widespread. They need people who can manage the land."

"And why do they suddenly think of the Reformed ?" Antoine interrupted.

---

(22) Béarn is an old province of France located along the border with Spain.

"For the reasons I just gave you. In fact, they were disappointed in the recruitments they have made so far by resorting to convicts in the kingdom's courts. Today, they would like to develop the island by relying on skilled settlers capable of responding to a farming plan that allows them to return to their hopes of profit."

"That sounds true", added Antoine. "And what should we do if by chance the experience tempted me ?"

"It's a one-way trip, brother. Captains of ships returning to Europe prefer goods to passengers. The *Compagnie de Saint Christophe* is heir to a mentality forged in the days of the *Compagnie des Indes Occidentales*, whose main sponsor was Richelieu [23] with whom Marshal Toiras had so many difficulties despite his success."

"But what do you mean ?" Antoine said impatiently.

"Antoine, these companies were created to enrich their owners, yesterday, Richelieu, today, the king. This means that the signing of a contract of commitment or the attribution of a home will oblige you to bring success and profits to the Crown. But this obligation, and the means you must deploy to satisfy it, are not customary to us. It is not like the old practices that we know with Monsieur le Baron. It is business, the way merchants of Beaucaire or Lyon do it. It is no longer about the collection of manorial dues by a feudal lord who cares very little about the results obtained. The king wants results. He wants the island to continue enriching him, to increase his power and his influence in a part of the world that we, isolated in our *Cévennes* valleys, do not yet know."

"Do you mean that the people who founded farms on the islands no longer care about the right to collect firewood between the feast days of Sainte Camille and Saint Martin [24] and the right to feed pigs after haymaking ?" Antoine asked increasingly interested.

"You are right," answered his older brother. "As I told you, the *Compagnie de Saint Christophe* aims to develop these islands and make a profit in return. They don't care about the right to collect dead wood or the right to graze pigs. Perhaps these rights are enforced, out of habit, but the goal is very different from establishing the power of a lord. In the plantations there is a notion of "business", as I told you,

---

(23) Armand de Richelieu was a cardinal and a duke. His political action led to absolutism in France during the reign of Louis XIV.

(24) Between July 14 and November 11.

in which each inhabitant is asked to succeed in the name of the king and on his own account."

Antoine remained thoughtful. This conversation opened new perspectives for him, and he regretted that his older brother had not spoken to him earlier. He asked him the question.

"You needed to think. If I had told you this a few months ago, you would have thought I wanted to send you to America. The situation is complicated enough with our sisters and Samuel. Since our father died, I have been responsible for you. Our old world is changing, Antoine. And I believe that you are made for the new one that is now being born. You are intelligent and hardworking ; you can read and count. You have mastered both the law and the work of the land. All these qualities can only lead to your success. Your efforts will satisfy your king and not Monsieur le Baron. It is an opportunity. If you want to know more, I will approach the Ginestou family."

The candle was slowly extinguishing, and the flickering halo illuminated the end of an evening that finally brought hope.

"I wish you good night, my dear Antoine. Tomorrow I am going to Saint-Jean for three days. Take care of the little ones."

Antoine would have liked to have talked more about the islands and the *Compagnie de Saint Christophe*, but he understood that his older brother had told him everything. All he had to do was wish him good night and fall asleep, despite all the words spinning in his head.

Samuel and his sisters were already in bed and that was fine.

8

Three days later, Jean returned from his trip, bringing bad news. The harassment by the dragoons was a daily event in the great centers of the Gardon Valley, Saint-Jean and Lassalle.

The obstinacy of certain worshippers attracted reprisals and punishments of great cruelty that led the most determined to reject Extreme Unction as a sign of a last act of resistance. The punishment then consisted of dragging the naked unfortunate over a wooden frame until the body collapsed, accompanied by the barking of dogs and the invectives of the soldiers.

This military occupation pushed them to withdraw into themselves, waiting for the revenge that would naturally occur one day. It was enough to wait, as the *Treasure of Divine and Human Consolations* taught, while capitalizing on their hatred. In that respect, they did not follow the teachings of their parents.

They were preparing for the future in silence. The king's representatives only saw submission when they should have detected in the keen eyes of the Reformed, the weapons that fifteen years later would set the valleys ablaze and turn pale the sun of Louis XIV.

> Proud Babylon who reduces everything to ashes,
> Blessed is he who once may return to you
> the cruel evils that your hand has caused unto us
> Happy he who will destroy you forever !
> Who snatches your children from the breasts,
> and will crush their unfaithful heads !
>
> Psalms of David, 137

All members of the family reacted in the same way to the news brought by Jean. Only Marguerite Roux, their mother, remained silent, locked in her widowhood, walled up in her thoughts, and physically paralyzed by her age. They all avoided dwelling on these issues in her presence.

But their mother was not passive. She discreetly supported the younger ones by transmitting the information necessary for their endeavors, teaching them innocently the geography of the *Cévennes*. Jean understood the maneuver well but did not object. His mother belonged to an ancient Huguenot family, originally from Boucoiran. Her family bond with Pastor Alméras, a refugee in Lausanne married to her cousin Gervaise de Fabre, whose family had been the lords of Montvaillant, underlined the distinction of her origins and a certain authority. Without the Revocation of the Edict of Nantes, these families would have achieved a significant degree of renown.

Indeed, many of them knew how to patiently insert themselves into the twists and turns of feudal society, to the point of becoming indispensable both to the aristocracy and to the poorest, through the rigorous application of the Christian principles that the Catholic Church had forgotten. They therefore only revitalized Christianity by undermining the foundations of the Church of Rome.

While it is necessary to pay a fervent tribute to the Catholic hermit in the medieval forests, by whom everything will be reborn one day because, thanks to him, nothing ever dies out, it is important to also understand the influence of the Reformed pastors who, with their actions, prevented the majority of the people losing their faith in the Gospels.

Whether believer or not, it cannot be denied that social evolution was linked to the institution of the Church, which while certainly important, was fragile compared to the monarchy. Therefore, it was the first target.

Furthermore, social theories were yet to be born. Only the increasingly marked affirmation of the individual was the bearer of evolution. The erasure of the institutions in the face of emerging individualism or at least the challenge to the institution is the important political act of the Reformation.

Under these conditions, Marguerite Pintard's attitude towards her youngest children could not be criticized. To the extent that they knew they were in a minority and always under threat, a consequence was the solidarity of women with men. Thus, women took on a social role that also flourished in decision-making within the community.

9

The north wind had risen, blowing away the clouds. However, the sky seemed laden with strong omens. The sounds of the gunshots had echoed as far as *La Cabanarié* : the dragoons were not far away. Jean was alarmed, immediately checking that the youngest were close to the family home. Antoine saw his mother's contrite face and the concern in her eyes. Suddenly the room seemed too dark. He had to go out. The bright sun calmed him a bit and he enjoyed walking around the property, listening, nonetheless.

Samuel was absent. His sisters were busy in the henhouse, near a building whose frame, new at the time, still exists today. Antoine checked inside but Samuel wasn't there. But he knew it was unnecessary.

His brother had left *La Cabanarié* to clean the spring that supplied them with drinking water, situated at the top of a small gulch covered with dead leaves and gloomy in all seasons. Its lack of charm underscored its usefulness because, had it not been a water catchment, no one would ever have ventured for pleasure into this damp place, inhabited by toads and traversed day and night by wild boars. The distance that separated them from the water source was short and he wondered if he would find his brother there, busy with his tasks. As he approached the spring, he called out but only received the echo of his own voice. He walked towards the rock from which the spring gushed.

He knew the place perfectly and found only silence. Worried, he ran back to the family home to report Samuel's disappearance.

Jean did not like Samuel being away from home. He suspected that he was part of a chain of contacts that sent information on where and when the devotees could meet on a pre-established date. The technique was based on the multiplicity of links that avoided placing the organizer in contact with the recipients. In this way, they protected the messengers by limiting their routes and increasing the number of relays. If that was the case, Jean and Antoine concluded that he would soon return.

The afternoon saw his anxiety grow. Samuel wasn't back home yet. Antoine was about to go out to look for his brother in a possible location when Samuel entered smiling as usual.

"But where do you come from ?" Jean asked him.

"I was not very far away," replied his brother.

"It's late," Jean continued, "you take more and more risks and so do we !"

Samuel was silent. It was true, he knew it. Jean did not insist, thus avoiding an inopportune dispute about the attitudes of the different members of the family. Each one had his own reasons, understandable to everyone else, and no opinion prevailed. Samuel's decisions were based on free-will fostered by family upbringing. No attitude was universally true ; and everyone knew it. The only point of agreement was to ensure everyone's security. That is why Jean, as the household head, reminded the youngest of his siblings that certain limits could not be exceeded, even in difficult times.

Samuel nodded.

Everyone retired to sleep only in search of rest, like someone who is hungry and eats without relish, or someone who is thirsty and drinks without quenching his thirst.

The lightness of certain words seemed to have disappeared from their vocabulary. Hunger, thirst, sleep, replaced appetite and repose.

The words used responded more and more to their basic function because emotion also faded in the face of fear. The subtleties of language disappeared in the revelation of physical needs increasingly limited by the events that unfolded around them.

How to appreciate a dish, how to express a preference or a taste when the misfortune of the times suspended the existence of both by a thread. For what purpose ? What for ? The Pintards had to focus on the Revocation, the most important issue. Antoine was trying unsuccessfully to sleep, thinking that he no longer looked at nature.

Samuel no longer saw in nature anything other than unrelated elements necessary for his activity, or obstacles to his movements and quickly fell asleep.

Jean, who had often only converted the pretty mosaics of flower-filled meadows into manorial rights, continued his book-keeping. He was the one who suffered the least and therefore, he was the strongest of all.

Antoine thought it was fine this way and that it was natural for his brother to be the head of the family. He finally fell asleep, reassured.

La Cabanarié was silent, in a setting to which it no longer belonged. It was simply a forest, a clearing, and a house. People slept inside in their respective cells. They each had a name, a goal, an action to take. The only link that united them was their civil status just as the different elements of a setting are connected by a common ownership. But family membership alone was no longer sufficient to maintain the group's cohesion. Only fear finally brought them together, in a common attitude.

In his somewhat harsh words to Samuel, Jean had shown that he understood that his family was disintegrating. The only course of action to be taken required prudence in order to protect all its members until they dispersed forever.

10

The next day was Sunday. The inability to reach the Protestant church due to closure or destruction made the day unusual for people who had established an almost functional connection between religion and this day of the week.[25]

The monitoring by priest Montbel of the attendance of the Reformed at Mass came under the strict application of the controls ordered by the Chief Steward of Languedoc. But it is true that the high administrative origin of intolerable imperatives made everyone want to contravene them. The disappearance of the link with a place of worship had consequences on the ties uniting family members.

Thus, the religious character of Sundays had been undermined by the absence of Françoise, Suzanne, and Samuel from mass. Jean's presence, irregularly accompanied by Antoine, reflected the image of a shattered family and hinted at a degree of non-conformism that was not appropriate in the *Ancien Régime*.[26] The disobedience of the siblings underscored the loss of authority of the elders over the younger ones.

Lastly, the pretexts of age or fatigue raised by Marguerite Roux, their mother, to avoid the mandatory attendance at mass made the family susceptible to lies. Moral force certainly prevailed but during this period everyone was able to lie, contravene, test the resistance of one or the other, go beyond what was acceptable within the framework of family regulations, and finally to experiment. Each one was asserting himself, more than he had ever done before. The opposition to their king, the breach of the pre-eminence of the parents or the elder brother,

---

(25) Weeks after the Revocation, Protestant churches were closed or torn down.

(26) The *Ancien Régime* (the Old Regime) is the monarchical regime which lasted until the French Revolution (1789).

the weakening of religious practice opened a window to new horizons. And the sacredness of beings and things was altered as a result.

Antoine asked himself questions and the necessary answers were part of this new horizon. And he didn't dislike what he sensed : the operation of a plantation in Saint-Christophe seemed to be the focal point of all the changes that were taking place.

Jean, for his part, discovered that questioning the hierarchy also exempted him from certain responsibilities and that his abjuration had in no way altered his business or his relationships. Rather, he was allowed to strengthen them professionally and in a friendly manner. All of this happened without the wrath of God, or the sanction of the community. Some of the fundamentals were thus shaken.

This Sunday, Antoine accompanied his brother and his mother to mass in Saint-Roman. His sister Françoise decided to join them at the last minute. Spring was certainly no stranger to the good humor that washed over the small group. They walked alongside the cart in which their mother was sitting.

The first effects of the new season on nature made them want to talk, comment and have fun. The climb to Saint-Roman used to be like the road to Damascus. That day, it was a pleasant walk to the village from where they would see the distant horizons under a great blue sky and meet everyone for a few hours. The tender green shoots of larch and chestnut trees colored the surroundings. The environment changed when they went higher-up in the valley. Not because of the effects of height, although the slope was steep, but because of the increased sunshine during the day that warmed the land and trees for longer.

Antoine, Françoise, and their mother hardly ever left *La Cabanarié*. Now they felt as if they were joining the real world. The bottom of the valley suddenly appeared to them as a prison. They had spent the winter there, claiming the discomfort of the road as an excuse not to appear in Saint-Roman and thus be dispensed from being present before a Catholic priest with a satisfied smile. Isolated from society, they had locked themselves in their own world, without any link that bound them to the community. Everyone understood then that they shared at this moment the same feeling. The worries which might have arisen were largely contained by the beneficial effects they felt immediately. They were delighted in this moment of bliss that brought them out of the bottom of the hole, also out of a virtual world shaped by custom, a long and cold winter and the permanent sharing of the Revocation as the only event.

Antoine understood that resistance to injustice, violence and arbitrariness alone could not fill a man's life. Dedicating one's existence to combat these scourges corresponded to an impoverishment due to the lack of implementation of the other senses. What he felt made him realize what he had forgotten. He remained silent to avoid disturbing his happiness and that of the others, knowing that the slightest comment could break the pleasure of the moment. Even though he was going to attend Mass, the minutes they spent together in communion with nature nevertheless represented a sufficient degree of elevation to serve as a Sunday service. The rest was a mere formality. He would have liked to explain that to them, but he didn't dare.

Saint-Roman stood out now in a blue sky, solidly glued to the top of its ridge. He understood why the monks had founded this community and realized that stationing a lone prior in this place was not necessarily a bad thing. Suddenly, the steps up to the church seemed more tolerable.

A small and plump man, the parish priest of Saint-Roman was undoubtedly a man from Gévaudan, who had been able to retire from work in the fields at a young age and been allowed to study. Only two hands and two tiny feet protruded from his cassock, which contrasted with the desire to be authoritative that came from his gestures and his voice. The desire to ensure dominance of his flock was concentrated in short, sharp, jerky nods like a rooster in the middle of its pen.

Antoine chuckled to himself and shot a mischievous look at Francoise, his sister. He understood that the bishop had done a good job of pastoral activism by sending this fanatic wrapped in a sharp accent. The amateurism shown by the Catholic church, in its eagerness to regain control of the Reformed, never ceased to amaze him. He suddenly remembered the tone and the vocabulary used by the pastors, the same gestures that accompanied their sermons and he couldn't help but see in this man's attitude a calculated and ridiculous administrative procedure. Antoine suddenly felt stronger in his convictions and his presence in the Catholic church was simply a moment in the week where he could satisfy his curiosity. The priest spoke for a long time about the misfortune and the wrath of God, but this conventional language no longer had any impact on him. He had become a spectator eager to act. In that moment, the desire for action prevailed over all other feelings.

Antoine was not a fanatic. His father had instilled in him from a very young age the need to consider with caution the rigid implementation of religious precepts like those that some members of the consistories applied against unfortunate sinners. The sanctions dispensed by the Reformed religious courts had often seemed severe to him, like for example the prohibition to dance. It alienated the most vulnerable faithful from the bosom of their young churches and comforted Catholics in their belief who proclaimed : "we dance despite the Huguenots !". He did not approve of the administration of popular justice where certain members of the community could use biblical inspiration and rigidity to establish their power over all others. They only reproduced, on a small scale, the great Episcopal courts of the Catholic Church. He felt as an outsider in meetings where the least educated in everything gave free rein to backbiting and stupidity through punishments propped up by the desire for domination and the inability to read a text with the necessary insight.

Community justice frightened him, and he would have liked the existence and development of a justice for men adapted to the changes brought about by the Reformation.

Antoine stayed away from the repressive arsenal of the religious law, as his father had done during his lifetime. He was convinced of the need to maintain a degree of elitism as a fundamental means for the implementation of safety for all. He knew very well, like all educated men of his time, that brutality had not disappeared and that the destruction of authority, even morality, would only propel the greatest number of people into uncontrolled actions motivated by envy, intolerance and violence. The work done by centuries of Catholicism could not be erased in one fell swoop by sermons or simplistic writing. He knew the usefulness of the ruling classes of the kingdom who, with their presence and emerging detachment from religious passions, prevented the situation from degenerating. Antoine thus blamed equally the priest, blinded by his fervent militancy and some members of consistories. He wished that royal decisions had never upset the order of an evolution that was nevertheless underway throughout the realm. The harshness of the Revocation edict had only created tension and favored the emergence of a radicalism leading to extreme positions on both sides and the chaos that he anticipated.

Antoine was coming of age. The ferocity of the parish priests' comments and the echoes of his religious community, the content of which he knew beforehand, now left him unsatisfied. He wanted priest Montbel to finish his service so that he could leave this Catholic Church where he had nothing more to do. However, he was apprehensive of the meetings that were surely going to be held in the square, marked by speeches that he knew too well, loaded with Protestant pessimism and alarming news that he no longer wanted to hear.

At that moment, Antoine was quitting his world ; alien to this parish, these speeches. The parish priest, brandishing his sermons like a sword, forged the conviction that nothing was going to go well and that the moral help that membership of a group provides would falter, because it could not lead to anything in this universe of opinions forged by accumulated hatred.

In the end, leaving the church seemed more pleasant than entering it. He suddenly realized the distance that separated him from events. He felt an individuality born in him that seemed hardly compatible with belonging to his lord, obedience to his king and submission to the government of his religious community. He turned to the horizon, toward the setting sun and remembered the conversation he had had with Jean about America. Seeing a small herd of goats that seemed to gaze back at him with their heads bowed, he smiled as one smiles at those he loves.

The return was made in a good mood, everyone pretending not to have lived the moments in the church. Denial of reality, even of time, took Antoine back to the legend of Sion. By going to Saint-Roman, everyone had experienced the climb from the bottom of the *La Cabanarié* valley as an aspiration towards life. Antoine had felt it despite all the injustices suffered by his family and his entire community. The exit from the abyss brought them back to reality whereas locked in their certainty and paralyzed by the injustice committed against them, they had the impression that they were surviving in the depths of the silent valley. He realized that the following days would be empty because he had almost finished his *Way of the Cross*. Penance at this point seemed like pride, a collective pride and, therefore, less susceptible to criticism, but pride nonetheless.

A few days or weeks earlier he would have felt guilty for having such thoughts but today he did not blame himself. He rejected this way of distinguishing himself from the community through accumulated suffering, the certainty of being right of being victims, of also being alone against all, even though he knew that his neighbors were in the same situation. But the difficulties in meeting people from other hamlets and the suspicion raised by the dragoons during each trip plunged them into an unbearable loneliness.

Upon his return from Saint-Roman, Antoine finally felt the moment to speak had arrived. He addressed his brother, avoiding talking about pride or making any connection between the sanctions imposed by the consistories and the sanctions that the family inflicted on itself.

"Jean, I thought of the *Compagnie de Saint-Christophe*. I want to sign a contract. That is to say …"

"That's what it's all about," replied his brother.

"Jean, this morning at church …"

"Don't say anything," interrupted his brother, "I think we all feel the same." Jean resumed with authority.

"Antoine, you're determined. You simply lack someone who will tell that to you and give you the confidence to continue the path that you are secretly contemplating. Because habit means that obedience owed to the head of the family prevents people like you from asserting their will. The events that afflict us lead me to a greater tolerance towards you. It is an opportunity. Your thoughts are no secret to me, but don't talk to me about them ; in a way I envy you because you are on the threshold of a new life that is not meant for me. You are younger and it is an opportunity for those who have ambitions, because, although they are bound by the obedience that they owe to their father or older brother, circumstances weaken this bond today. Do not tell me anything else about this morning, the Revocation, our attitude, what we shouldn't do because I have no solution or opinion that I do not immediately criticize when it comes to my mind. My attitude is the best I can do given time constraints. I envy you because if this is your plan, you will escape all these questions and fully experience what is new for people in our condition. You will not break free of the law because it is necessary, but the possibilities that the new world will give you, even if it is full of danger, will allow you to have an opinion and to express it. Because in the New World there is still nothing, and the events and the ups and downs and the misfortunes that I do not wish for you, but that you may find, are unknown. It will then be necessary to implement new means and solutions, move forward and just invent your own society ! You will continue to serve your king and the king needs new men to attend to his business. He will recognize innovations in attitudes and behavior all the more easily as they will be favorable to him and will increase his greatness. You have the ability to do so and you have my authorization."

"This is the last link that still connects you with the old world as it is sometimes called among us, among men of law, it is the world of Monsieur le Baron, of feudal homage that no longer represents much. A world of declared fidelity between men who no longer have much else to do with each other. However, this still constitutes the content of our professions and the basis of our organizations in our mountains. This is the world of our parents, and it will last a long time. I fully intend to play a role and participate in its development. Our Protestant faith is there to bear witness to this. We simply want these links to be as real as in the beginning, thanks to the Catholic church that consecrated them, but whose moral vigor has weakened. The violent questioning of the whole could one day be the result as it has already happened in the past."

Antoine was amazed at the frankness of his brother's words and willingly accepted the support of his family.

"Thank you and I assure you that I will not forget you. My absence cannot be final."

"These are the words that our mother will want to hear when you leave."

"I won't forget to say that to her," added Antoine.

"Good," concluded Jean.

11

The following days passed as usual. Antoine was anxious. He would have liked things to go faster but Jean could not reach the prosecutor of the Marquis des Vignolles, who was the only one in a position to provide information about the signing of an indentured servant contract with the *Compagnie de Saint-Christophe*. Antoine was waiting for his older brother to return. He understood what patience meant and why this quality was a virtue.

Between the disastrous events he faced and the personal and family consequences of his departure, a grey area remained that needed clarification. With the essentials defined, many details remained to be resolved. Patience was the necessary means to achieve his goal ; it was inscribed in the *Treasure of Consolations* as an indispensable virtue in the face of the afflictions that came from God.

He made efficient use of this long wait by reading and re-reading the passages devoted to *patience* in order to find the true meaning of the word. This quality could not be reduced to submission alone. It also had to be seen as the mental preparation for his inner development. Such a discovery satisfied him and reinforced his conviction that this path was the correct one ; a path made of experiments where old and immutable solutions became obsolete, a new path of endeavors and reflections where everything remained to be invented. He felt that in this emerging world the need to build would require much patience but that this patience would no longer be exercised in fatalism. He thought fervently of that passage in the *Treasure of Consolations* where God, manifesting his substance, included the Creator, the Master, the Father and the King. He now knew that he would not go alone on his American adventure. He would take with him the means necessary for his success, the only ones he knew thus far.

Disturbing news circulated while Antoine was still waiting for information on life in the American colonies. The opposition between two ongoing events underscored the state of mind he was in. On the one hand, he knew that he was restricted in his actions, victim of the Revocation, subject to the authorities, just like his parents or neighbors; on the other hand, in this feverish period of waiting, he found himself in charge of his own destiny, possessing the power to change his life. This realization filled him with joy. He had finally reached a state of mind that he had not known before, a state of mind that he had noticed in certain merchants of Anduze or Saint-Jean at the annual fairs. Their confidence, their direct and firm bartering had always surprised and delighted him. He couldn't help but compare them to the permanently cautious and respectful attitude of his grandfather, father, and brother. These differences took on a new meaning now, and the desire to act, to react, to move forward with freedom, finally formed, in his eyes, the certainty that he had lacked for so long : the impatience that he felt was the counterpart of action. He assessed the magnitude of the task in a society that would no longer be frozen. Here, in France, he could not act. There, in the New World, he knew that novelty would give birth to solutions. He understood during this long wait that the key was to increase the virtue of prudence to control the impatience that took hold of him.

The days that followed were dedicated to his domestic activities and to juggling between virtues that were complementary rather than mutually exclusive. These intellectual games were familiar to him. Antoine knew that he was well-equipped intellectually and would have liked to put his knowledge to use for the justice of men. He regretted the difficulties of the time because his departure compromised his projects. He reassured himself by thinking that the teachings received would be useful for much more.

Antoine found out a few days later that the *Compagnie de Saint-Christophe* no longer existed. The king had put an end to the development of the island by the aristocracy. In fact, their inability to meet the financial goals he had assigned them had once again led him to take matters into his own hands.

The island of Saint-Christophe was now attached to the royal domain. The introduction of sugar cane, which was in the process of supplanting tobacco, required many skilled hands and people of good health and good character. The latter could aspire to a comfortable life to the extent that they agreed to abide by the rules decreed by the ordinances of Colbert, Controller-General of Finances, and his nephew Senneçay, particularly with regard to the unique exercise of Catholic worship. One king, one law, one faith.

"The contracting conditions for emigration are regulated by the notaries of La Rochelle," announced Jean, who had the information from the *Bayle*, the manager of the Marquis des Vignolles. "That's all we know", he added.

"Then I'll go to La Rochelle," exclaimed Antoine. 'I can't wait to learn more, but it's a long journey".

"I will do everything in my power to help you. But you are right ; it is a long and dangerous journey. I suggest you take some time to think it over."

"I've been thinking about this trip for weeks," added Antoine. "It is time to decide."

Silence fell in the family home. The silence that lingers, the silence as an indispensable airlock between the valley of family memories and the animated shores of the province of Aunis.[27]

"I'm going."

Jean placed a hand on his shoulder. They stayed like that without a word for long seconds.

"What is the best way ?" asked Antoine. "Through Saint-Flour or Languedoc ?"

He did not wait for an answer from his older brother and continued :

"I thought that the road through Toulouse was safer than that of Gévaudan and all the surrounding Catholic lands. If necessary, it will be easier to find help among the Reformed in Languedoc than among the Papists of Auvergne."[28]

Jean suddenly appreciated his younger brother's decision-making and realized that he had reflected on the matter, a guarantee of his new autonomy. He was satisfied and reassured at the same time.

"Well thought through !"

Marguerite Roux, their mother, had been silent, sitting by the fireplace. She hadn't missed any of the conversation and nodded silently. The boys had got it right. Her presence had not bothered them because, in addition to the obedience they owed to their mother, it

---

(27) Aunis is an old province of France along the shore of the Atlantic Ocean whose main city was La Rochelle.

(28) Auvergne is an old province of France.

prevented them from resuming the discussion in the hours and days that followed with new and inappropriate words. It suited them that way.

It was Antoine's decision and the silence of all of them would put a final stamp and family seal that could only support him in his future endeavors.

Antoine left *La Cabanarié* in early September 1687.

Map of Languedoc.

12

The ascent from *La Cabanarié* was made in the direction of the Baume valley located on the other side of the ridge. The day was shaping up to be hot. The chestnut grove was dry and Antoine couldn't help but wish for a little rain to give the fruits of the trees that were the *Cévennes'* bread a good size.

The serrated leaves crunched under foot in the undergrowth, the leaves of yesterday and today, old leaves, all mingled while awaiting their final union with the humus that smelled so good in the autumn showers. In some places, a blackish furrow divided the uneven carpet, marking the passage of a wild boar in search of last year's chestnuts. Blackened branches covered with still tender green moss sometimes crossed the tracks left by the boar, indicating the depth of the excavation made by its long hard snout.

Antoine, turning around, realized that he too had left his footprints on the vegetation cover, tracks that were shallower and less black, more difficult to detect. Footprints of a man that the breeze would carry away and that a little rain would erase completely. His passage through the valley floor would leave memories only among his own people. He had built nothing so far and had only maintained the heritage of his parents.

His departure would not change the fate of the place that might one day return to its solitude. He was the first of its occupants to leave. He had a feeling there would be more. After reaching the top, he crossed the Baume valley and greeted in passing tenant farmers, his distant relatives from this neighboring valley. The blood ties facilitated the analysis of events, enabled him to avoid gossip by retaining only the essentials to which they adhered and excluding the sentimentality that leads to despair.

The Exile Pass had not yet acquired its name nor the mystery that still surrounds its origins today, but it is a safe bet that Antoine had to hurry as would others, more and more numerous in later years. They would come from the farmhouses beyond *Saint-Roman*, terrified by the barbarism of their king, blackened with the ashes and smoke of the great burning of the *Cévennes*, thus adding with their resistance one more tier to the King's crown, that of impotence.

Crossing the pass, Antoine took the gorge towards *Saint-Jean*. The French Valley fell behind him along with its legend of the battles fought by the Franks against the Saracens eight centuries earlier. The Catholic church of Moissac, transformed into a Protestant church, was erected in ancient times to commemorate the victory of the Christian knights over the Mohammedan horsemen. This epic continued to be the subject of conversations by the fire in the folds of the valley where the country houses were harmoniously dispersed, surrounded by their stone terraces like the immense steps of a staircase to the Almighty God.

The *Gardon* Country now spread out before his eyes. The Bermond d'Anduze family had been their lords, until the crusade against the Albigenses. [29] All that remained of their feudal magnificence were the watch towers visible in the distance atop the ridges overlooking the Gardon River. They guarded the borders of this *seigneury*, the remains of which genuine and fake nobles had divided amongst themselves. The immensity of the fields, cultivated in terraces, reminded him that this country was a place of settlers brought, centuries ago, by Benedictine monks from *Saint-Gilles* [30] as a new medieval frontier.

The considerable efforts made by all to make the country inhabitable were visible on all sides, the testimony of a people on the move who could never avoid injury and bloodshed.

Saint-Jean stretched pleasantly along the Gardon river at the bottom of the valley, joining its tributaries downstream, it would gather over and over the same information and the same dramas until it merged

---

(29) The Albigenses (Cathars) were followers of an unorthodox Christianity that thrived in Western Europe and in Languedoc (France) in the 11th century. The Albigensian Crusade led to the persecution of Cathars by the Catholic Church and to the end of the quasi-independence of Languedoc in the 13th century by Philippe le Hardi, King of France.

(30) Saint-Gilles is a monastery in the South of France known for the beauty of its church's tympanum duplicated by Andrew Carnegie, " the richest man in the world " on a scale 1:1 and installed in the Museum he founded in Pittsburgh (Pennsylvania). During the Middle-Ages, the Saint-Gilles pilgrimage was as famous as Santiago de Compostela's.

into the Rhone that also flowed through Geneva, the capital of the Refuge.

The same geography, the same events that marked the fate of the Protestants, he thought. He understood that all this could only end in the immensity of the all-engulfing sea.

He crossed *Saint-Jean*, occupied by dragoons with eyes swollen from exhaustion and past drunkenness. He felt like a settler at that moment and saw nothing but the ocean, in the blue of the sky and the soldiers' eyes.

13

Antoine reached the Anduze gorge without incident and then headed on to *Saint-Hippolyte* after a further day's march in the Bailiwick of Sauve. His passage was uneventful and nothing could hinder his progress as he took the royal road out of town, in the direction of Montpellier. He discovered the great scrubland of Pompignan bathed in light with its sparse kermes oak thickets which creaked in the sun. Antoine had his back turned to the mountains. He was heading towards the southwest taking a U turn, a necessary route through that configuration of places buttressed by the *Cévennes Mountains*. This mountain ledge sealed the definitive break with his country and, therefore, his pace had to slow down to give a mandatory and fraternal greeting to these mountains.

"Stop right there !" suddenly cried a man's loud voice with a foreign accent.

Antoine, awakened from his reverie, stopped short.

"Where are you going ?"

"I'm going to Montpellier," replied Antoine to the police officer.

"Do you have permission to travel ?" Antoine handed his pass to the sergeant. The latter frowned as he examined the document, then added

"Are you from the mountains ?"

"Yes," answered Antoine.

"And what are you going to do in Montpellier ?"

"I have to meet Monsieur de Payen, counsel at the Court of Aid."[31]

"You Protestants always know someone who can be useful to you for something ... And what exactly is this something ?" Antoine was amazed that the sergeant could so quickly distinguish between a Catholic and a Reformed, but this was not the time for analysis.

---
(31) The Court of Tax Appeal.

"Monsieur de Payen is a friend of my family and will undoubtedly be of some use to me in my business."

"You didn't answer me, what is your business ?"

"To serve my king," replied Antoine, emboldened.

"You would serve him much better if you stopped all your cruelties there !"

"What are you talking about, sir ?" asked Antoine, who didn't understand.

"Not Sir, Sergeant ! Of the abuses that you Protestants commit every day, of the murderous ambushes against the dragoons, of the murders, of the plots you have with foreign powers, of the prohibitions that you transgress, of the misfortunes that you impose on everyone."

"I haven't heard anything like that so far, Sergeant, and yet I come from there. I want to go to Montpellier. What should I do ?"

"And how do you plan to serve our king in Montpellier ?"

"I have to meet with Monsieur de Payen to obtain an additional pass from the stewardship to continue my journey to La Rochelle."

"And why do it ?" persisted the sergeant.

"To go to the American islands," said Antoine.

"To preach the lies of your religion ?" The sergeant added.

"Work on the development of *Saint-Christophe*," Antoine corrected.

"I hope you don't ever come back. The kingdom doesn't need you now or ever."

"Sergeant, I will serve my king with as much dedication as you do now, and only he will decide my return as he decides everything. Our destiny is in his hands and when we act for better or for worse, we act for or against him. That's all I know and it's worth all the passes. The conduct of each person can only be dictated by the will to serve him and to serve him well. I know that the king needs competent people to carry out his business. I give myself to his service."

The sergeant was dumbfounded by this assurance, and the clarity of the words Antoine spoke made him think. Certainly, these presumptuous Reformed are as dangerous as they say everywhere, reasoning and misleading ! he thought.

"Get back on your way !" He snapped at Antoine.

They parted quickly, the sergeant grumbling under his breath at the Protestants. His subordinates, who had been silent during the interrogation, were now laughing.

Antoine had just left the bastion of the *Cévennes* and the dwarf oaks easily exposed him, especially since he would now have to walk two whole days through dusty vegetation.

The rest of the journey to Montpellier was uneventful. In other seasons, this truly wild place must have been beautiful, Antoine throught as he examined the spire of *Pic Saint Loup* that rose in front of him, like a tidal wave, a relic of the geological surge that created the Alps and the Pyrenees. Antoine at that moment would have liked for an identical wave to shake the entire Languedoc again and more *Pic Saint Loups* to emerge from the immense scrubland, carrying on their summits crenellated white heavenly cities like the fortress of Montferrand, their capital in the sky.[32]

> The Almighty will rise
> The weak will be oppressed,
> And in his greatest anguish,
> It will serve as a fortress.
>
> Psalms of David 9

This vision finally saddened him because he realized that it had hitherto corresponded to the reality of the strongholds reserved for Protestants by the Edict of Nantes for their protection. The Revocation had removed from such cities their function of stronghold.[33] The hilly terrain had also done its job, and between the edict of tolerance signed in 1598 and its revocation in 1685, the topography had been shaped like sand on the beach after waves. Only small mounds remained for still some time, which the king's last centralizing blows would soon crush.

The remains of the treaty were not found at Aigues-Mortes whose architect had been Saint Louis. [34] There too, Antoine thought, time had served its function. Between the father of the Crusaders and his very Catholic descendant, only silhouettes remained. But the wind of history would end up reducing them to twilight colors, until the

---

(32) Montferrand was an important castle built during the Middle-Ages on a rocky outcrop about 20 kilometres north of Montpellier. The castle is ruined now.

(33) The Edict of Nantes (1598) had confirmed many cities as safety places for Protestants in order to stop Catholic riots. As of 1622 Aigues-Mortes was no longer one of them.

(34) Saint Louis, king of France, sailed from Aigues-Mortes when leading the 8th Crusade (other historians say 7th) in 1270 against the Hafsid dynasty of Berber descent in Tunisia. John Locke visited Aigues-Mortes on Tuesday 24 March 1676 and depicted it with care and interest.

vermilion of the setting sun that sets the sky on fire, announcing a day of north wind, erased them forever.

Antoine fell asleep in a limestone fold of a great white rock, lying there for all eternity like another piece of hard foam among all the others with which the scrubland was strewn. Montferrand disappeared at the peak of the *Pic Saint Loup* erected there, like a pike in the fiery light.

The Tide.

14

The next day, approaching Montpellier, Antoine passed through the sleepy village of Assas and saw the shadow of the castle of Castries in the distance which John Locke had nicely depicted on Tuesday 26 March 1676. He had decided to leave very early to enter the former seigneury of the kings of Mallorca at a reasonable hour, which would allow him to find his way to the Hotel de Payen. Assas was a pretty village, round and tucked up like a chestnut boletus, perched on an elegantly designed promontory, and surrounded by full-grown trees whose beautiful vivid green stood out in the Mediterranean setting.

This name was familiar to him. Assas was a family of old nobility, who in the fourteenth century had left, for unknown reasons, their historical area of influence and their presence at the court of William of Montpellier. They had settled in the barony of Hierle at Le Vigan.

The priests, knowledgeable in all matters, postulated that this family could have been hostile and physically threatening towards the Bishop of Maguelone, who was the great dominant lord of Montpellier. The hypothesis had its coherence since the Assas had spread into younger branches that were, for the most part, endowed with small manors in the *Cévennes*, devoid of judicial courts and guilty of the worst attitudes and provocations likely to revive a forgotten past. Irreligious behavior often highlighted the independence of nobles. The Assas had probably not been an exception and the lord of Marcassargues, whom Antoine had approached in *Saint-Jean*, had given him the impression of being an angry man, whose Huguenot faith came after his patrimonial ambitions.

Antoine, through these memories lamented the lack of consistency of the nobles in their adherence to the Reformed Church. It was conceivable that such an attitude was based both on the advantages to be derived from adhering to Calvinistic ideas and the disadvantages occasioned by direct opposition to the king. Along the way, he couldn't help but think that the nobles, the last to enter the Roman Catholic Church, might also be the last to leave.

The tide, always, turns.

The towers of Montpellier appeared in the distance, their battlements mingling with the spires of the churches of *Saint Pierre* and *Notre Dame des Tables*. The commercial city drew closer, bringing the echoes of its activity to the suburbs, as it had always carried out its trade far and wide by mixing its accent with those of the men of Jacques Coeur, [35] the king's financier in the 15th century, as well as those of Jews and Moors, Protestants and slaves.

Montpellier is not a port and yet, at that time, its wealth was built on the sea. Montpellier is not a Roman city ; it was founded only around the year 1000. Montpellier is a feudal lake city, standing on large stilts that float on ponds with geometric shapes and still waters bordered by foam that shines in the sun which, at sunset, transforms salt into gold.

Antoine entered the city where the sky is blue and where the women have deep black eyes. This mosaic of colors and riches surprised him. He quickened his pace and walked without looking around through the vast confusion of the markets, towards the Hotel de Payen. He couldn't help but think about the little provincial piece of land that he had just left. The vast white stone facades gleamed in the sun that lowered toward the horizon. He recalled other commercial facades that marked the prosperity of *Saint-Jean* and *Lassalle* and noted that the aspirations of some are sometimes reflected in the wealth of others. It is fortunate that our Lord, he thought, put sometimes so much distance between his sheep that he often prevents the wolf of fortune and envy from absorbing them all to the point of making the world unbearable.

Antoine finally arrived at the Hôtel de Payen which, despite its modest architecture, hid treasures of comfort.

He fell asleep thinking about the soft and fragile light that would be surely illuminating his family table at this moment of communion while, mired in an uproar that had not yet ended, he struggled to focus for his evening prayer which he sent to heaven, piously, like the last link that would unite those above with those below across the stars.

---

(35) Jacques Cœur (1395-1456) was a merchant born in Bourges (France) who established himself at Montpellier and initiated regular trade routes between France and the Levant (Near East). There, he began gigantic operations that made him illustrious among the European financiers.

15

He spent the morning at the Hôtel de Payen waiting behind the stained-glass windows whose colors rippled in the irregularity of their material.

Brought by the Crusaders to the coast of Provence, like black holy women stranded a few centuries earlier on a beach in the Camargue, these glassed windows had made the fortune of some of the Languedoc nobility, previously ruined by successive wars. The king, in his great wisdom, had elevated the profession of glazier to the rank of art, thus allowing the nobles to become artists and not mere craftsmen, while maintaining their rank.[36]

As glassmaking was not a trade, some thirty glassmakers appeared in Languedoc armed only with their talent and their will to work and earn money, thus chasing the drafts in their castles and giving a new shine to their crests.

Antoine listened enthusiastically to Jean de Payen, inspired by the sight of a horse-drawn carriage bearing the Girard family's arms, crossing the alley.

In secret, he concluded that kings, unmistakably, had great power to deal with situations without altering the rules and that the magnifying glass effect should be constantly applied to analyze the designs of our majesties.

He shared his thoughts with Monsieur de Payen, who appreciated them.

Antoine, flattered, embarked on the natural downward slope that leads to self-satisfaction.

---

(36) In France, noblemen lost their rank when entering business or becoming craftsmen. In order to hold their rank, the king decided that glassmaking was an art and not a craft Thus, the noble Crusaders who returned ruined by the expenses of the crusades became glassmakers without losing their privileges.

He couldn't help but think back on the gloomy and sometimes stubborn attitude of the Assas. Realizing his vanity, he began to have doubts about the proper behavior to adopt in a city, in a world in which he did not know the rules. He thought it best to resume his trip to the west coast of France in the next few days.

16

The following days were spent meeting important people in the city. The gentlemen of the *Cour des Aides de Montpellier*, graduates or doctors in law, poorly concealed their desire for social recognition behind their showy clothes and hats that artificially made them appear important. Many of them moderately demonstrated their Huguenot faith, listening to Antoine's projects and their connection with events taking place on the heights of the province. Antoine was not fooled. He sensed the lukewarm nature of the comments owing to the proximity of the General stewardship of Languedoc, which was located near the *Place de la Canourgue*, the center of the aristocratic and judicial life of the city, standing on its promontory wrapped in a temperate climate. The serious and religious exchanges that he had listened to for years disappeared in an unctuous tone devoid of spontaneity. This suavity worried him. He waited for a brotherly blessing as he recounted his journey, but the words, albeit full of encouragement as addressed by his brothers in faith, sounded like an extremely listless Last Sacrament on the eve of his departure.

The last night he devoted largely to after-dinner discussions with Monsieur de Payen's friends in the presence of their ladies. His rustic and rough attire did not harmonize with the refined clothes which this already established bourgeoisie and, in certain cases, aspiring nobility, flaunted as the steps that they had already climbed to reach the much-desired heights. Antoine secretly noted the divergences in all their objectives. He perceived the abyss that could separate the discussions and attitudes expressed by the notables and nobles from the *Cévennes* and the way they exercised their social function as they moved to Montpellier.

At the foot of the *Cévennes* mountains stretched the dry and thorny thicket that held in its claws the ceremonial ribbons of the people seated in front of him. Such ribbons would never adorn the button holes of his father or his brother, nor those of his religious brothers in a protective overarching canvas covering the entire Languedoc.

The end of the evening passed in economic comments dealing with the tobacco industry that these gentlemen had recently discovered and whose unequaled benefits had reintroduced Antoine into the heart of the general discussion. Those who cited figures drawn from the reports commissioned by the king were filled with pride as they compared them with economic data from the businesses of the merchants of the eastern Languedoc capital. Antoine, initially bored, ended up taking an interest in the discussion. His eagerness to understand, to focus on ambitions and goals, aroused their curiosity, to the point that some members of the friendly meeting openly questioned the strong religious views that they sensed in the rigor of Antoine's clothing and speech.

He did not want to expand into this area, nor did he want to start a discussion on the topic. Monsieur de Payen understood this and often came to his aid, pretending to be interested in a fragment of the sentence thrown by his colleague like a hook that Antoine did not want to bite on. He had abjured and was officially no longer a Protestant. His faith vibrated secretly in the ambitious projects that he wanted to carry out on the shores of the West Indies. His new ventures blossomed into a religious dream that he could not as yet clearly envisage.

However, there was no stopping the enthusiastic commentators. Antoine surprised them, by slipping into a language bordering on ungodliness. They suggested to Antoine, all the difficulty that well-born souls could encounter, given the affirmations of the Catholic Church. The discourse was to quickly fall in line with the protestant questioning of purgatory with the nuance that the demonstration was fully revealed in nascent disbelief.[37] Antoine understood that the

---

(37) "20th May 1676 : Mr. Bertheau told me that there was little piety or religion about their people …". John Lough, ed : *Locke's* travels 1675-1679 ; Cambridge, 1953, 28, 41. This note is quoted by Philip Benedict in *The Huguenot* Population of France 1600-1685 : The Demographic Fate and Customs of a Religious *Minority* ; American Philosophical Society, Philadelphia, 1991, p.2. Locked spent three years and a half travelling in France. He sojourned 18 months in the city of Montpellier. Another entry of February 1676 notes that the Huguenots " and the papist laity live friendly enough in these parts ".

John Locke's travels have been translated and annotated in French by Guy Boisson and Marie Rivet. *Carnet de Voyages à Montpellier et dans le sud de la France* 1676-1679, Les Presses du Languedoc 2005.

evening would be long : his status as guest prevented him from retiring early.

After returning to the Hôtel de Payen, he fell asleep without having participated, for the first time ever, in universal prayer, with his brothers on the summits.

17

Antoine left the Hôtel de Payen the next day, after warmly thanking his hosts. Their wishes for success would accompany him in his new life. He held tight the precious passport to leave the province that Monsieur de Payen's friends had obtained for him from the authorities of the administration. In the heart of the mercantile city, Antoine crossed alleys and squares full of food and provisions displayed in makeshift stalls where abundance competed with a variety of perfumes and smells.

The continuous stream of ordinary people, dressed in different shades of clay colors, rose and fell through the alleys of the old town, as if fed by a giant and invisible water wheel. This uniform current of earthen hues was punctuated by successive bursts of deep black from the cassocks of the Catholic priests who had invaded the city again. The soft creak of the waxed and colored sedan chairs announced arms wrapped in summer damasks and hands placed with sensuality above the carriage door, crowned at the wrists with light embroidery in the form of dazzling lace.

Arriving in front of the old Guilhem Palace, Antoine made out in the midst of the assembled crowd, three men dressed in white, heads wrapped in brightly colored scarves, their ebony hands like the figures of the three wise men.

As he approached the group, he discovered that the three men were barefoot. Their dark eyes did not seek to avoid the gaze of the others, which seemed to be acceptable those who were staring at them. This spectacle aroused Antoine's curiosity. His amazement certainly showed, since someone said to him.

"Slaves, sir, that's all !"

"But I thought this practice was gone."

"Not quite, because of the trade." Faced with Antoine's questioning expression, the man explained :

"The Turks make our seas unsafe and the taking as hostages of our sailors to Algiers or Tripoli needs the intervention of the king and of the Catholic Church to pay for their release."

"And when will all this end ?"

"When the king's fleet has control of the coasts and the high seas and our sailors are no longer kept in barbaric slavery."

"Will that ever happen ?" Antoine asked him.

"In any case, I believe that the Ministry of the Navy is doing everything to achieve this and that the development of the French Galley Corps in Marseille provides for this undertaking. It is also said that more and more Protestants will have their feet in the sea !" Antoine didn't answer, guessing the danger. He broke away from the group, hastily saying goodbye.

He left Montpellier. The people of the city, unaware of the conditions which had forced his departure, were far from the concerns of the people of the *Cévennes*. Although he knew of the important events for the Reformation that had taken place in the Languedoc capital, it was difficult for him to compare the causes of the actions of the Reformed here with those of Saint-Jean and its surroundings. The conditions necessary for an action full of purity, and perhaps naivety, he suddenly thought, were inconceivable in the midst of a parade of lawyers, merchants and marquises, particularly given that the last Protestant Church had been torn down in 1682.

Suddenly he was glad to leave the city, in search of solitude again among the rocks, as white as foam, warmed by the daytime sun, dotting the immense thicket, in which he would huddle at dusk.

18

Antoine's walk to the village of Fabrègues went smoothly. Monsieur de Payen had a residence in the parish. So, he had taken it upon himself, in case of difficulty, to show Antoine the path that led to Aniane along the Cournonterral mule trail. From there, he assured him, it would be easy to take the road to *Vieille-Toulouse* and reach the judicial capital of the Languedoc. This route, shorter than the passage through the city of Carcassonne, went through villages totally on the Reformation side. There it would be possible for him to receive help and assistance from Protestants and new Catholics who maintained very strong ties with their former religion. Antoine was not afraid of the police with his passport, but he preferred to travel on Huguenot land rather than risk having to endure unpleasant allusions to his previous state or harassment from vindictive or suspicious people. He enjoyed crossing unknown lands, swept by winds whose names he did not know, inhabited by people with the same accent but rolling their r's. He was curious about these lands, which were not so alien to him, populated by people who resembled him, whose language and customs were close to those he knew. He walked with a firm step enjoying, with all his senses, the countryside and the busy traffic of the surrounding villages. Antoine had discovered for the first time an important route between two great cities.

Muleteers, mail trunks, travelers on foot : he was stunned by all the encounters, the unfamiliar faces, the carriages and their postilions, the different outfits and garments, the packages of goods overflowing from the too tight straps. He saw the entire Languedoc pass by, every day. That name suddenly took shape, in front of him, through the wide variety of vehicles transporting a working population. He felt, with regret, a stranger in all these endeavors and understood that until today he had also been a stranger in his own province. He discovered unsuspected aspects of it even as he was leaving it. He thought that traveling should be recommended for young people, as it gave peace of mind and a lot of satisfaction. As he progressed, Antoine sometimes saw names of places on the road signs that seemed familiar to him, followed by the advertisement for inns that took over the names such as *Saint-Guilhem, Gellone,* or even *Saint-Pons.*[38] Antoine noted that all these destinations were linked to the religious history of the region and that it would be so until he reached La Rochelle. Such a strong trace of religion did not displease him and his journey turned into a beautiful procession on the way of the cross. Each town he passed through corresponded to a station and the scenes he could see reminded him of how men are sinners. The concentration of goods on a major road attracted greed and robberies were daily. The simplicity of the manners of the local people, who lived poorly in the depths of their beech forests on the slopes of the *Espinouse*, contrasted with the good looks of the mule leaders and their employees in elegantly knotted red scarves, and wide-brimmed black hats. Their gold earrings sparkled in the sun. They emitted blinding rays of light at intervals, adding sparkles to the silver reflections of the chiseled blinkers that their animals wore attached to their eyes roving shop signs, making it easy to identify the leader and the owner of the convoys.

Some of them, of noble origin but having lost their rank, displayed their coats of arms gilded by road money. Others, of obscure origin, highlighted their past in an ostentatious way that did not fool anyone. The last, philosophers or *bon vivants,* underlined with their mule plates their limited aims in life : "Love makes time pass - time makes love pass". They all yelled at each other, made fun of each other, laughed at each other. Antoine couldn't help but think of the scene from the first of David's Psalms :

> Blessed is the one who does not walk in step with the wicked
> or stand in the way that sinners take
> Or sit in the company of mockers,
> But whose delight is in the law of the Lord,
> and who meditates on his law, day and night

---

[38] John Locke visited the bishopric of Saint-Pons on Monday 1st March 1677 whose inhabitants living in the surrounding valleys were protestants.

Antoine's memory was full of verses, their rhymes and stanzas. He knew entire pages of them and the music that accompanied them. Each stage and each stop were an opportunity to recall a passage from the Psalms of David that the pastors taught their children and families sang together. Everything was seriousness, the fight against sin and the wrath of the Eternal. The violence of words and situations did not appear to them in their physical, carnal reality. It was a sky full of principles that collided, tore apart and ended up destroying evil. The fight had to be led by the systematic application of the rules and precepts that these verses conveyed, even if in the process it meant breaking some skulls that represented only error and lies. The force of the words and the simplicity of the musical accompaniments could make the exercise of this art as terrifying as a primitive universe. And there was in the Psalms an obvious connection to a failed beginning of the world ; its renovation could not be accomplished without an inner work on oneself prior to the realization of the eternal city.

Antoine traversed lands that had been Christianized a long time ago, whose dense monastic life had quickly plunged into selfish *deviationism* by acquiring feudal rights or granting loans on pledge.

He knew that such behavior was the cause of the Reformation and he measured the consequences by contact with these busy populations, totally devoted to their trade. Greed was only a consequence of more developed economic activity than in the *Cévennes*. He would have liked, despite exhaustion, to get close to the people on the peaks whose poverty would remind him of his parents. The complexity of the enterprise made him feel dissuaded, all the more so since, as he got closer to the mountains, he was told, he would only encounter a population, very often without a Catholic priest or Protestant pastor, uneducated and abandoned to their fate in the absence of religion, eager to live in solitudes still snowy in the month of May.

Antoine continued the road to *Vieille-Toulouse*, accompanied by psalms in fortuitous encounters and the chaos of the road, amid the waves of vehicles and travelers that connected the two provincial capitals.

As he approached *Toulouse*, he crossed the Guyenne convict's chain gang that was headed towards the sea in Marseilles and which had made him look down.

Antoine entered the city of Parliament, already beautiful and imposing, to which the works in progress, excavating and removing the surrounding countryside, were destined to bring opulence and extraordinary fecundity. The sun fell on the pink brick facades, inlaid, molded, ribbed, highlighted with architectural reliefs and topped with chimneys that accentuated the beauty of the decoration. The great avenues traced by the pencils of the artisans hired by the City Council, promised a future full of promise and sensuality. The city of Law, Antoine thought, would become the city of pleasures at one of the gates of the province while the *Pont-Saint-Esprit* and its centuries-old hospital work, at the other end of the province, would keep alive the memory of the distant east and a Jerusalem overflowing with charity.

Antoine fell asleep thinking of his loved ones, of the protection of the Lord that he had felt along the way and also of the heavenly city that he imagined, in line with the haughty facades, erected in the sky of Toulouse as a reminder of the Law.

19

Antoine stayed two days in Toulouse. He was thus able to freely roam about the *Place du Capitole* and the adjacent streets, where he saw great commercial, artisan and judicial activity.

Appreciating the wealth and the bustle of the city, he detected in this congestion the gap that separated the educated and worthy souls of his poor *Cévennes*, from the assemblies of the people of the capital of Languedoc. He felt all the misunderstanding that the people of the mountains had harbored until then, seeking in their distant capital the aid Toulouse was not prepared to give. Here, it was all business and services, the writing of deeds that were advertised on the many plaques of lawyers. Payments and collections were made in the street itself!

Toulouse was the judicial capital of the province whose members of Parliament could sometimes oppose the Absolute King's edits in conflict with the Romanist law of Languedoc. Montpellier contributed to the administrative management through the Stewardship and the Court of Aid and Auditors. Toulouse was bigger, more sumptuous, and more solemn. The complexity of life in the big city, he thought, especially when it is the judicial and political link in the chain of the kingdom, distanced them all from the purely spiritual concerns to which he had so far dedicated his existence. His practice in the field of law had only served to consolidate an established order, an organization of society where hierarchy prevailed over all other considerations, the king being chosen by God. The observation of his compatriots in Toulouse returned him to a horizontal world where the notary and the lawyer forged regular links with artisan and merchants, which went beyond the signing of marriage contracts or the establishment of wills. The mutual trust in this social bond suggested habits, a certain degree of familiarity. The discussions and transactions were marked by a certain levity, and the absence of solemnity in the moment of closing the deal opened the way to a world of abundance and competition. Toulouse was indeed a capital entirely dedicated to its trade that had taken over the quays of the Garonne. The brown canvases that covered the merchandise mixed visually with the muddy, almost dirty, water of the river. A river that had been, at its source, transparent and crystalline.

In this city, full of life and exchanges, Antoine lost his way. He found nothing of the pride, the reserve, of those in the mountains, of those who had forged his education. The freedom and recklessness he discerned behind all this coming and going transported him to a whole new world, made of calculation, anticipation and speculation.

Whereas he had always lived in a rural society, preoccupied with the uncertainties of the climate and only considering the future to fear it, he now discovered that the future could be counted in joyous arithmetic by rubbing hands, sometimes even forgetting to shake hands. Lawyers, at times, had to intervene between people with ferocious appetites and solve financial crises that for Antoine were similar to crises of faith. Finally, this world was alien to him, not because he rejected enrichment - Antoine had plenty of ambitions of wealth - but because the accumulation of fortunes could be detrimental to religious rules. The powers of evil could only be secret agents, offering their covert services at the gates of the city markets, invisible in an infernal subcontracting.

All this reminded him of the villages he crossed on the way to *Toulouse*, where opportunism and petty theft was rife, perpetrated by a population which counted among the most deprived people of Languedoc. The trips to the places of trade corresponded to an identical search and the degree of morality necessary to access wealth was the variable. Antoine judged such behavior harshly and saw in it only greed. For him, petty theft could not be opposed to fraud as one was only the offspring of the other. He reassured himself on the basis of the education and moral principles transmitted by his parents and *Cévennes* pastors. And he suddenly understood that the rules he had been taught could only flourish in a new world where rigor and virtue, obedience to the established order, and responsibility would have the force of law.

Antoine left the *Marché des Minimes* convinced that the bright future he envisioned through the Psalms would only be built on virgin land, free of ancient foundations. Antoine needed purity and it was with a joyful heart that he left Toulouse, thinking of the Benedictine monks who had once spread out over the Languedoc to build their order, as monuments to "the glory of the Lord".

The excise office of the city receded behind him, marking with its ugly limits the entrance to the mercantile quarter enveloped in a tumult of carts and animals that would always remind him of the dark designs of its inhabitants leaning over their accounting books.

20

The river was clear and transparent. All was calm and quiet in the fields tended with care by the peasants. The vineyards extended in a gentle slope until they met the waters that flowed, crystalline, at their feet. The sun-drenched bunches of fruit heralded a happy and bountiful harvest. The meadows, warmed by the late summer sun, offered glimpse, through the tall grass, of a second healthy cut that in some places accentuated the absence of grazing animals. This variation, made by the tenants according to the qualities of the plots, formed a harmonious chessboard, underpinned by the property deeds. Antoine noted the importance of tenure. He thought about the small size of the Cevennes parcels of land, which was reflected in the thickness of the county registers.

These Old Regime tax records, which were kept throughout Languedoc, were supposed to make surveys of the agricultural production in each parish and were used to assess taxes. And they swelled like the bunches of grapes in September during the revisions, witnesses of the successive divisions made within families. Only the increase in size of properties through the grouping of plots reduced the importance of these records, like a deep breath of air.

Antoine had often looked at the maintenance of the Moissac parish register and had even once participated in its updating, helping the surveyors commissioned by the Languedoc Stewardship. In these documents, the whole life of the community was detailed. Churchmen attached great importance to these tax collection records which were also the source of their income, but the advance of Reformation ideas had led Protestants from the beginning to oppose tithing.

Antoine, always involved in the resolution of appraisal disputes, a source of difficulties between relatives or neighbors, saw similarities in these geometric drawings, with other figures drawn in Palestine where the Old Testament reflected the ancient echo of Israel.

The evocation of the Holy Land made the road tremble under his feet. He knew that from now on, the land being the only wealth, he would not resist dividing virgin spaces like a restart of a biblical cadaster[39] where he would establish his City of Joy.

---

[39] N of T : A cadaster is an official register showing ownership, boundaries and value of real property in a district, for taxation purposes.

21

Antoine had gone out early in the morning crossing the countryside still full of promises of crops to be harvested. The poplars cast their cool shadows which dotted the path with the outlines of their leaves, shimmering in the light breeze of the rising heat. The air smelled good. The pack beasts were all at their morning meal, nodding their large heads to help the flight of little flies with transparent, fluted wings ; hawks animated the sky with their predatory yet graceful flight. Antoine felt very good. He walked briskly through the welcoming fields, randomly dotted with the church towers of the communities and towns through which he passed. Bridges crossed streams of singing water in places where their unfathomable depth did not allow fording. A frog, tempted by the hover flight of dragonflies, would sometimes take an acrobatic dive into small chasms littered with aquatic weeds. Antoine was now far from the austere confines of Gévaudan, permeated by silence, animated only by the movement of hot air between the peaks and depths of the valleys, like a slow and steady breath.

He discovered unsuspected landscapes, exciting, like children's running, beaded like their foreheads, and throbbing, like their reddened temples, with the blades of the small water mills placed haphazardly and resounding like little drums. Joy spread through the meadows and streams harmoniously drawn by God or an ancient creator who would have known how to preserve the art of proportion. Antoine felt the harmony of the approaching Guyenne and the end of the Languedoc that nothing disturbed at this fragile moment of the day. He understood all their significance because he sensed all the sensuality and goodness that grew with each step he took. Perhaps he was discovering happiness for the first time in his adult life, a childish happiness like irrepressible laughter restrained for too long by habits. He kept walking, looking straight ahead, without expectations or questions, without preparing answers, without analyzing. He kept walking and wishing it would never end.

Antoine knew that there was still a long way to go to America, and that thought appealed to him. He now began to dream of "after America" and he understood that in this "after" there would only be him and him alone as a plowman in a huge field. A shiver of happiness overcame him and made him stray a little from his way. He realized the effect of his thoughts on his balance and could have wished to stop them, but he preferred just to keep walking, free and smiling, accelerating his pace.

22

The Languedoc grew farther away with each step and while the people he encountered still spoke a familiar language, the physical characteristics of the population slowly changed as if they were being put through a sieve that let some of the peoples that had passed through its mesh leave their mark in this province, and others not.

Neither the Romans nor the Jews, nor the Saracens, nor the Vandals, nor the Alans had left visible traces here in the names of the places or on the faces of the Celts, just as the Iberians or the Visigoths had not marked their passage with many descendants. Antoine, of course, was not in a position to take an inventory, but the very absence of diversity or the simplicity of the racial mixtures brought about by history perhaps made these populations more apt to tranquility, none of them ever needing to construct barriers or to defend themselves from others.

Business was not absent, but it seemed to be asleep, limiting itself to more or less bottled fruits.

The estuary of the Garonne, which Antoine had left on his left as he entered the Saintonge, [40] welcomed overflowing and meandering rivers as in an immense lake. It seemed like a benevolent basin preceding the ocean, shared by all and so useful to all that its very existence seemed to be the result of a secret agreement and a wise collective decision. Antoine thought that identical areas must exist in other parts of the world and that they were ideal places to establish a city of hope ; a city founded solely on all its members sharing the same principles and working together for its prosperity.

"It's wide !" a passerby said in wonder.

"Yes," Antoine answered in his reverie, noticing for the first time in

---

(40) Saintonge is an old province of France whose main city was Saintes.

his life such large ships coming down the estuary.

"And it widens more and more from here to the ocean."

"Do you know the estuary ?" Antoine asked him.

"Yes, and even Bordeaux upriver !"

"Must be a beautiful city ?" Antoine asked.

"Ever more beautiful. It is because commerce is flourishing there and people are full of ventures, especially the Protestants."

"With the Windward Islands ?" Antoine asked, trying not to bring up the subject.

"Yes, but also with England and now with Africa."

"Africa ?" Antoine questioned the man, puzzled.

"Yes, they say they buy blacks like the Dutch and the Spanish do and take them to the Islands."

"What for ?" asked Antoine.

"To work in the sugar cane fields. They seem to be more resilient than the others."

"But who are these people ?" asked Antoine.

"Slaves, they are said to be black-skinned, but I have never seen them in Bordeaux or on the ships that pass along the bank of Blaye."

Antoine said goodbye to the passerby and resumed his journey. The estuary now disappeared behind the growing vegetation, placed there perhaps by the signatories to the agreement to hide its secrets. Only the royal citadel under construction could be seen.

Antoine traveled three more leagues before finding shelter for the night in a place where he could also hide. He thought of the Bordeaux merchants who, at this hour, on the edge of the estuary, were lying in their comfortable beds behind the elegant facades of their houses, making and remaking their accounts after having cut short their daily conversations with God. He wondered how it was possible to maintain moral standards in a world that grew bigger by the day and in which the temptations were now called Luck or Fortune.

Psalm 16 then came to mind in response :

> *I love the saints, I help the virtuous,*
> *whom we see enjoying and singing your praises,*
> *But evil after evil will settle upon the ones we see*
> *following strange gods.*

23

Antoine arrived the next day at *Saint-Jean-d'Angély*. He liked the name of this *senescalade*.[41] He was well informed of all the actions taken by the King of France against the Reformed community and perceived much bitterness in the words of their members. The fall of the city in June 1621 resulted in the abolition of communal privileges and the destruction of its walls, thus opening wide the gates of La Rochelle.

Perhaps, he thought, the term "Saint John" attracted misfortune as a kind of destiny ? The relics of John the Baptist were kept in the parish church as if to protect it from the demons and the numerous Protestants nearby. The dismal and partial exposure of the Saint was indeed proof of the attachment of the Papists to the skeletal remains of the Christian religion rather than to its founding principles. Antoine thought again of the strange gods in David's Psalm who had helped him fall asleep the day before.

He attempted a comparison between this little city and the small town of *Saint Jean de Gardonnenque*, which was less the capital of the Reformation in the *Cévennes* than the gateway to the *Hautes Cévennes*. A region that would completely commit itself to the resistance a few years later, in a shattering of arms and heads, punctuated by the haunting singing of psalms, but Antoine didn't know it then. *Saint-Jean-d'Angély* still exhaled revolt. Too landbound to find in shipping companies the palliative to her failed emancipatory religious concerns but nevertheless rich enough in her lands to continue thinking, she remained unfortunately too much attached to law to take risks, like *Saint-Jean-de-Gardonnenque* did fifteen years later. But *Saint-Jean-*

---

(41) N of T : *Senescalade* are lands under the jurisdiction of a *Seneschal*, a court official of high rank.

d'Angély was like the gateway to the great port of the Atlantic. Antoine gathered as much information as possible about his departure from an organized Protestant community of new Catholics,[42] eager to promote mutual aid and relief among their members.

Antoine lingered in *Saint-Jean-d'Angely* for two whole days as if he also wanted to delay his unavoidable embarkation, as if the fear of the unknown were already born on the outskirts of La Rochelle which he hesitated to enter, in the heart of a cosmopolitan crowd, at the end of an inlet connected to the kingdom only by a navigable river thin as an umbilical cord in the middle of its swamps.

Antoine knew that he was reaching the end of his journey. La Rochelle approached as the holy city of the Protestants, holier than Geneva, Nimes, or Montauban. He knew the pain and suffering endured by the people of Aunis. While the city secretly prided itself on its intellectual past, thanks to the printing press, and on its insubordination, throughout the four wars it had fought against the king, it was all the same subdued. The crashing waves and the violent winds drowned the voices of the trustees and their humiliating resignation to the king in 1628 despite the unsuccessful help of the naval forces of England. Nevertheless, its natural role as "gate to the ocean" remained.

La Rochelle was, for a long time, one of the most populated and richest cities in the kingdom. The privileged relationship it maintained with books, associated with an entrepreneurial population, made this city unique and exemplary in many aspects. The Huguenots would remember this when they founded New Rochelle in the province of New York in the late seventeenth century.

Antoine was still concerned about his departure. The information obtained in *Saint-Jean-d'Angély* on the role of notaries was confirmed to him on the spot. He wandered in front of the scribes' offices for a long time before crossing the threshold : it was the natural fear that comes from insecurity, he thought. Unless it was just one more step to take, a step towards a departure, well desired, but whose break with the past was impending. Antoine was not feeling very well. All that coming and going of sailors, street vendors, auctioneers, and busy people, in the middle of great businesses conducted silently behind the beautiful facades of the houses of the bourgeoisie and the shipowners, made him

---

[42] Catholics who had recanted were called new Catholics. They kept in secret their protestant faith.

feel tiny. Preferring to momentarily delay his action, he stepped away from the bustle to observe his surroundings and take in its rules. He sat for a long time, scrutinizing the men and their faces, trying to uncover some logic in all this disorder.

Antoine saw the activity of a great port for the first time in his existence. He felt the same misgivings as in *Saint-Jean-d'Angély*. Ports are not ordinary cities, he thought suddenly. Their inhabitants are without attachment and ties beyond their business goals. Antoine surveyed with fear the diversity of the people he met : Bretons, perhaps English, white settlers from the West Indies. He didn't understand their language and couldn't always easily tell where they came from.

Lost in his own kingdom, he watched, over and over, trying to understand the organization. He knew very well that the traces of this society, invisible to the naked eye, would ultimately become discernible through behavior or through certain usages which would become visible by wearing out eyes and ears in observation and attentive listening. Antoine discovered complexity.

Here there were no lords or clergy or the Third Estate. Everyone seemed to be on an equal footing that went beyond the simple familiarity found in Toulouse. It was all pushing, screaming, invective, force, noise, strong smells and vulgar laughter. Everything here radiated freedom, the freedom to come and go, to leave or stay, to obey or walk the line. La Rochelle, the beating heart of the French Atlantic coast, flourishing in a stimulating climate, was conducive to adventure. The city, long rebellious and raised in the Calvinistic spirit that imbued its elite, had imparted indifference to its people in everything.

Criticism of the Catholic religion had not been the object of long and patient studies by all the port dwellers. The only lesson they retained from the religious unrest was the relativity of things, which suited them well. The most obvious result was the unscrupulousness Antoine saw in this vast mix of social classes and origins. The defeated elite had no further lessons to teach, as they were the only ones humiliated by the king's victory. The populace didn't care and had risen to the next level, in their arrogance and vulgarity. The King of France was far away and a stranger to this state of affairs. These people, whose universe was made up of confusion and resourcefulness, were equally satisfied with a world without pastor or priest. They wore their dignity in their arrogance and their insolence clothed their poverty. Antoine finally understood the rules of this disorder. He knew that he should never forget its significance in building his City of Hope.

At five o'clock in the afternoon, Antoine pushed open the door of the office of the lawyer Guillaumont.

The study was cluttered and dusty, but it seemed organized. He was greeted by a clerk who was quick to remind him of the ecclesiastical origin of his title, perhaps to underscore its sacredness. Antoine felt more at ease here, in this unattractive arrangement of furniture and shelves that marked, by their dissimilarity, the limits of good taste at the heart of a modern practice. The conversation with the absent lawyer was postponed until the next day pending his return.

Antoine found shelter for the night in a makeshift cabin located near the Protestant Church converted into the Catholic Cathedral where Calvin's spirit still blew for Antoine despite the glances, the mixed smells of wine and cider, and the indecent cooing of the homeless.

Grand Protestant church in La Rochelle
before it was partially burnt down in 1687

24

"You know, sir," interrupted the lawyer, addressing Antoine, "it is said that our king declared in 1661 when he took over the state affairs at the end of his mother's regency, that disorder reigned everywhere. He is resolving the problem both here and also in Saint-Christophe."

"And how ?" asked Antoine.

"In his own way," replied the notary, "consisting of determination and plain orders, without adjectives or embellishments, aware that his lofty point of view is only the result of an order of things that he has decided to put in place once and for all, as a necessary tool for the realization of his project for the greatness of the kingdom. When he deprived the Protestants of their churches, the King was not posing as a defender of the Catholic Church, he was simply imposing his own order. And if he punished you, it was not because you committed a fault but because you delayed his plans, and your attitude, according to him, only showed that you did not pay sufficient attention to his words. He may also fear that this kind of behavior may spread and thereby devastate his entire kingdom. Thus, he punished the lack of attention more than the fault that, perhaps secretly, he does not even think exists."

Antoine thanked him for his frankness and noted that the notary, through his enthusiasm, was supporting the king's views.

"That's why," he continued, "you need not worry about your project. You have recanted. The king does not care if they are Catholics or Protestants who will develop the cultivation of sugar cane on the islands. His only wish is for the business to succeed. With respect to the exclusive exercise of Catholic worship, it responds to the attention he expects from his subjects. As long as this rule is followed, he knows that he has been listened to and that later phases of his plans and views will be understood and executed with the same obedience."

Antoine would have liked to answer, but the lawyer didn't give him time.

"If the said adventure does not suit you, you are not obliged to embark on it."

Antoine understood the coldness of the words and departed disappointed by the lack of importance given to religion, the mention of which entered only as part of the overall strategy of the king.

Antoine was visibly entering another world where the commercial reality tied to the Islands prevailed over all other considerations. Strong in his beliefs, Antoine was strangely puzzled by the royal designs, which necessarily went beyond him and translated into a distancing from religion or even a form of irreligion.

After what the lawyer had told him, he realized that the venture was appealing. He decided to put aside his own concerns and see the lawyer again the next day since the latter had other matters to deal with right now. He told him this politely. Master Guillaumont nodded, not without adding that an honest man must have greater ambitions than the mere signing of an engagement contract which they had discussed during the conversation.

"Come back to see me again tomorrow, I may have something else for you."

Antoine wandered for a long time along the docks crowded with gangways, freight, and sailors, wondering what the lawyer's enigmatic statements might have meant.

Not knowing how to solve the puzzle, he recalled word-for-word the conversation they had had. He couldn't think of anything. The judgment made on religion seemed irrelevant to the proposition that could be made to him. This was just good advice and a warning at best. It was a matter of principle. There was no room for discussion. The solution was not in a loophole of the kind that lawyers like to exploit. The stones of the Saint-Christophe edifice were perfectly even and the polishing of each of their faces left no relief to cling to. Everything was structured, immutable. This was a project emanating from the highest authority in the kingdom, built for the mutual enrichment of all parties involved. Antoine concluded that the enigma lay only in the quality of the men and the bond that would unite them to the enterprise.

He walked for a long time towards the suburbs of La Rochelle until he came across smaller houses with blue-painted shutters. The alignment of the houses formed a long ribbon that was reflected in the drainage channels of the surrounding marshes. The irregularity of the excavation of the ditches sometimes transformed the course of the waters, invisible to the naked eye, into a deep green sewer under the September sun. It went down to the heart of the swamp, where the channels stopped suddenly as if barbaric surgery had put an end to the vital irrigation of the Huguenot land. New and mysterious constructions appeared in the distance as if perching there for no apparent reason.

A fisherman, who had seen Antoine from the shore when he was going to his work, interrupted him in his reverie.

"Sugar refinery ! Does that remind you of anything ?"

"No", answered Antoine.

"The sugar cane comes from Saint Christophe, in the American islands. They bring it here and turn it into sugar. It seems to be very good."

"And what does it taste like ?"

"I don't know, I never tried it, it's too expensive, but well-to-do people love it, it must be good. I don't even know its color. If you are interested, you can get some downtown or in the city of Nantes, they seem to have the same there."

"Nantes, why Nantes ?" asked Antoine.

"Oh, I mentioned Nantes because I see that you are not from here."

"No, actually not." Antoine replied.

"And what are you looking for in the area, there is nothing here !"

"Yes, there are sugar refineries."

"And that's what you were looking for ?"

"No, not really ; I was walking without realizing that I was leaving the city."

"And inadvertently you left it", continued the fisherman, "and here it ends unless you are one of those damned hired hands who come back sick from the Islands and who wander around here without knowing where to go."

"No, I'm not an indentured servant."

"And you know what an indentured servant is even though you're from somewhere else ?"

"I know what they told me", answered Antoine.

"If you have been told something, it is because you have asked questions". Antoine realized that he would not get rid of the man so easily.

"I met people in the port who told me about the shipping conditions for our compatriots who want to try their luck in America."

"Compatriots ? Most of them are Normans or Bretons, we don't understand what they say but we know where they come from. When these people come to our swamps, it is because they have lost everything on the Islands. They come back sick and thin and sometimes they live with us in the reeds. From time to time, we find one that has died."

"It's a shame", added Antoine.

"Unhappy people, continued the fisherman, as you say."

"And why are they coming back ?" Antoine asked, suddenly interested.

"Why ? Because between what they were told before hiring and reality, there is no comparison."

"Is life difficult on the Islands ?"

"Yes, especially if you work a lot for a planter who lives in Nantes or La Rochelle because these gentlemen prefer to settle their affairs here, it seems that it is more convenient. You seem to know a bit about it and are also interested in knowing more."

"Any information collected is good", answered Antoine.

"You're probably right but take a good look at these buildings here, they are sugar stores as they call them, and take note that all the profit is for them. Think about it before committing yourself, I would not like to find you dead in my fishing net, due to illness or whatever, now that I know you. Be careful before working for foreigners !"

"Foreigners ?" asked Antoine.

"That's what they are called."

"Why ?" Antoine continued.

"I don't know, but they say they're Irish."

"Irish ? But what are they doing here ?"

"They say they were kicked out of their homeland ; I don't know any more ; we never see them anyway."

Antoine thanked the fisherman and left him. The sugar refinery gave away part of its profits that would never go to anyone and would only cover the smell of the decaying body of an indentured servant returning from the West Indies, from time to time.

Antoine left the land of salty, stagnant waters that served as a refuge for men who did not know where else to go. Their engagement sounded like a one-way ticket since they no longer depended on anyone after their return. The link, dissolved by the clauses of the lease, made them new men and the termination made them free but lonely. The badlands became their only refuge. There they could die without disturbing anyone but the fishermen, at the foot of the thick smoky chimneys, wrapped in the fine mist of the setting sun that would hover all night over their poor heads full of their failures.

The tide.

For the first time, Antoine thought, more men free to be entrepreneurs would also mean more men prone to disappointment. The inevitability of agricultural calamities will henceforth disappear in the face of deficiencies and incompetence unless men resorted to other misfortunes to protect themselves. He took a quick look at the flat landscape that appeared as he emerged from the swamp. According to the fisherman, it also served as a refuge for outlaws who carried out their business there. The chimney breathed with a breath full of youth and vitality that brought relief to its architecture.

25

The next day, Antoine went to the notary. The day was shaping up well. The docks were resuming their usual animation. The towers were illuminated, standing there, haughty and an essential component of the landscape. Although their construction formed part of the defense policy of the kingdom, they underlined by their height the vigor of the opinions of the La Rochelle shipowners and the importance of their business.

Antoine did not feel alien to the maritime and urban environment and he was surprised by that. He was eager to make a deal and feared any delay in departure. He walked the docks in a state of excitement, impatience and doubt on the eve of a great decision. He expected a lot from the lawyer. He knew that he was in his hands and depended on his words to blow the winds of hope and one day carry the echo of his fortune beyond the oceans.

Antoine was at a turning point in his life. He was aware of it. The towers of La Rochelle hid the inlet and masked the open sea. He could guess at its beauty through the masts of the ships at anchor that had not been able to enter the harbor the night before. He, too, was waiting for an opening, a window that would open the door to his journey, except that he would sail, perhaps, when the big ships had safely entered.

He was full of the promises of his enterprise while the large sailing boats already displayed their success through their heavy bellies resulting in lower waterlines. He would become a captain whereas the commercial tall ships had theirs already.

The task was great, but Antoine was confident when he approached the lawyer's study and inadvertently went past it, deep in thought.

"I thought you had changed your mind," said the clerk, still jovial.

"No, here I am", answered Antoine with a smile. He couldn't help but notice the employee's behavior, perhaps more respectful or affable this morning, when entering in the office that smelled of ink, dust, and paper.

"Master Guillaumont will receive you."

The notary appeared a few moments later, happy with all his business, which must have been good.

"Monsieur Pintard, I have a suggestion for you." Antoine gave his full undivided attention to the notary's words, which took on a solemn character.

"I hear you."

"Yesterday, when we met, I saw in you, the result of my experience, certain qualities that are not usually found in our clientele. You seem to be an educated and decent man. I don't think a contract of indentured servant is something I recommend for you."

Antoine let him speak. The room was empty and had a crucifix on one of its walls. He saw a nautical chart spread out on a simple table. A carpet was placed in front of a rectangular chest as if to soften its shape and provide touch of affluence to a functional unit that lacked it. An unlit fireplace in the room still smelled of soot.

The notary informed him about the conditions of the contract and the absence of a salary due to the need to pay back the shipowner for the journey. He further explained that an enlisted man signed a three-year contract at the end of which he was free to return to France or settle permanently on the islands.

Antoine interrupted him to ask if there was any possibility of avoiding this intermediate state. He now knew the conditions of the unfortunate hired hands and did not wish to submit to them himself.

Antoine was surprised at his own audacity and keenly awaited the answer.

"I was right, said the lawyer, we're coming to that. This is what I have to offer you," he announced as a conclusion to his analysis.

"The policy of repression undertaken by the King against the Reformed had led some stewardships to review the question of the treatment that should be applied to them. Our administrators are aware of the quality of the Protestant subjects. Their departure abroad entails a loss of skills that should be remedied."

"But I abjured," Antoine interrupted him.

"I'm getting to that," replied the lawyer before continuing.

"A development policy implies the installation of a large population on the islands and the establishment of colonies. Therefore, it is necessary, in order to fulfill the King's ambitions, to bring to the colonies virtuous people with agricultural skills and, if possible, also skills in other matters that facilitate their administration. You have all three."

"I'm not a Protestant anymore, sir," Antoine interrupted.

"That is correct, but you have preserved all their virtues. That is why you are an attractive candidate!"

Antoine discovered that the lawyer was going fast, but he didn't dare interrupt him again.

"Because I understood that agricultural work is not alien to your education, and that it is carried out under difficult conditions in your mountains. I do not know this personally but can measure the patience and care required. Finally, I am not mistaken if I affirm that you received an education that was not restricted to reading the Bible."

"That's right," Antoine said.

"I was not wrong," added the lawyer. "So, in my opinion, you are an ideal candidate."

"Yes, but in what capacity?" Antoine interrupted again. The lawyer did not respond immediately but continued with a positive analysis of Protestantism through the teaching of the virtues by pastors and families, which was not as widespread as believed among Catholics. He defended himself against the audacity of his words by attributing or sharing this opinion with a large number of the members of the Catholic nobility, the bourgeoisie of the towns, and even with people of the Stewardship.

"It is a fact," assured the lawyer.

"What should I do?" asked Antoine

"Think carefully!" the lawyer replied. "I don't think your beliefs as a New Catholic are very strong, and I would go even further. I'm sure of it."

Antoine did not interrupt him and let him speak.

"I am sure of your abilities, but now you are no longer a Protestant." Antoine didn't quite understand where the lawyer was going.

"It is possible, I say quite possible, that within the framework of a policy of implantation of the Reformed in the islands, your file is considered magnanimously by the authorities of the Stewardship in charge of transporting the Protestants. For this, it would be necessary that you appear as Reformed, therefore you should not declare having recanted."

"What do I have to gain ?" Antoine asked in amazement.

"A plantation !" the lawyer replied.

"Meaning ?" asked Antoine.

"Meaning the award of a field of several arpents [43] that will allow you to exercise your talents without depending on anyone else other than you, in the service of your king."

"But why should I keep quiet about my past abjuration and identify myself as Reformed again ?"

"Monsieur Pintard," replied the lawyer, "within the framework of the implementation of this policy, it is necessary that we obtain only successes, and finally when I say "we", I mean of course the people of the Administration. Your request is of interest to me, in fact to us all because it perfectly meets the criteria of the people we are looking for."

"But then, I lost everything by recanting," sighed Antoine.

"No sir, it brought you here safely, and with a passport."

Antoine had nothing more to say.

"But what is your role in this matter ?" asked Antoine.

"The one I'm performing right now."

"And what should I do ?"

"Some formalities we could discuss tomorrow."

Antoine noticed that the notary's words took on a solemn character again.

He left the study and walked slowly towards the docks, trying to synthesize the entire conversation. The lawyer had shown a cynicism that Antoine did not expect to find in a man like that and he was surprised. How are we to understand such reasoning ? he thought suddenly. What should I do ? He ended up wandering once again beyond the city walls. Before leaving the city, he saw at the end of Chef de Ville a small industrial building against which leaned workers' houses. Old sheets were spread out in the sun. The courtyard was empty and silent. Antoine, motivated by curiosity, crossed the threshold expecting not to meet anyone, lacking coherent explanations ready to give if someone had asked him the reason for his presence there. However, he realized that the sheets must have already been dry for several days, and possibly longer. The buildings seemed abandoned.

---

(43) N of T : Arpent is a French or Swiss pre-metric measure of the surface of the land still in use in Québec or some areas of the United States that were part of French Louisiana.

"Are you searching for something ?" Antoine quickly spun round in the direction of the voice behind him.

"Hello, I was just wondering what all these facilities are for." The man noticed with a glance that Antoine was dressed modestly but correctly, which reassured him. Besides, he wanted to talk.

"It's a sugar factory, a sugar refinery !"

"But it's closed," Antoine continued.

"Of course. The season is over," the man added.

"And when does it open again ?" asked Antoine.

"They cut the cane in February or March on the islands, and then comes the refining work," the man continued,

"It ends here in the summer."

"But yesterday in the swamp a fisherman showed me a chimney in the distance and told me that it was a sugar factory."

"A smoking fireplace ?" the man interrupted with a smile.

"Yes."

"I don't know what he showed you, but the season is over ; the refineries are not operating."

"Are there others ?"

"I only know about this one."

"It is said that …"

"What else have you been told ?" … interrupted the man.

"That the owners were unknown."

"Ah, that's true since they rarely come here."

"Irish ?"

"Indeed, you are well informed . . . yes, they are people who are running away from something. They say they come from Brittany [44] and were previously in Ireland."

Antoine approached the man with great attention. The latter noticed it and, emboldened by the interest he aroused in him, continued the conversation.

"They would have been expelled for their faith as Catholics by a usurper who reigns in England. But some came to Brittany a long time ago, where they are apparently doing good business."

"But are Catholics being expelled from England ?"

"Maybe ! But are you not a Reformed ? I find that you express yourself well for someone of modest means."

"I'm mostly just passing through", answered Antoine, a bit puzzled.

---

(44) Bretagne in the western end of France.

"We are all passing through, continued the man, Catholic or Protestant, we all end up in the same place."

Antoine assured the man of the veracity of his words, wishing to put an end to the discussion.

"Be careful of what people here tell you. La Rochelle is a port, and everyone takes pleasure in pretending they know more than their neighbor. It is like that in areas where people are passing through the truth does not matter. What counts is to appear important amid all the wealth that unfolds in the docks and that has nothing to do with us. Things are not as simple here as they are at home. Everything is calm now, but it was not always like that and then there were the English, and many battles. Well, that's another story."

Antoine said goodbye and turned around so as not to enter the swamp and meet again with the speaker from the previous day who had informed him about things that he had no idea about.

On the way, he thought that he should exercise caution with the lawyer the next day. He spent the evening like the previous ones, alone and not wanting to share anything with the characters who roamed the port and the surrounding streets. He now felt a certain attraction for La Rochelle.

This commercial city had in addition the prestigious title of the most important seaport for the colonies. The locals were not versed in legal or judicial matters. The practice of law was often reduced to issuing bills of exchange, to intermediary activities associated with receiving orders and accepting goods. The law appeared in practical and everyday aspects. The city did not have the vantage point of Toulouse or Montpellier, but it was not secondary either. It was content to be a port and that utilitarian character filled its days and all the ambitions of its inhabitants. Antoine liked this a lot.

He sat for a long time contemplating the great bay dominated by the towers, awaiting the daily closure of the port, by order of its captain, by means of a heavy chain. This obstacle, he thought, could have been the result of an old sentence condemning the rebellious city that had stood against her king.

At the foot of the towers chained for the night, old sailors played Two Truths and a Lie.

26

Antoine had decided that, before beginning the discussion about his trip to the West Indies, he would question the notary about the sugar refinery he had seen the day before, to satisfy his natural curiosity and at the same time to give a less solemn tone to their new meeting.

"You had been correctly informed," stated the lawyer. "That refinery belongs to the Irish."

"The Creagh family operates this industry. They came from Ireland ; they were driven out by Cromwell after the Battle of Drogheda which took place near Dublin in 1649."

The lawyer, satisfied to be able to provide the details that apparently interested his client, continued in the same tone.

"Cromwell is a usurper as you have been told, but he is above all a regicide."

"A regicide !" exclaimed Antoine.

"In fact, Monsieur Pintard, he is responsible for the beheading of Charles I, King of England."

"And why was he beheaded ?" asked Antoine.

"Simply because he was against the Puritans [45] and a king, but Cromwell himself is dead now."

"If we could get back to our business ?"

"I hear you." Added Antoine somewhat hesitantly.

"Monsieur Pintard, you know that notaries are aware of many things. Don't ask yourself and don't ask me where I got this information from, I have it because in business you meet people who know things. Our role is also to connect together worthy people who may not otherwise know each other and to ensure that the demands of one meet precisely the needs of the other."

---

(45) He is sometimes referred to as a crypto-Catholic or a peculiar Anglican.

The lawyer went on for a moment in that monotonous tone that perfectly matched his preamble.

"In addition, I must inform you about the special relationship I have with Sire Du Poyet, whose name is not familiar to you, but whose activities in the American colonies are very important. This family, originally from Lyon, has established part of their business on the island of Saint-Christophe. However, since 1684, the creation of additional sugar refineries in the West Indies has been prohibited. From now on, their establishments must be in France. The Poyet family recently allied with the Angennes family, of Norman nobility, whose title was Marquess de Maintenon. Maybe this means something to you ?"

"No, not really !" Antoine replied.

Seeing Antoine's questioning expression, the lawyer continued.

"This family has been well established on the islands since Saint Christophe became part of the royal domain and this family has the support and trust of the king. These gentle folk, as you can see, have the will to develop companies to increase production in the Antilles and to refine sugar in their factories in France. This means that they surround themselves with competent people. All of this follows on from what we have already discussed."

"That's right," Antoine agreed.

"Consequently, I am doing my best to facilitate your journey to the islands and to your settlement. But there are conditions."

"Which are ?" Antoine asked with interest.

"It is, above all, necessary that you agree to join your religious brothers who are detained on the island of Ré while they await their departure to the Windward Islands."

"Where is the island of Ré ?"

"It's the island in front of Chef de Baie." [46]

"But why should I join these unfortunate people ?"

"For the reasons I mentioned when we met."

"Put yourself in my place . . ."

"I will not insist !" interrupted the lawyer. "Monsieur Pintard, in other times you would have left La Rochelle for Saint-Christophe or Martinique without difficulty because you were a Protestant and your education met the Company's recruiting criteria when it still existed. Today things have changed. You need to go through an additional process to comply with the penal policy implemented after

---

(46) Chef de Baie is a district of La Rochelle.

the Revocation. This is the consequence of the annexation of Saint-Christophe to the royal domain."

"I must proclaim myself a Protestant again ? Because that's what it's about. I recanted. And now I must say out loud that I am a Protestant again ! How absurd !"

"You won't have to say anything. Sometime before, you will join the Reformed who are waiting to be transported to the colony, in order to be numbered along with them. In return, you will obtain a pass until you take possession of a house on the island of Saint-Christophe."

"Put an end to your scruples, Monsieur Pintard. You entered this office for the first time as a man willing to reorganize your life, owing to the suffering you endured in your province ; you did not say anything to me but I understood perfectly. You returned this morning with information about the processing of sugar that has allowed you to discover that Catholic people are as badly treated in England or Ireland as you are in France. What do you want ? Our kings have ways of acting that sometimes seem incomprehensible to us and against which we can do nothing. This being the case, believe me, look only to your interests and do not forget that the colony is far from France and that, judging by what they say, the conditions for those of your religion are much better there than here."

Antoine thought that the lawyer lacked ideals, but that his words were not without common sense.

But the brutality with which he was asked to renounce certain fundamental principles made him want to take time to respond.

"Can I see you again tomorrow ? I need to think about it."

"Take a few days, there are no immediate departure plans."

Antoine thanked the lawyer and left his office stunned. It was a hard blow, and the truths he had been taught did not seem to him in the end as firmly attached in the sky of the realm of ideas as the stars in the firmament.

Antoine took time to think over it. He understood the mechanism that had been proposed to him and he also understood the reasons. After its dissolution, the *Compagnie des Îles* had been annexed to the royal domain in 1674. The Revocation occurred in 1685. Thus, it was totally judicious for the general government of the American islands to promote the development of the colony while making the most of a statistic that would benefit the King and his entourage.

Accepting a cunning plan, without batting an eyelid was, after all, nothing more than a renunciation of his faith as a New Catholic, as retracted Protestants were called. And from that point of view, Antoine had no regrets. But the cavalier nature of the proposal pained him. The recanting was the result of threats. How could he accept a reverse request issued by the same authorities ? The question he was asking himself suddenly revealed to him the answer.

Antoine realized that it was not the same authority. He was in La Rochelle in the hands of those responsible for the administration of the kingdom, the people of the Stewardship as they called it then. These people who demonstrated their loyalty to their King were as eager to serve him as they were to satisfy their own interests. Their ways of reasoning did not exclude them from taking into account the expected development of the Windward Islands. They simply had the intelligence to insert the proposed policy into all the available gaps in this great mechanism. They affirmed thus their presence, their existence, and wanted, very likely their share.

Antoine was not very comfortable with the proposal. First, he considered the risks involved in asserting his Huguenot faith. They were considerable because at any moment he could be classified as a recidivist if, unfortunately, something went wrong. He imagined himself confronted by investigators and did not see how he could preserve his good faith amid the titled families and the lawyer. In addition, being confined to the *Ile de Ré* seemed an irksome stage to him, to which he could only submit by convincing himself that only pride commanded him. Finally, he admitted, without actually taking any decision, that the situation could be seen as a slight to the Languedoc Administration.

Antoine continued deliberating.

He let several days go by in this way, not knowing what decision to make. He felt very lonely and saw in the possibilities that opened up only a series of moral difficulties that he had to overcome. The principles of virtue, honesty, and patience were confronted with the goal of survival that had motivated him during his journey through the kingdom. He could not decide whether the principles should prevail over the objective or the contrary. He was looking for a referee. He turned to God in his prayers, to his brother, to his parents, but he got no help. The sky was empty. Only the principles waited in repose for his spirit to animate and revive them to project them one against the other, in an immense clash, and finally unravel the truth out of this entanglement.

He walked a long time through the city and the docks, looking for a situation, a look, a conversation that would provide the beginning of an answer. Nothing came, no perception, no signal.

Do I really have to go ? he suddenly thought. What do I have to gain from that ? He was amazed at the use of such a word in a process that he had hitherto believed to be essentially religious. Now I end up reasoning like all these people, he told himself. This city is transforming me. Am I protected enough to face temptation ? I received a good education, but what good is it in the world of selfishness ?

Antoine was far from the *Cévennes*, his family, and his roots. He knew that the holy city had succumbed to the allure of the open sea. Perhaps his brothers in the faith were still for the most part faithful to their teachings, but temptations lurked among La Rochelle's piles of merchandise, tarpaulins and ropes, the forest of tall masts, and all those sailors who had seen so much.

Antoine kept doubting.

He understood that no matter what he decided, he couldn't stay long in La Rochelle. The city was now a commercial port, and the appeal that it held for him since his arrival was partly tied to the tales he had heard about the past of the city, considered to be heroic in the eyes of all Protestants. La Rochelle did not turn her back on her past but, while she looked towards the ocean she turned her back in part to the city's beginnings, to the closed doors of the small Protestant churches that dotted the Aunis countryside, to her Huguenot roots that were now plunged into the swamps and in the Holy Scriptures that were sometimes lost in the accounting records of the shipowners. The peoples of various origins who roamed the docks, ignorant of past struggles and only concerned with the tasks ahead, could not revive the faith that was fading behind the palisades of ships and ropes. La Rochelle had become an active city devoted entirely to its trade.

Antoine couldn't back down. The disappointment would be too great, he suddenly realized guiltily. But it's too late, he thought. The damage is already done. I am no longer the same. This trip and my stay here have made me discover so many things that now I cannot give up. I have to leave.

Antoine understood that the search for his own interest could only be a challenging of the principles contained in the teachings of the pastors of the *Cévennes*. He wished he could have talked to one of them. He was in no condition to decide for himself. He did not feel ready to choose, burdened perhaps by scruples, by taking literally the precepts of his Church. Antoine was alone but he no longer wanted to be so. The fight was uneven. He needed enlightenment in this world that he was discovering and which he perceived everywhere as the world of tomorrow.

He suddenly thought that riches inevitably create a state of mind alien to the simplicity of the end of the day when the animals are taken to shelter, and the folks can enjoy all together the last rays of the sun, the fruits of their land and their work.

Antoine discovered on the docks of America that the opulence he had never known made men greedy for the pleasures available to them, beginning with the consumption of food that they did not farm themselves. Measuring then the degree of trust that one must have in one's neighbor to feed oneself in this way, he understood that it is a reality that men of the city have to entrust themselves to the care and services of others. It could be a fault, he thought, unless, ultimately, it was their main quality which he still lacked.

Antoine let his gaze fall on the tangle of ropes and fishing nets that the men deftly untangled. Their sharp eyes never left the work, straightening and loosening their nets.

The work was thankless, and yet the men seemed happy and joking. There is an order in all things, Antoine thought. One only needs to unravel the difficulties that *a priori* seem inextricable. For that, you need a starting point. Antoine understood that, confronted with the open sea or the great emptiness, he needed to be accompanied. He was well equipped by his education, which would one day provide him with the means to build a new world ; but to leave the old one, it was necessary to seek help, to have a guide. He suddenly reacted to such recklessness on his part and blamed himself for not seeking a pastor sooner.

The first nights he spent in La Rochelle near the Protestant church should have inspired him had he not been faithful to his recanting.

Tomorrow he would go to the Protestant church and try to find the pastor.

27

The morning was turning out to be a beautiful October day, like when summer does not want to end and rejoices in the sea breeze in a prelude to the end of the season. The towers, largely lit by the rising sun, framed the deep blue that colored the bay. The big wooden hulls in autumn colors had some difficulty integrating harmoniously with the whole. The waves, identical to those of the Mediterranean, retained against their will the sailboats built for ocean travel. Antoine felt the same. The city and the port transmitted its oceanic energy to his body while he was paralyzed by the struggle between the principles wedged under his skull. He was eager to meet the pastor. He had the same impatience that seizes men in anticipation of a strong wind that would drive away clouds after too many days of heavy rain. He hoped the pastor would clear all that sky up with a vigor that would provide clarity even long afterwards.

The pastor was a red-headed giant with wide shoulders and the face of a fighter. His voice resounded like a hunting horn at Saint Hubert's mass, uniting strength and harmony, the voice of a preacher. Antoine felt the security emanating from his bulging chest. The clarity of the words full of strength and courage penetrated his brain like arrows that always hit their target, interspersed with criticism of the king's entourage and the Papists. He remembered his encounter before his departure, with preachers who still roamed the slopes of the *Cévennes* supporting the Reformed and pushing them into revolt. Antoine knew how to appreciate these characters but he also knew their limits. He remained attentive to his words and his questions, seeking to extract from the man all the intelligence that he knew was reliable.

"I understand your expectations and concerns, Monsieur Pintard ! And I must tell you that I appreciate them and that they honor you."

The pastor had started pacing the room, returning every few moments to the seat he had just left and leaning against its red velvet back, he talked like a lawyer full of convictions.

"This may surprise you, but you have no other options", he said. Antoine remained focused, watching out of the corner of his eye the sway of the hands firmly attached to the arms that protruded from the shoulders like the sails of a windmill. He had expected wind and there was a lot of it !

"You speak of loyalty, loyalty to your upbringing, loyalty to your principles, loyalty to your parents. It is not through loyalties that you will find your way. You build an impregnable wall around yourself, and then you are surprised that you cannot cross it."

"However, they are elements to be considered."

"I agree", replied the pastor, "but on the condition that we measure how much does it all weigh given everything that is happening now. The King of France has questioned all the rights that our ancestors had achieved during the last century and has done it so well that now we no longer have many options but to exercise our rights in secret. Otherwise, we do not exist. That is, neither you nor I can practice what we were made to do or what we were trained to do, or what we had a strong desire for. In addition, everything that makes our individuality, our person, that is to say our faith, must disappear if we want to reappear again in a form acceptable to the King. And only in this way can he allow us to act and live as we want, except of course worshipping God in the way that suits us best. Thus, everything else is subordinate to the recanting of our faith. That you have done !" added the pastor, raising his eyebrows.

"So, if you have the right to keep your religion private, and that us the case since it's written in the Revocation law ! insisted the priest, you remain, always a Reformed."

"What do you mean ?" asked Antoine

"That you can embark for the Windward Islands as a Calvinist since you still are such."

"And for the rest ?" Antoine added.

"For the rest you complied with the demands contained in the Edict of Fontainebleau but, as you correctly understood, these demands were accompanied by civil penalties against those who did not recant."

"Consequently ?" Antoine dared to say.

"Consequently, sir, you have recovered all your rights and even that of becoming a rich landowner in the islands ; for the rest, you will act according to your conscience and your courage. That is, it is up to you to remain faithful to the Reformation, knowing that worship is forbidden but prayer is not. This will help you to learn to be your own guide through daily Bible readings if you have one. This, sir, will allow you to act as a judge by weighing the pros and cons and not being satisfied with the first interpretation that comes your way, but instead seeking to discover others, the most interesting because they are the least visible. You will learn, sir, that the answers are sometimes hidden in syntax and grammar, in short, you will learn to be intelligent !"

"What if I apply your words to my concerns ?"

"Go ! Go away, sir ! You are a Reformed in the depths of your soul. It is as a Reformed that you will pass through the offices of the governor of Saint-Christophe and these gentlemen of the Stewardship, who have decided you were a Protestant before embarkation, and so you remain faithful to all your commitments."

"But those conditions are like recognizing an aberration," Antoine said.

"Which one ?" The pastor interrupted.

"That there are two people within us !"

"That is correct and well-reasoned, continued the man of God, but this is imposed on us by the Revocation, that is to say, by law ! exclaimed the pastor, hitting the back of his chair. Please understand. If the law divides each person into two people, one civil and one religious, let's use this to build our reasoning and guide our actions !"

"But it goes against the teachings of our Church !"

"In any case, it is the law, and moreover, it is the applicable law here in La Rochelle as elsewhere in the kingdom. Know, sir, that the law will be more and more prevalent, I hope you have understood . . ."

"Yes, of course," said Antoine.

"Under these conditions, our role is to infuse as much religion as possible into the construction that is imposed on us, in the absence of building a totally religious world. Believe me, when you make the journey, you participate in it. It is said that there are already a great number of possibilities for us in the new world, we have to be there now. I think I've told you everything, sir."

"Thank you."

Antoine left the pastor reassured. He had regained a certain degree of pride that he did not intend to erase, at least not right away. He walked around the city in a different spirit than he had an hour before. He felt like a pastor. He discovered that everyone could speak of God in order to draw all closer to their Creator.

Suddenly he felt like a missionary and he sensed emerging in him the desire to exercise his mission in a changing world, in a new world. At this instant the teachings that would later spread within his family likely took shape.

Antoine felt he was born morally and spiritually in La Rochelle. Maybe that's why he always claimed to be from there.

The October breeze had strengthened, releasing one by one the great brown boat hulls that now would set sail, crowned with their banners of new white sails flapping happily in the wind.

The sea, liquid before, was transformed into a vibrant and invigorating swell that took over the entire bay and exploded in a multitude of white sails. The air was fresh and healthy, his thoughts were all in order. Antoine was smiling. He returned to the center of the shipowners' town, walking with a determined stride. All the world, all the riches suddenly seemed to be made for him. He was totally enjoying what he was seeing for the first time. The streets were livelier, the goods more beautiful in their stalls, the porters suddenly seemed like decent people doing their transporting, the lawyer's facade, welcoming. He opened the door forcefully, which surprised the clerk a bit, who immediately resumed the facial expression that his natural joviality imposed on him.

"Monsieur Pintard !" he exclaimed.

"Good morning, sir !" Antoine responded, openly extending his right hand in the direction of the employee.

"I want to speak to Maître Guillaumont."

"I'll see if you can see him."

The lawyer appeared moments later through the door of his office. He was smiling and obviously pleased to see Antoine again. He held out his hand vigorously.

"Follow me, Monsieur Pintard, and please have a seat !" Antoine gladly accepted. The large table with the charts was to his right and close enough to guess the titles and the pretty representations of the West Indies, which formed a vast archipelago shaped like a constellation of stars. Antoine would have liked to have taken the maps in his hands to leaf through them, in delight, and savor the strange names, especially Hispaniola which was written in bigger letters than the others.

"You'd like to take a look at them ?" the lawyer dared to suggest.

"With great pleasure !" exclaimed Antoine.

"Come closer, please do !" the lawyer insisted, delighted with the effect the nautical chart had on Antoine.

"I find this very beautiful," said Antoine.

"And it is, sir," added the lawyer.

"I'll explain how it is all presented." The lawyer spoke for quite some time about the islands, the new world, the progress achieved in cartography, the new information collected after each trip, the sugar, the struggles between European powers. Antoine listened carefully, trying to remember everything the lawyer told him, happy in his turn to discover America.

The great ships that he had seen departing moments before now sailed proudly in spirit over the navigation charts [47] between the Antilles and France, solidly built to carry cargos of exotic products that would make their owners a fortune and brighten the tables and palates of the nobles and the bourgeoisie.

Antoine felt that the old world was gradually disappearing and that the emerging modernity had difficulty integrating into the old structures. He felt all this in front of the table where the charts were spread out, while thinking of the Baron de Moissac, of the Ginestou family.

Europe was small in front of the ocean, and the distant America, of which neither the contours nor the extent was known, seemed already very large.

The Cevennes were invisible. Antoine felt slightly dizzy at the vastness and suddenly realized the possibilities that the new world offered him. He felt that he should not keep this to himself and that he should share his enthusiasm with others and especially with his brothers and sisters.

"This surprises you, Monsieur Pintard !" exclaimed the lawyer, who had been noticing Antoine's distraction for a few seconds.

"Yes, that's the right word," answered Antoine. "I feel far from my country when I listen to you."

---

(47) N of T : Which represented the two hemispheres on the same map as was usual at the time.

"You know, added the lawyer, when I speak like this, I am well aware that we are also far from La Rochelle and the whole kingdom, we are in the colonies. The last few sugar seasons, Monsieur Pintard, have generated returns of about 25 percent !"

"I cannot imagine what that represents," Antoine told him, "I only know the meager returns of our lords."

"This is all over, Monsieur Pintard, no matter how long it lasts, the future is no longer on the often-ridiculous piles of rights in exchange for equally ridiculous rewards ! You are young and educated, I see that your decision has been made and it is the right one, if only I were twenty years younger …"

"Indeed, my decision is made," said Antoine satisfied. "I am leaving under your conditions."

"Congratulations," added the lawyer. Antoine left the lawyer after agreeing to meet him again to inquire about the upcoming sailings to Saint-Christophe. He waited for long, idle and purposeless days. But the situation could not continue because the means for his livelihood were diminishing day by day. Antoine was counting the days.

28

Days followed with no more information than that gleaned at random from casual encounters on the docks. Antoine usually visited Maître Guillaumont, the lawyer, twice a week seeking news that would illuminate his seemingly dark astrological sky. Antoine did not adhere to beliefs that were more widespread than one might think, despite the religious times, but his questions sometimes led the clerk to suggest unexpected interpretations or advice.

"You should pray for someone !" the latter had once told him jokingly.

"Pray for someone !" Antoine was surprised.

"Yes, perhaps one of your relatives has sinned !"

"Probably ! but go on !" added Antoine

"So, if that person has sinned, it is a matter of redeeming him with a prayer."

"And thus, get him out of Purgatory !" Antoine continued.

"That's right !" affirmed the clerk, happy with his irreligiousness. "It is the Communion of Saints !"

"But how will that improve my current situation ?" Antoine asked him.

"If you take him out of Purgatory, your wish will be granted in return. Remember that Purgatory is a temporary hell that you can only get out of if you have redeemed your sins. And how do you expect the deceased to redeem their sins in Purgatory ? It is not like a sentence of imprisonment. He is in jail and there is nothing there that allows him to obtain a pardon. Somebody else has to do it for him !"

"I don't believe in Purgatory," Antoine dared to say, annoyed.

"You're wrong," replied the clerk, who obviously wanted to continue the conversation.

"Because what better hope than to be out of Purgatory ! Think about it ! You won't find any ! It is a necessary step between good and evil. Evil is condemned by all religions, but men practice it regularly, as if the temptations are so strong that they cannot avoid it."

"But we can avoid temptations, or in any case repress them, with prayer or with the help of the Scriptures," added Antoine.

"I agree with you, but if we do not succeed and fail, the sinner is marked for life."

"That's what you have confession for", Antoine insisted, thinking the speaker was Catholic.

"Yes, but it does not erase sin, the soul will always carry the scar and upon death, the destination will be purgatory. Next, we have to get out from there and for that, we have several solutions."

Antoine noticed the "we" used by the clerk, which confirmed his membership of the Catholic religion, and the use of the word solution that sounded strange to him in the discussion. He left him free to respond in any way he saw fit and carefully let him continue.

The clerk was devoted to his business, and the experience of his professional life took his words far from religious affairs. He seemed to be secretly amused by the torments of others in the face of their existential anguish and their fear of death.

"Think, Monsieur Pintard, of all the means at our disposal to redeem our sins. You see, it is amazing ! Even without confession and prayer, which are already part of a high degree of civilization, we are left with indulgences and spiritual testaments."

"I know these practices !" Antoine dared to say.

"But have you ever investigated the content of any of them ?"

"No, I have not."

"Sir, *The Treasury of Indulgences* is wonderful, but this is primarily the responsibility of the Church. [48] All sins are listed and penances

---

(48) Note of Author (Matthew 16-13-20) : " Who do you say I am ? " questioned Jesus. Peter's Confession was clear. " You are the Christ, the Son of the Living God ". Jesus replied : " Blessed are you, Simon, son of Jonah…I will give you the Keys of the kingdom of heaven ; whatever you bind on earth will be bound in heaven, and whatever you loose on earth will be loosed in heaven ". According to this verse, the Catholic Church granted full or partial remission of the punishment of sin to diminish the time spent in Purgatory by the sinner. The Keys of Saint-Peter are seen on the papal coats of arms as a symbol of spiritual and temporal papal authority given by Jesus. They are also seen on the coats of arms of the city of Avignon. The state of Avignon in the south of France was the capital city of the Catholic Church during the 14th century. The business of indulgences gathered more importance, there, in connection with the financial needs of the Church during the Hundred Years

are charged for a full or partial, albeit temporal, pardon of the fault committed. What could be fairer in their application than these codes in use in Ireland or La Rochelle ? Recognize that the Christian world, therefore, has a standard applicable in all places and regardless of the sinner !"

"With all the abuses that this entails and that were denounced in their time !"

"You will never prevent abuse, but how effective !" replied the clerk, full of admiration for the technique employed.

"I prefer the *Treasure of human and divine consolations*", Antoine risked, "because it is a manual that instructs every Christian on the attitude to adopt in life, so as to avoid mistakes, based on simple virtues such as caution or patience."

"I follow you, but if that is not enough, recognize that something is needed to redeem sinners because if you do not redeem anyone, it means that we are all lost. Differences must be created for all this to work because it is by taking the example of the repentant that one can raise or hold everyone to a sufficient level of Christian morality. And for that, we need the law ; this is the object of canon law and for this we need money." [49]

"But you do not intervene in these matters," interrupted Antoine.

"No, of course not, but we can advise sometimes as we do, and have done for a long time."

"Namely ?" Antoine asked interested.

"People who are aware that they are going to pass from life to death welcome us into their homes to express their last wishes and distribute their assets among their children and their surviving spouse. Apart from the attribution to each of part of their estate, we intervene to note their desire to have recorded in their will their purchase of indulgences or alms delivered to the poor, and finally the anniversary masses that they wish to be said in their name according to a calendar that they decide."

War. The indulgences were sold to different Catholic institutions in Europe which can be regarded, nowadays, as wholesalers or dealers. These institutions sold them back to the faithful with a profit. During the Avignon papacy, England like Spain did not ask for as many indulgences than France or Italy thinking the money was embezzled by the King of France. The aggressive marketing practices of the selling of indulgences led to the Protestant Reformation in continental Europe. (*Les concessions pontificales d'indulgences d'Honorius IV à Urbain V (1285-1370)* ; Presse Universitaire de Rennes 2003).

(49) Nowadays, state fines or community services.

"But all that does not appear in the Gospels !" Antoine intervened.

"No, of course, but we are responding to a request from the dying. The laity has a lot of experience on the subject, I assure you. We took the initiative in devotion to the dead long ago. It is part of our role to help the dying and their families. Who could blame us ?"

"Luther did it in his time," Antoine replied. [50]

"Yes, but this practice continues and it will be difficult to get it out of one's head. Death is scary !"

"The question that arises," Antoine dared to say, "is the effectiveness of such a technique that is only realized after death ! The deceased should have worried about their salvation earlier."

"Perhaps", answered the clergyman, "but we are not the judges. We only register, very often, the expenses that will be paid after death. The will takes this into account."

Antoine was thoughtful for a few moments.

"In a way, accounting for the afterlife !" He dared to say.

"Yes, that's provided for ! But you can buy an indulgence while you are healthy," the clerk replied.

Antoine remained thoughtful for a few more moments, regretting that the word clerk, whose source was religious, was associated with such procedures, satisfying the taste for mysticism of many of his compatriots and the mercantile character of such practices.

"Everything can also be measured, added the clerk in an apparent desire to conclude his reasoning. Otherwise, why assign different inheritance values between an eldest child and the younger ones, a boy or a girl, a legitimate child or a bastard ? By doing things this way, we place a value on each of them. You see, things are not that simple !"

Antoine was unsettled by the clerk's words and didn't know what to say. His unattainable ideal of purity had long since turned into a rigorous application of principle. Suddenly he discovered their conversion into value, moreover a monetary one. Each mass had a cost and he understood that this was ultimately what it was all about.

---

(50) Luther is the author of " *Disputation on the Power and Efficacy of Indulgences* " known as the Ninety-five Theses (1517). The Disputation was related to the sales of indulgences to rebuild Saint Peter Church in Rome. The sales started with Pope Julius II (Born Giuliano della Rovere, former archbishop of Avignon) and was continued by Pope Leon X (Born Giovani di Lorenzo di Medici, son of Lorenzo di Medici known as Lorenzo the Magnificent). The Disputation was the origin of the Reformation of the Catholic Church.

The selling of indulgences

Antoine was about to leave the study when the secretary exclaimed :

"Ah ! I think I can hear Maître Guillaumont !" In fact, moments later, the lawyer did push open the door of his office.

"Monsieur Pintard, you are in luck ! I was looking forward to your visit."

Antoine recovered immediately and abandoned the thoughts in which the secretary's words had plunged him.

"Dear Monsieur Pintard ! Can I talk to you ?"

"With pleasure," answered Antoine.

"Please come in !" added the lawyer, indicating the door of his office.

Antoine shot a quick glance at the Crucifix on the wall. It was medium sized, in the order of two hands high, made of dark wood without ribs or reliefs, enhanced with yellow brass screws. The body of the martyred Christ was carved from a white material that Antoine did not know.

"Ivory !" exclaimed the lawyer.

"It is very beautiful !" Antoine added he had never seen one like that before.

"And with good reason," continued the lawyer, "they were once objects for our princes ! Now they are affordable and decent people can buy them ! The history of ivory on Christian soil, Monsieur Pintard is already ancient and from the beginning, linked, of course, to travel, crusades, discoveries, and trade. Different worlds can be found, understood, and appreciated, as can other religions !"

"And this is what Christ on the Cross suggests in this place !"

"In part only and in a very small part !" the lawyer dared to say, evidently not wanting to go too far.

"Please enter !"

"I am sure, Monsieur Pintard, that you will love the new world and you will love its commerce, he said as he sat down. You appreciate the essence of beauty at a glance. You will also appreciate the goods, their quality, and the needs that they could arouse in a population that still ignores them and that, therefore, does not even suspect they even exist. This is commerce, Monsieur Pintard, and it's wonderful !" The lawyer continued, "such an attitude and such a usage can be associated with beauty, with beautiful things, in a word, with art."

"Art and commerce, in a way ?" Antoine dared to suggest.

"You are right, knowing that commerce is itself an art since it transforms into an object of admiration, just as you a moment ago admired the crucifix, something that was intended to remain in nothingness. Imagine the passion of Christ without representation for seventeen centuries, without images, without crucifixes, there was little chance that we would be still talking about it. And if sometimes we take out Christ, we keep the cross, then ..."

The notary out of politeness did not go further in criticizing the arguments propagated by the Reformed against the religious Catholic images.

Antoine was not very comfortable with these discussions. As a Reformed believer, he would have liked to respond. But, on the one hand, he needed the notary, and on the other, his Protestantism was largely embedded in an ethos rather than blind fanaticism. Antoine was not as skeptical as the lawyer. He exercised his faith with moderation.

"Monsieur Pintard, I need your services."

Antoine listened in surprise.

"The business is active at the moment. Travel to the American colonies is growing, transactions are increasing, and the sugar industry is bringing new legal needs. Besides, I don't know when you'll be able to get on board a ship."

Antoine feared bad news.

"So, I have a proposal for you. Your resources are not inexhaustible . . ."

Antoine noted the free expression of opinion, which brought him back to the courtesy of the exchanges between his father and the Baron de Moissac.

". . . and not being inexhaustible, you probably need to work !"

"That's right" agreed Antoine.

"I would like to focus my activity on legal matters related to business development here in La Rochelle. One day my secretary will succeed me in my position and from now on, he will have to assist me more significantly in everything that constitutes the drafting and signing of current notarial acts, receipts, marriage contracts, wills, etcetera. He will need help. So, I thought of you ; believing that you meet my expectations. Of course, you will be able to leave me as soon as you are cleared to board."

"I need to work ; your proposal interests me and I accept it with great pleasure." Antoine was surprised by the frankness and speed of his own response. He was changing and he was learning fast.

The notary, satisfied with his response, asked him to come in as soon as he could early the very next morning. Antoine left the studio in a state of mild euphoria. He would have liked to share the moment with someone, but there was no one to listen to him. He walked for a long time, waiting for the end of the evening, satisfied with the nascent social bond that would weave itself tomorrow.

He fell asleep thinking of his family, perhaps more than any other time. Were they unhappy in the *Cévennes* mountains, lying alone, under a plain, empty cross nailed above the bed and carved from ancient wood ?

29

Antoine spent months waiting to depart, relegated to a corner of the room, under a wood carving of Christ the redeemer. This location did not bother him too much, since the firm's clients, as well as the lawyer and secretary, had no particular deference for the crucifix. It was enthroned, so to say, in majesty, recalling by its mere presence that all the deeds were confirmed with reference to the year of the Lord's birth, and to the reign of Louis XIV as an extremely simplified calendar that marked the beginning of the counting. This reference accorded with the echoes of the often-selfish words of the families, of the dying and their occasionally cunning heirs.

The resolution of confrontations, which originated in the small and great misfortunes of people, made Antoine tougher. He learned a lot about the family codes of a big city and felt the looming weight of the rapid conversion of situations into silver. Of course, he had previously had access to the precious metal out of which Louis or Franc coins were formed, but never in such quantities.

The *Cévennes* Mountains were not exempt from hard currency transactions, but they were few and far between and scales to weigh precious metals were often absent at fairs. As in all parts of France at the time, exchanges were often limited to barter because money was scarce.

During the last few years in *La Cabanarié*, he had observed the increase in currency circulation. This was still a key event, like the crossing of a threshold into a new world. This had not been fully integrated into the minds of his contemporaries who maintained a great distrust of this means of payment. Perhaps, the difference between the size of the beast sold by the farmer and that of the coins that could fit in the hand, quickly encouraged the exchange of these coins for more tangible goods or animals.

In any case, Antoine was able to verify in La Rochelle that societies absorbed in the pleasure of counting money, were also in a better position to respond to the difficulties of the time. Once the trust in the monetary counterpart was established, then also followed the opposite excess of not wanting to take coins out of one's pocket or have them, like children, clutched in one's little hands. Sometimes, the refusal to break piggy banks led to litigation involving bad debts, often for no apparent reason, resulting in profits for the lawyers.

Antoine knew the reaction by which the years of good harvests in the Cevennes multiplied conflicts like a thirst for justice which ended up in chicanery, the culmination of the aspiration of a people towards a judicial mysticism. In all cases, the people opened their closed fists and dumped gold and silver coins into the pocket of the lawyers' robes. The thirst for justice was truly a wave of mysticism that, as always, was closely linked to spirituality. In lieu of paying the priest for the novena mass, it was necessary to pay men of law for exercising the arithmetical piety demanded by their clients. Antoine thus learned accounting.

He also found that the dematerialization of transactions materialized relationships. The remarks gleaned here and there through his legal work took him a little further away from the thoughts that preoccupied the peasants, totally focused on their subsistence and their prayers. Opulence made people from La Rochelle focus only on their business, anxious not to lose what they had accumulated. Secretly, Antoine dreamed of a world of abundance where men, freed from material limitations, could finally dedicate themselves to improving their behavior and beautifying their souls. This society should be somewhere further west. Its reflections were shown in the purchase orders that the notary verified and from which echoes sometimes reached him.

Antoine was simply discovering reality.

Thus, passed months of his apprenticeship. He enjoyed the job and knew that the education he was receiving would serve him well. However, he was eager to cross the Atlantic. He would have liked to set sail before Christmas so as to mark his departure in the days of the new year. But that was not to be.

On the day of the Nativity, he wandered around the churches all in full celebration. The Protestant churches were closed or torn down. Antoine guessed that the furniture was covered in dust and the Bible had perhaps been left open to let people think it was not all over. The lone pastor had found no provision in the Revocation edict to contain his scruples and circumvent the prohibitions. Worship was prohibited, and a royal ordinance dating from November 1685 swayed in the wind behind the protective grating of the wooden frame reserved for notices. The document, protected against bad weather and not from the passage of time, had found its own reliquary under the portico of the Grand Temple partially burnt in 1687, finally leaving the expression of the royal will to the winds.

The Reformed prayed and shared the Christmas feast in a fellowship where concerns linked to their sovereign were absent. Their prayers stressed the intensity of their faith and their warm words were full of hope. Rochelais Protestants were not hopeless. Economic conditions were good, the land was fertile, the surrounding landscapes consisted of fertile lands, and the city looked out over the vast open sea. Their resistance was rooted in time and developed its strength in patience, while their way of life, of reasoning, of calculating, of trading, of doing business flourished every day and in broad daylight, plowing, transforming, disfiguring the old world, to the point of making it unrecognizable.

The Rochelais were aware of their importance but without boasting or showing triumphalism. They built in silence, improving their well-being and secretly knowing that their success would be envied. Their Protestantism was nothing like that in the heights of the *Cévennes*, which was closer to the Scriptures because it was closer to heaven. They had managed to discreetly integrate themselves into the developments of their time, becoming actors, whereas in their search for truth and purity the Reformed from the *Cévennes* had managed to create an impressive dignity. The father of the family, poor but upright, sometimes lacking in everything but demanding nothing, exercised justice a little more every day, beginning by treating his daughters as his sons and his wife as himself. He thus built a humanism where the postures did not hide yet what was just and good.

Antoine navigated between these two visions of Protestantism. Like a native of the Cévennes, he maintained the dignity of his lineage but, educated and curious, he came close to the approach of his brothers from the Aunis.

He felt all this on this Christmas day, in the company of the clerk and his family, gathered in the family communion to which he had been invited.

After spending a few weeks together, the clerk had confessed that he belonged to the Reformed religion. He had explained to Antoine both his recantation out of necessity in order to pursue his professional ambitions and, at the same time, the recantation by the notary in an already distant past. To Antoine, who was astonished by their cynical words the clerk had replied that by acting like this they both maintained a necessary distance from all things and, therefore, a certain degree of reason. It was a question of survival, understandable to all, that could not lead to condemnation. In saving themselves, alone among others who had retained their Huguenot faith, and despite their recantation, they all participated together in clandestine but more effective work, namely establishing contacts based on shared principles.

In short, a network had been formed that, in lieu of struggles and confrontations, maintained privileged relationships among its members for the enrichment of all. Sharing the same interests while respecting the same rules could only lead to general salvation and pre-eminence sooner or later.

"Business here is too important to camp solidly in indefensible positions these days". The clerk told him. The fight is uneven. The speech reminded him of his brother Jean. He understood the meaning. He had always understood. The clerk went on to assure him that, in this new world that he had discovered since arriving in La Rochelle, it was better to share religious principles than a place of worship. Criticism of the Catholic Church could not be resolved in the greater or lesser importance attributed to relics, Christ on the cross, or the communion of saints.

The place that each could have in the kingdom was predominant and the objective was already fueled more by principles of action, the results of which were evident every day, than by endless theological disputes. Antoine understood the message of this urban Protestant. He kept it in mind for the rest of his life.

The visit to the Catholic church, essential for people who held legal positions, ended in a moment of contemplation in front of the representation of the Nativity that the priest of the parish had installed in his church. Both men were too rational to be surprised by the simple and reassuring humanity that radiated from the Adoration of the Shepherds. They thus remained, pensive, absorbed by the poetry that emanated from the place. Silence united them all.

Antoine received his authorization to embark at the end of March in the year of Our Lord 1688.

Book II

THE PLANTATION IN SAINT-CHRISTOPHE

30

The sky and the sea were immense. They met on the horizon in an infinite gradient of blues. The wind blew in from the sea with rhythmic regularity. The ship, creaking everywhere, expanded vigorously by sails, ropes and masts, was running at full speed amid the rain and wind that stretched the rigging already under great tension.

Antoine was free, at least he felt a sense of freedom for the first time. At times he had galloped across the limestone plateau close to his home, but now it was something else ; he wanted it to last forever.

"So, the earth is round !" shouted a sailor to Antoine.

"Oh yes", Antoine replied, happily, who was feeding on this new roundness.

"And yet they took a long time to admit it in Rome."

"Why ? Was it decided there ?"

"You have to believe it ! They were not all in agreement, someone had to proceed with a decision."

"Yes, but why the Pope ?"

"I don't know," replied the sailor. "If the Pope says so, we're fine. But if you had asked me !"

"Sure", Antoine added, with a smile.

"It's like the calendar. We, in the navy, use the calendar for the logbook, well I don't but ... well, we use the Gregorian calendar, which is in better agreement with the sun, it seems. Well, the English refuse to do so, because they prefer to disagree with the sun rather than agree with the Pope. You see, there are weird people everywhere !" The sailor walked away, satisfied with his little conversation. Antoine realized that on the high seas deference and obedience were due solely to the captain.

A second sailor approached and passed Antoine, still in his reverie, and asked him :

"So ? Is the earth not round ?"

"Yes, yes, it is round !" Antoine replied, laughing. An officer came to meet him and asked him to return to his bunk. He was embarrassed at the request, but he hid behind orders to justify his disagreeable behavior.

"Last year, the vessels for the transport of the Reformed were less comfortable," he confided in a diplomatic tone. "It is not that we like to mistreat people of the Reformed religion, but the usual trips, combined with the Protestants, made things difficult."

"Many have left like this ?" Antoine asked.

"Yes, a few hundred since the end of 1686. And more and more in addition to cargo and regular passengers. In other words, their fate waiting them on board was not pleasant."

"And what is the reason for this resurgence ?" asked Antoine.

"After the Revocation, the Crown tried to populate the islands with competent and honest people, then a man named Michel Bégon who had been stationed in the corps of the galleys in Marseilles took advantage of this practice to improve the fate reserved for the Reformed. They were competent and honest."

"And it worked ?"

"Yes, in the beginning ; you will also find Reformed in Saint-Christophe, but the number of transportees has lessened considerably in recent weeks, perhaps because the number of Protestants sent to the galleys is decreasing since they massively recanted," the officer said.

"You should go back to your deck", he added.

Antoine did so, saluting the officer politely and disappearing through the hatch. The wind whistled off the halyards, a bracing wind raising waves that soon broke up scattering like sparkling confetti. This prevented giant waves of salt water from crashing on the deck.

When leaving La Rochelle a few days before, they had come across a heavy swell which combined the waters of Brittany with those of the Bay of Biscay in a powerful mix. The sick passengers had vomited their meager ration of food filling the ship's hold with a foul-smelling dough edged with salt yellowed by the spreading seawater.

Antoine had not escaped the sea sickness and his nausea had not brought him closer to the other passengers. Each one remained crouched and lethargic in his own silence, having nothing to share except exile. The reasons for the voyage didn't matter. They all shared the same fate and the lack of respect for their wishes, notwithstanding what was written in the preamble of the notary acts that registered their departure, did not give them any additional confidence. Most viewed their deportation as a failure and the injustice inflicted on them made it feel worse. They were ashamed. They did not feel that they were victims. They did not forgive themselves for their weakness, for being tossed between two stronger forces. They remained suspended over the Atlantic emptiness like the clothesline stretched across the hold, swinging between two shores, from where most of them would never emerge victorious.

Antoine was silent, alone. He secretly observed, this departing humanity, rocking in a giant hammock of damp canvas stained with stale vomit, without fear or terrified gaze, immobile in expectation and dwelling on its past ruin. He needed to go out on the deck and he willingly respected the time allotted for that, as a leap into another world whose contours he sought to imagine. Leaning for a few minutes on the railing of the small deck made him think he was getting closer to the islands. He smelled the wind, imagining finding already in the changes and nuances the aromas of the land, the strange and natural variations of the new world.

Antoine was halfway between Aunis and the Caribbean. He couldn't dwell on the plight of others, having so much to do for himself. "Exile is not an easy thing" he thought, "it is even more difficult at the bottom of a hold". That is why Antoine liked to go outside, where he held his head and his ideas to the wind in the direction of the ship's navigation. Otherwise, he found the shadows of his fellow-sufferers in the bottom of the boat, fraying a little more every day with bones sticking out from under their used shirts, visible in the dim rays of dusty light. The humidity and heat were unbearable. The humidity invaded the pocket of stale air in which they lived, constantly fed by the water bubbles that oozed from the caulking like the drool of a toad.

Antoine was tired, and despite the supplementary food he could buy, he felt his strength was failing him, like those of his fellow unfortunates, shadows groaning in the tangle of hanging canvases. He too immersed himself in them. His thick shirt prickled his skin and his wet neck and back. With his mouth parted for more breathable air, he sought to sleep to pass the time, his lip hanging in a degrading smile.

Death, the officer had told him, is inevitable during a crossing. "I'm counting on you to warn us because passengers are sometimes too weak to climb up and inform us in time. It is urgent to react in these latitudes as all bodies are tired and infections spread rapidly".

The journey was just beginning. Death could be the very next step. Antoine wasn't expecting it. But he knew that it would come given the condition of some passengers, immobile, in their shirts stiff from dry perspiration. He couldn't have prevented his jacket from hardening with the accumulation of sweat deposited every day in equal layers that ended up becoming a rough shroud like a jute sack. This death wrap hurt his back, drawing red veins like spider bites where all kinds of small insects were housed.

Antoine knew his state of health but did not react. He had to wait and pray for it to stop. He knew that all this would continue until they reached the Antilles. It was the price to pay for leaving the old world. A shedding, driven by the friction that occurred with each glide forward of the ship on the waves, rising and then plunging in an apparent effort to tear away the aged skin of its human cargo.

Antoine thus traveled thousands of miles, scratching his back with his too long nails that sought in the red veins, now hollowed out, to retain the wet rot that was embedded there.

Each itch brought back its cargo of swarms of black insects whose invisible juices destroyed him. Hunger consumed him as he tugged at these creatures, irritating his poorly emptied stomach that released bitter gases, making him feel nauseous. Antoine was very sick.

His head was spinning at times and his hard, dry stomach also gave him the impression of an internal transformation.

Antoine was delirious. He spent many days thus, surrounded by the meager care of other passengers who forced him to drink not knowing what else to do. Antoine, too exhausted to realize the seriousness of his condition, kept a stern expression, thus showing that he was still alive.

The wind had died down. In the depths of the night, when men and beasts slept, seeking relief from the aches and pains of the day, the ship fell into a strange calm. A sky and a sea made of flat and smooth waves, always impressive in these stretches of water, kept the passengers asleep. Silence reigned. Only the voices of the crew echoed like in a huge grotto where the sounds bounced between the arch of the sky and the flat of the ocean.

The moon, hidden behind the bobbing clouds of the tropics that lined the sky, cast its rays of thin celestial light in the direction of the great liquid lake. It indicated the entrance to the landscape at the top of the seemingly underground scenery.

Antoine was no longer sleeping. All the days he had spent in sleep had enabled him to perceive the smallest changes. His body was now rested. The sound of water hitting the sides of the ship at long intervals had awakened him. The tall masts creaked like the rapid pecks of a woodpecker, followed by a long silence, until the surf shook the ship again.

Strangely, Antoine felt better. He was hungry, but mostly he was thirsty. He had a strong desire to drink from a source of fresh water to cleanse his insides and return to the open sea what the ocean had taken from his old skin. His intestines still retained debris that began to purr again. He tried to get up from his hammock starched with dried grime and succeeded. He felt his strength reborn in this enclosed space with a surprising vigor that drew him toward the upper deck.

He ignored the prohibition to go up on deck at night in the open air outside the agreed hours. He had to get out and breathe again.

Antoine climbed the steps that separated him from the outside and his former life, pulled by the emptiness of the open sea. He breathed in slowly to savor the moment, inhaling through his nostrils ; one breath after another, which he blew out through his now recolored mouth and his lips once again full of life.

31

The calm remained over the sea as if an invisible hand leaned against it with an immense force that stilled it. It seemed as if the water from the day before was just moving there in front of him today, without rejuvenation. Antoine had difficulty breathing and was thinking about the consequences of his indisposition of the last days. The sun was rising timidly in the distance, under the clouds. He would have liked all this to get excited again, the clear sky to invade the ocean floor, and a saving breeze to scatter the dew in a benevolent shower that would cleanse the deck and his face. None of that was happening. The ship stopped, stuck in the ocean that the salt from the tropics and the rising heat was turning into a slimy broth. He felt his neck and forehead beaded with an unpleasant sweat that heralded the discomfort of the sticky heat. A few minutes later, he wiped the backs of his hands against his pants ; the day would be hot.

He stayed leaning as long as possible, delaying the time when he would have to seek shelter, as the temperature made the heat unbearable. The crew remained inactive and reluctant to watch the deck. He, in turn, succumbed to the warmth that rose from the red depths of the ocean and was reactivated by the heat rays that pierced the clouds. Last night's cave had turned into a furnace.

The captain was nowhere to be seen, probably preferring the stuffy gloom of his cabin to the piercing light of the new day. Everything was as strangely quiet as an early August afternoon in a garrison city. The men were waiting for all this to end.

Antoine was better. He was able to quench his thirst and eat. But he felt empty, without purpose or enthusiasm. This state, which he had never known before, seemed strange enough to attribute it to his recent illness. He remained like this not knowing if the mild cold of the night would eventually revive his being and make him want to do something.

At night, nothing in his attitude showed the expected changes. The furnace became a damp cave again and Antoine remained in the same state. He wasn't worried, maybe a little curious. He took stock of the days and weeks that had elapsed, trying to carefully identify the flaw in the plan he had put in place to undertake his journey, both physical and religious. But he couldn't think of anything. Antoine was quiet but awake. He told himself with a smile that perhaps he himself was the cause of all this trouble and tried to sleep. He had a hard time unrolling his prayers for his family and sisters ; they were not light or fluid enough to get out of the cave.

Antoine was also stalling.

The following days went on in the same conditions as the previous ones, filled with the emptiness of waiting for the humidity of the night and the heat of the day. He was in a giant cauldron.

One morning, as sweat began to soak into his shirt, Antoine felt a breeze, a barely perceptible touch that brought him a few moments of relief. This light touch did not last.

Antoine expected other breezes, other drafts, but nothing else came. In any case, things could evolve ; the weather could change. Not everything was inanimate. The ship floated on the water, waiting for a spring that once again would give some tension to the whole.

He strained his eyes looking at the horizon, scrutinizing the imperceptible, the air moving in the immensity of light. The clouds had disappeared as if they had been caught one-by-one by the entrance of a cave. Antoine did not know this cloudy phenomenon. All these budding masses of clouds were alien to him. He did not know how they formed or how they disappeared over the ocean. He couldn't understand what he hadn't been taught, nor what he hadn't ever been confronted with before. Antoine was discovering a new world. He felt this way for the first time. Little by little his whole being turned towards the sunset, unable to understand a state made of new sensations, strange perceptions and curiosity. Antoine was being reborn.

"The captain wishes to see you in his cabin !" yelled a sailor who hadn't bothered to address him personally beforehand. Antoine did not understand the remark nor the tone used. He wondered what the captain wanted from him, but he headed there anyway.

The captain made him sit down. He asked him how he was. Antoine was visibly better and reassured him about it.

The captain was a handsome man, elegant in his merchant marine uniform. He had an intelligent look and, in his eyes, shone the curiosity and the alertness of a person adapted to his time. He showed no signs of despondency or concern, much less despair.

"I'm glad you are better !" the captain told him.

"Thank you, captain," replied Antoine, "the journey was really hard these last few days."

"It just shows that 'crossing' is not the right word," added the captain, "and yet it is the one we use regularly."

"You are right, it is a journey, perhaps a deportation, in any case it could be a test for me."

"I realized that and I had you in my sights during your indisposition."

"And I appreciate it," added Antoine.

"Oh ! Don't thank me, I had instructions to do so, apparently you are protected cargo."

Antoine, surprised, did not answer but smiled back. The captain was relaxed and was looking at him intensely. His frank and direct gaze showed confidence and great benevolence. The ship moved slightly and then stabilized.

"I believe that, finally, the weather will change Monsieur Pintard, we are reaching the end of our difficulties. We are about to leave the temperate world except that sometimes, in this part of the Atlantic, one can fall into a calm, like a transit zone, mandatory between Europe and the tropics."

"The tropics !" Antoine dared to say.

"Yes, it is an imaginary line useful for navigation, a line of latitude that marks the switch to the torrid areas of the planet ; from now on things will not be the same, you will have to get used to it."

"Is it so different ?"

"It certainly is ! The world you are about to enter is a new world, Monsieur Pintard ! You will be in Saint-Christophe, far from France, far from everything, but nevertheless closer to Europe than in your province."

"How is that possible ?" asked Antoine.

"Here you will hear about foreign powers every day, nations, the King of England, the King of Spain, the Dutch, and more. This is Europe on a scale model in the middle of a huge sea. All the conflicts, all the tensions that appear in Europe have local repercussions and each of the islands can in turn become the scene of military and maritime operations where our admirals exercise their skills and leadership. It is a whirlpool whose magnitude you have never suspected ; your perceptions will change and your concerns will change even more. You must prepare for it. I wanted to warn you because a good number of the transportees experience problems in Saint-Christophe. Exile is a state of mind. You better think about it before we get there."

"Thank you, Captain !"

"It's also part of my mission."

Silence fell, then the captain began to speak again.

"I wanted to educate you personally since this is your first visit to the tropics. Forget about the king, about the king as you perceived him during your life in a religious framework that was not always a happy one." Antoine was surprised at the captain's freedom of tone. The latter noticed it immediately and added,

"Don't be afraid, I'm also a Reformed. Many of us are in the merchant navy. Forget the past and seek to work for the greatness of the kingdom. Here, the conflicts in your province are of no interest to anyone. If you remain locked in your memories, you will be there alone and for a long time. Your transfer to the colony would be a failure."

Antoine said goodbye to the captain, impressed by his common sense, and descended the steps of his cabin, the comfort of which he had not even noticed, absorbed as he was by the fresh look at reality expressed by the captain.

He crossed the deck and stood for a moment in the shadow of a black mast. His fragile figure merged into the shade. Antoine was now one with the ship and no longer wandered like a lost barrel that would have broken its hoops and emptied its contents without order or reason. There he remained for a fairly long time, understanding better and better the slight shudders of the ship that he felt were more and more brief but regular. Life seemed to return ; the ship would soon resume its course. Antoine remembered the preceding days and the great calm that had followed his days of delirium. He thought about the words of the captain and understood their meaning. Antoine had anticipated his advice. Without realizing it, King Louis had disappeared from his foremost preoccupations, which surfaced instantly upon awakening and continued uninterrupted until evening prayer. The monarch who had completely occupied his youth and his adult mind was now disappearing almost entirely into the depths of the Atlantic.

But Antoine was not calm. This emptiness was horrible, terrifying. He discovered that he had lived only for the King and that his existence had been shaped only by reference to this distant monarch who had filled his entire being. Antoine was now alone, with no one to love or hate and no-one to fear. His principles ran the risk of losing strength, having nothing and especially no-one to trust or put them to the test. Their confrontation, in the future, would take surprising forms if the king was not replaced : a kind of weapons room where an endless training session was going on. The wind seemed close now. The breeze, light as it was, produced drafts. The sails would soon be filled with good, hope-laden winds, and Antoine would soon be sailing toward the king's island in the middle of the Caribbean Sea.

With the breeze that was now driving them, Antoine spotted on the horizon the masts of another ship, also undoubtedly immobilized for days, that revealed itself when suddenly unfolding her sails. She was heading back. The thought of it amused him. The return to where ? the King of France or the King of Spain ?

The Antilles were like so many ante-islands, before the European continent. In fact, it all depended on the directions the ships took. Christopher Columbus had believed that he was approaching the islands situated before India.

Antoine realized the relativity of things for the first time ; and his blood circulated more strongly in his veins.

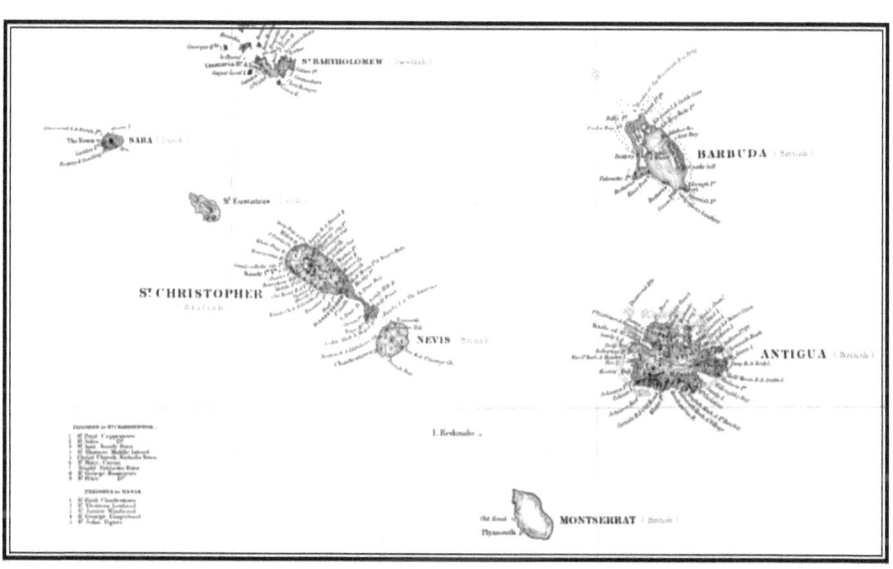

Saint Christopher and Nevis in the Leeward Islands

32

The sunshine was fierce and sweat dampened the torsos and backs of both the indentured workers and the black slaves. Free white people roamed among the workers and were subjected to exactly the same trials and hardships.

The sugarcane harvest had ended several weeks ago and the slopes showed the remains of dry and yellow plants. Even the smallest parcel of land was used and not one piece of land was left untilled.

Antoine was discovering the utilitarian aspect of things and had a hard time getting used to it. The plots were all similar, drawn to the same overall pattern. They consisted of a multi-acre strip of land, longer than they were wide, stretching from the shore to the foot of the hills like a coarse ribbon unwound by the Saint-Christophe administration. Only the crowing of the rooster in broad daylight added a touch of fantasy to the facilities. In fact, it was difficult to speak of farm or estate.

The island was divided into sectors without having sought to avoid the irregularities of the slopes on which the cane grew, while the land near the shore was more fertile, and easier to plow for growing fruits and vegetables. The few rocks gave way to small hills, providing a pleasant view to the whole area but receiving the curses of their owners. The buildings, almost all the same, had a functional look.

Ventilation was essential in a latitude where the sun invades everything and quickly. The whole evoked the practical aspect and the search for efficiency. Colors were missing. The tropical woods compensated for the harsh climate and withstood the hot sun well, making exterior treatment unnecessary.

There were no cultivated flowers, only wildflowers, no decorative touches, other than nature, reduced and concentrated on the top of the island like a sentinel always ready to resow the land after the intruders had left.

Nor were there women anywhere, at least not ones one might like to meet. Only slaves or exiles, lost or orphaned girls, accidents of history. But also, men off the ships, crippled, uncivilized or crazy. The island was well suited for its primary purpose ; namely to work and generate profits or to wait for escape or freedom. To recognize that, sooner or later, was the only way to tolerate these conditions.

All day long, without interruption, the men loaded the cut cane into sacks on their backs. It was the middle of May 1688 and work on the cane harvest was coming to an end. Antoine hadn't had time to rest or to explore the island. As soon as he arrived, he was taken without explanation to a dwelling near the huts where the black slaves were staying. He had to start work the next day without knowing exactly who he was working for. The cutting of the cane, with a few weeks' delay, had to be done in a light and soft soil, not too wet, before the beginning of the rainy season or before the end of Lent, which marked the end of the dry season. The explanations would come later, they had told him. Antoine did so without complaint, curious about all the porters of canes that traversed the slopes of Saint-Christophe like a multitude of ants laden with great baggage. The island was like a great mound of termites, hot, humid, and smoking with the fumes of the last boiling of refined sugar.

Workers in single file climbed steadily and confidently to their cane plantations where they would spend the day working in the scorching sun. The alignment of men moving forward was reproduced in each juxtaposed strip of plantation on the hillside. Conditions were almost always harsh, but occasionally clouds from the upper part of the island blew over the slopes below. This gave relief to the men who, regaining their courage, began to speak louder. Voices then echoed strangely against the soft-looking wall of clouds, which reverberated the sound as at the bottom of a cave. Antoine felt once again isolated as in the calm that he had found in the Atlantic. The sun or the sea breeze soon dispelled the thick mists that returned throughout the day, alternating good and bad moments. Antoine understood that, on this island, it would often be like this.

The mode of production and organization was different from what might exist in the kingdom's provinces. An experiment was being carried out here in Saint-Christophe. It was conceivable, perhaps, that this nascent society would experience advances and setbacks, attempts and failures, hopes and revisions for a long time, before stabilizing and settling down. The line of black men was dotted with bright spots in this slow procession. The backs of the white men who shared their destiny thus put wings in the ebony procession, like termites with transparent elytra that would undoubtedly take flight one day.

With their feet they heavily pressed various shovels and picks that the workers had carried to the foot of the hills on their shoulders. The earth was good, it stuck to the tips of the forged tools, greasy and compact red that they cut into cubes, heavy as a loaf of sugar. Each man had to dig a hole six inches deep and eighty inches long, at the bottom of which were placed two cane cuttings with about eight buds. The terrain had been fertilized during the previous harvest by scattering and burying ash, blood, manure or rotten cane leaves.

Antoine arranged the two cuttings in orderly fashion at the bottom of the hole, anticipating with his thought the buds and flowers to come. He carefully covered the buds with a light soil that he had been careful to first aerate between his fingers. He knew that three weeks later the plant would point its little head in the direction of the West Indies sun. Each hole was aligned eighteen inches apart while each row was one meter apart. Planting density was important.

"Where did you come from ?" a white man who had come near him by chance during his work suddenly asked.

"From France", answered Antoine.

"Where from ?" the white man insisted.

"From the *Cévennes*".

"And, where's that ?" the man inquired.

"In the Languedoc," answered Antoine.

The man walked away from him to dig his hole and continue with his line. Antoine was sweating a lot. He drank in small sips, as peasants used to working in the fields tend to do. He had regained all of his strength and made sure not to get into too much trouble by over working. He was looking for a regularity in his tasks, a cadence in his gestures, a habit in his hand movements in order to endure the climatic conditions he was facing.

Ever since he had started working, Antoine had set these goals so that he would not rush in without taking precautions and put himself in danger. He had observed, over the days, and due to the work on the slope, the damage caused to the people's bodies by work and the physical pain that deformed and swelled them.

Antoine quickly understood that the important thing in those latitudes was to endure. To protect the body was to avoid going into a hole from which you would never emerge, wading through the decay and muddy water of excess rum, the abuse of which emptied eyes and faces. The important thing was not to fall, not even to start slipping, so as not to have to exhaust yourself in vain in a dangerous ascent, with your hands scratching the overturned earth and grasping the fragile reeds that broke with the pull.

Antoine would finish his day around five in the afternoon so that he could go back down to the shore along paths still lit by the sun. The men were tired, the women too. However, they were all glad to return to their huts amid the growing coolness.

The efforts made during the day were so great that the abrupt stoppage brought with it a deep relief that released the effects of a mysterious alchemy. The dazed men had no concern whatsoever for the evening, their wives or their neighbors. Many of them, happy and smiling, were already exchanging incoherent comments about other peoples' wives, while downing cane extract.

These men sunk more and more into stupor.

Antoine kept his distance seeing that he had nothing to gain, nothing to share. He sought sleep in the cold trade winds. His day was projected again before his closed eyes through images of gestures repeated thousands of times, which emerged again and again as the beginning of a punishment that would rob him of part of the night. The days followed one upon the other until the sowing was finished with the total burial of the cuttings.

Some twenty days later, the slopes were covered with thousands of dots that inevitably transformed the hills into a green carpet. The rapid revival of the vegetation cover gave Antoine satisfaction. The result of his work became apparent without having to wait too long. The natural impatience that possesses men found a sure ally in the climate and the fertility of the soil ; this too was beginning to invade him, to unroll its mat to show him the way. He did not try to suppress this new feeling, these new sensations. He did not want to disturb his existence with reflections acquired in another life. He discovered, snorted, sniffed like a young dog tied up for too long.

He wandered the island in his spare time in search of something new, a new vantage point. His natural curiosity led him to evaluate the work of others, to examine their quality, to supervise their organization, to learn how to manage this intensive farming that had nothing in common with that of his province.

The captain was right, he thought, when he discovered at the bottom of a small valley a hummingbird feeding on flowers in long hovering flights, this world is different. He resembled that bird whose name he did not yet know, savoring everything airy, light, and carefree in a ravine that had never been touched by human hand. Large green plants covered the slopes in a mysterious and fragrant mix.

Here the island did not resemble a cultivated area, turned over, scarified, exploited. The trees were tall and the earth black. Numerous and colorful flowers bloomed, revealing their broad petals crowned with slender stamens that fell gracefully in cascades of plump red bells. Their invisible roots under the foliage fed the plant and plunged into the appetizing soil like a fresh blood sausage, sprinkled in places with soft, plump tubers. The beneficial humidity invaded the small depression located between two cultivated slopes, providing a slight freshness like whipped cream. The place made you want to sit there and quench your thirst and enjoy some pastries. Antoine tasted this moment with gluttony and recollection. He swayed between these two states just as the little valley swayed between the two slopes that also resembled a deliberately sloping plateau into which a diamond had been inserted. So much beauty gathered in such a small space gave the impression of sitting in a living room, in a safe place, in a corner of the citadel of Saint-Christophe, needy in many senses, but lively. Everything was quiet here, as under the vault of a Catholic church or in the corridors of a Protestant church. He sat like that, in silence. A long time.

The trade winds at times cut through the natural bays outlined by the curves of the trees. They left sweet smells that mingled with the babbling of a fine stream of water that flowed from the bottom of the valley. Sometimes he would go there and discover a basin of clear water large enough to bathe in. The water was cool and clean, dotted with round rocks that formed a miniature archipelago where freshwater crabs lurked.

The place was still deserted, which led Antoine to think that no one had an interest in it. He took to coming there regularly and, in the weeks that followed, he became a frequent visitor to the place to the point of monopolizing it. He enjoyed the moments of relaxation, the long minutes of bathing and the silence. The sky glimpsed at the back of the dark brown canopy resembled a constellation of blue stars through the thousands of tiny glowing eyes created by clumps of foliage.

Young women were sitting on an islet in the middle of the pool when Antoine reached the bottom of the valley. It had been a hot afternoon, and their light outfits underscored their desire for coolness. Confused, Antoine withdrew, trusting in his smile. The youngest ones burst into laughter, fiddling with their toes. The oldest girl looked at him with a calm and kind look. Antoine buttoned his shirt and turned away. She must have been eighteen years old.

He left the valley. The air was still warm. The trade winds were weakening. He regretted his missed swim, but only partly. He had been caught unawares and the last few weeks of solitude had made him awkward.

Antoine returned to his cabin near the huts of the black workers. The day being a Sunday, there has been less work. The men behaved in a more reasonable manner and he was able to exchange a few words with them. Antoine didn't know their names. Blacks didn't have any and the whites called them whatever they wanted. He was thus addressing strangers who would remain such for a long time. Most of them had no hopes or ambitions. They responded to orders, to an organization that was based on a great mechanism that had its base on both sides of the Atlantic and sometimes moved its pawns towards Africa to renew its workforce.

Antoine had understood the mechanism well when he arrived on the island. The planters ordered black or white men according to the needs to be covered, according to the difficulty of the tasks and the skills sought.

Whether a cooper or day laborer was needed decided the origin and therefore the color of the skin ; the stewards of the province of France or the kings of Dahomey did the rest. Everything was regulated here like a business. Saint-Christophe was a trading company whose production would cover the world with sweetness. It valued its suppliers, just as its customers discussed with it its prices, caring only for the success of its enterprise.

"Where do these ships come from ?" Antoine asked one of the men sitting next to him.

"English colonies in the north", answered the man.

"And what are they doing here ?" Antoine continued.

"They are looking for sugar and molasses."

"There are none over there ?"

"No. They don't know how to make them. Now, we know how since the Brazilians came here", said the man.

"Brazilians ?"

"Yes, that's what we call the people who contributed the technical knowledge".

"And where do they come from ?" he asked again.

"From the coast of Brazil in the south !"

"Why, are there other islands further away ?"

"Islands ? A whole continent as big as Christian Europe !"

"And why did they come here ?"

"The Portuguese drove them out after they chased the Dutch.[51] They say they are Jews."

"But why did they come here to Saint-Christophe ?"

"Because the king welcomed them, like you", added the man with a smile revealing toothless gums.

"But they are not prisoners, they could go elsewhere", Antoine insisted.

"Why ?" added the man. "Business is good here and while it lasts, they will stay."

"Are they here only for that ?"

"Yes, like everyone else !" he added in conclusion.

"But…"

"Only for that I'm telling you and nothing else, like everyone else, and if everything stops one day, they'll abandon us and we'll have to get by without them."

"And what will become of you ?" Antoine dared to ask.

"I don't think anyone thinks about that. But you are in the same boat."

"That's right", added Antoine, who didn't want to persist too much.

"But, if tomorrow we don't send any more sugar or stem waste to France or anywhere else, you will still get up when the rooster crows at four in the morning."

"You're right", added Antoine.

"I know I'm right, but whether or not I am right, we have to get up tomorrow. Go to sleep !"

Antoine said goodbye and returned to his cabin. The air was fresh.

---

(51) In 1654.

Everything was calm. He said his prayers quietly, barely disturbed by the little frogs which sent their throbbing croaks skyward. He knew that for a long time they would make regular waves in the bowl of their nocturnal moonlit pond, like the legs of the young Creole girl he had just met drew circles in the water.

33

The island had become round by the planting that looked like a successful seeding. The buds had grown, masking the roughness of the landscape and camouflaging the large irregularities. The heat was at its peak. It was August 1688. Antoine had acquired a bit of independence thanks to his ability to assimilate the new techniques that had been entrusted to him and to his ease in adapting to the customs and language of the community. He understood the meaning of the orders and their usefulness and immediately incorporated them into the general plan that he had drawn up from the beginning.

Antoine was thinking about the organization devoted entirely to production ; he quickly inserted himself into the gears and into its hierarchy. He sometimes accepted its meanders as a river tolerates the plain of its delta that slows its course towards the sea. The main thing was to move forward and not waste time. He knew that the canes would finally mature, heralding a satisfying cash flow for the planters and the hope of a re-sowing. The successive improvements in the fortune of everyone strengthened his own function in the plantation, which allowed him to have dreams and even pretensions.

Men are made that way, he thought. What's the point of fighting such a powerful and complex machine ? "Things will get better here", he told one of his co-workers, "when no one will need us. In the meantime, each one had to face his destiny."

"And how ?" his neighbor had asked.

"Starting by giving the best of oneself, learning, repeating the same gesture a hundred times, a thousand times until you become essential for the success of the plantation."

"But it is not easy and sometimes even impossible."

"You're right," Antoine answered, "but that will be your destiny."

"And then ?" the day laborer added.

"Then you will know what you are worth, how far you can go, how far you want to go. You will know yourself," Antoine continued.

"But what use will this be to me ?" the man asked him, intrigued.

"Nothing perhaps, or to be happy maybe," Antoine continued.

"Nothing ! I don't care about all that," the man concluded.

"Then choose another goal and accomplish it," Antoine suggested.

"Well, you disappoint me," said the man boldly.

"No, since you can talk to me whenever you want," Antoine concluded.

"And when ?" the man asked, anxious to continue the conversation.

"When all this will have entered your head, when you will have buried in your brain the cuttings that I give you and when, after a lot of care and attention, you will see them grow and bloom, then you will appreciate what I've told you."

"And all that, how long does it take ?"

"The time it takes depends on the person, patience is needed."

"Yes, but that doesn't tell me anything !"

The night was mild as it is usually in the tropics, where the overwhelming climatic extremes of the day gradually fade into the early dark. These moments of respite were also essential for rebuilding his strength. Antoine didn't waste them. He looked forward to them as times of intimacy essential to his moral survival in a collective life that could reach a high degree of crowding and lack of privacy. It was an opportunity for personal recollection, reflected in thought and prayer, which allowed him to fall asleep quickly, like reading a psalm or a poem. Antoine recited a prayer, lingering over each word in his head in order to bring out all its meaning, just as plucking at a stringed instrument, pushes and stretches the vibration to unknown heights. Antoine loved to climb the fly system of this great theater where he found the purity of sounds and the intelligence of concepts. This was essential to avoid descending or exhausting himself in futile fights with those around him, whose existence revealed the fragility of their education. Others' lives sometimes wavered and he needed to withdraw so as not to get lost.

Saint Christophe was also a prison. Antoine had known it from day one. The people weren't there of their own free will. He had seen the huts of the blacks on the very first night. He had shared his house for weeks with other workers who were bound by a three-year contract.

The free workers were so consumed by greed that they shut themselves up in comfortable houses in which all self-examination was absent.

Antoine protected his body but without forgetting his mind. He knew well that the degree of addiction to confinement or to money was determined by the emptiness that filled your mind ; a bad habit that prevented you from fighting.

34

In this month of October 1688, Saint-Christophe would not take on autumnal colors. The millions of heads of sugar cane would continue their ascent to the sky, shaping the curves of the island. As the groundcover thickened, moisture would be more easily trapped between the rows of young shoots, facilitating their growth and overall beautification. The harvest to come would one day perhaps give bad ideas to the captains of the ships that roamed the Caribbean Sea. Apart from this always possible contingency, nothing heralded profound changes in the routine that had developed in recent years.

Antoine knew that there was no autumn in these latitudes and that the difference in seasons was barely perceptible, almost invisible. The islands had enjoyed peace lately. The economic boom had been facilitated by time devoted exclusively to production, organization, and trade. The old islanders claimed that things had improved and that peace and security were the cause. Anyone could work toward his own goals without fear for his person, his staff, his property, or his merchandise. Everything was calm, reasonable, weighed, written.

The Kalinago Indians had received a treatment that satisfied both the English and the French. By granting them the islands of Dominica and Saint Vincent, the French and English freed themselves from their presence and committed them to peaceful behavior by signing a treaty of friendship on March 30, 1660. Diplomacy had used its rhetoric, barely concealing the big stick that it held, secretly, behind its back and that had finally been used at *Pointe de Sang* causing several hundred dead. Reason had done the rest, preventing these people from disappearing forever like the Arawak of the Lesser Antilles, their predecessors. The winding path started halfway up to the top of the island like a rough and stony *Cévennes* goat track, strewn with reddish thorn bushes, which resounded when crushed at every footstep by the displacement of stones. The tips of the bushes, sharp as forged leaves, held up pieces of cloth in places, remnants of the passage of fugitive slaves that the wind stirred toward the ocean like prayer ribbons.

Louisa, one of the young women he had met at the freshwater pond, accompanied him sometimes on his walks outside the plantations. These strolls put aside the conversations and worries of the coast that were renewed every day, identical to the day before.

Antoine had found his rhythm. He was improving his daily tasks and he was fully satisfied with them. He still didn't know what all this would lead to, but the pleasure of succeeding day after day filled him with joy. With patience and perseverance, he thought, surely there would be a result. In any case, he felt that he was where he needed to be. It was in these warm waters that the world was changing.

"Louisa is your name ?"
"No ! my first name is Judith."
"And then why do they call you Louisa ?"
"It seems like it is better suited to Saint Christophe."
"Why ?" asked Antoine.
"Because there is Louis in it like the King of France".
"Judith, that's a name found in the Old Testament".
"That's true, Louisa answered. You see, I too come from far away."
"What do you mean ?" Antoine added.
"I'm from Brazil."
"You too ?" Antoine interrupted.
"What do you mean, me too ?"
"I have been told that the Brazilians brought the technique of boiling and refining."
"That's right, my father is one of them."
"But you don't live with your father."
"No, because my mother is not his wife, she was a Brazilian slave, and I live with my mother who is no longer a slave."
"But your father is here."
"Yes, and it's a secret but his family knows who I am".
"But then your father is Jewish ?"
"Yes, since the Brazilians who brought this knowledge, here were Jews. They were expelled from Dutch Brazil by the Portuguese," Louisa continued, "and my mother followed my father's family."
"I know about the Dutch", added Antoine.
"So here I am."
"And what do you expect from this island ?" asked Antoine.
"I am waiting for Prince Charming" ! Louisa responded with a laugh.

"You risk waiting long," Antoine ventured, surprised by his audacity.
"It depends."
"On what ?"
"On Prince Charming !" They had reached the top of the island and found themselves side-by-side facing the sea. Antoine couldn't escape Louisa's gaze, who had been holding this conversation with him while they climbed one after the other. They chose to sit down, both looking towards the horizon.

"This island, Antoine, is special."
"I agree."
"You know the English are our neighbors. The French also live in the north of the island, up there, in that direction," she indicated with her amber arm as she slid it under his eyes.
"I did not know that ; how is this possible ?"
"The island was conquered by the English and the French at the same time and thus a partition was made, the north and the south for your king, the center of the island for the king of England."
"So, we can say the heart is missing !"
"Yes, we have the head and the legs," Louisa added," but it seems that is not very practical."

They both wanted to laugh and ended up giving in to the overwhelming temptation to pick up the pieces. They sat there for a long time, amazed and happy. The waves followed one another at regular intervals. Their vast dimensions stretched across the empty sea. Neither the rock nor the ships disturbed the rhythm, it was a beautiful arrangement.

Everything was silent again. The sound of the waves did not reach them. Their voices had fallen silent, carried by the light breeze that quietly ruffled Louisa's dark hair. The multi-colored birds that also had their abode at the top of the island happily granted them those moments of eternity by altering their flight at the last moment.

The landscape was immense. The languid island in the sun spread out to the north its round and sweet expanses, with undulating foliage and amber valleys, hiding the borders established by the kings.

Emotion, for the first time, had covered everything, like a great wave coming from the East that marked the change of season.

35

"What is the name of this mountain ?" asked Antoine.

"Which mountain ?" Louisa replied.

"Our mountain !" Antoine added.

"I don't know, but we could call it "our mountain"."

"We could do better !" exclaimed Antoine.

"We could ask what its name is."

"Also, but we could secretly name it just for ourselves," Antoine added.

"Mount Antoine ! Isn't that nice ? Or Mount Louis !" Louisa exclaimed !

"Oh no !" Antoine replied, "that is out of the question !"

"We'll call it "Louisa's mountain"," suggested Antoine, "it's a pretty name."

"In any case, I like "Louisa's Mountain" !"

"Louisa's Mountain", she repeated softly, grabbing a small stone that she had picked up on the way.

"What are you going to do with this stone ?"

"Save it as a memento."

"As a memento !" exclaimed Antoine. "But I am not a memento."

"No, you're stupid, but ..."

"But ... nothing at all," Antoine interrupted.

"Antoine ?"

"Yes ?"

"These islands always separate those they gather as if they were too small to house everyone. You see, there is always one that falls into the water and disappears. Afterwards it is too difficult to return, the winds and currents carry the castaways and if they manage to make it, they are so afraid that they never come back, so happy to have found dry land."

"Who told you this ?"

Louisa didn't answer him and kept talking.

"Here we are surrounded by water but nobody knows how to swim, much less how to navigate. Without the ships of France or England, we would all be condemned to stay here. The ships give us hope that we will one day be able to leave, but we do not command them, so we cannot decide our departure unless we have a lot of money. That is why Saint-Christophe is a prison like all the surrounding islands that I have never been to. Except, perhaps, the great island of Hispaniola."

"But what are you thinking of ?"

"Of the two of us ! I know that one day you will leave and you will not return."

"Can you imagine me as a castaway ?" Antoine joked.

"Do not laugh ! There are rumors that the English drove the French out of Saint-Martin."

"How do people know ?"

"Many men have arrived lately by boat. They found refuge here on Saint-Christophe and they all came from Saint-Martin. Some died of their injuries near the beaches before disembarking."

"And women ?"

"They keep them when they chase away the men."

"Maybe, but what are the risks here, the island is shared between the French and the English."

"You are right, but a few years ago, the French expelled the English so everything could start all over again."

"Yes, but it's not certain."

"No, but the French from Saint-Martin said that the English wanted to make them pay for the attacks by Louis XIV that took place in Europe. It seems that great coalitions have been formed and that the war is going to be long since the troops of the King of France devastated the Palatinate,[52] in any case that is the name I remembered."

"I don't know anything about that, Louisa, I only know you and that changes everything."

"What does it change ?"

"It changes that we are now two and that if you fall in the water, I'll search for you all the way to Hispaniola."

"Yes, but what if we both fall in the water ?"

---

(52) The southern part of the Land of Rhineland-Pfalz nowadays in Germany.

"I will search the Windward Islands and the Leeward Islands until I find you, Louisa."

"That could take a lifetime."

Antoine remained thoughtful, looking at Louisa. Her long black hair curled profusely and gracefully around her pretty face. She was beautiful like the silhouette of Ethiopian women against the setting sun of the Horn of Africa, wise, thoughtful and determined.

"You are my queen of Sheba !" he joked to break the melancholy.

"There is an island not far from here called Saba. Did you know ?"

"No," answered Antoine.

"Oh, I thought . . . It is said to be the island of women."

"That's interesting !" Antoine said. Louisa pretended to throw a stone at him, which she was holding in her hand.

"Then there is your island and your mountain," Antoine laughed, "this is paradise. I will never be alone anywhere. Come on let's go back !"

Antoine was proud to walk alongside Louisa. Her long hair fluttered gently around her long, slender neck. Her golden skin was smooth and flawless, amber and with a silver shimmer, enhanced by a gold choker that she wore in three tight circles at the beginning of her beautifully outlined and partially bare shoulders. Antoine remembered the passage of Kings in the Bible and the visit that the Queen of Sheba had made to King Solomon from where, dazzled by the splendor of the monarch, she had returned leaving him magnificent gifts. He didn't want his queen to leave. He wanted her to stay there forever as an unexpected gift from the confines of Abyssinia.

Antoine reached the shore, holding Louisa's hand in his own sunburned hand. This communion of color amused him and the pressure of their loving fingers returned the beat of their pulses, in unison, to the hollow of their palms joined in a last kiss before parting for the night. Now they were approaching the barracks. They could hear the voices of men and the barking of dogs near the fires lit to cook dinner, lined up like a garland at an equal distance from the beach, marking the foot of each plantation. The daylight was slowly fading, easing the pressure on everyone's eyes.

Antoine felt Louisa's hand move away from him. A few seconds later, she was nothing more than a shadow disappearing in the twilight. She whispered words laden with promise in his direction that would cling to the first moonbeams for a long time.

Antoine knew that he would have a hard time eating and falling asleep like a lonely nomadic shepherd. He knew that Louisa would also have difficulty falling asleep.

The little ledge where the huts had been built right up to the end of the small inlet was cold, black, and deserted like the great plateaus of Ethiopia.

36

The reddish moon lit up the sky due to the magnifying effect of the humidity suspended in the clouds. Soon the sun would rise and take the place of the night star. Antoine was not sleeping. He knew the day would be difficult without the rest that his body craved. Good or bad ideas invaded his thoughts like flowing water washing away the river banks, spreading out into flood plains long fertilized by the principles of his education, and separated into squares by the barriers erected by his forefathers for the exploitation of its riches, by people from the same land, from the same community.

This order, this organization, this very civilization, had always possessed something comforting, pleasant and worthy of attention and respect for him. But, in the middle of his dream, he realized that under the fragile fences, the bubbling that came from upstream was not delicate at all. Its force was not in any way ungainly. The acceleration due to the slope gave linearity to the apparently disorganized progress. The direction of the flow was the *raison d'être* of the flood. It was to sow the plains with the soil pulled from the mountainside as an expected appeasement, a necessary stop before taking their overflow to other shores and other destinations. Those below were receiving the beneficial mana from heaven while those above were already rehabilitating pastures and property boundaries. Life thus resumed its course, each finding in the fertile mud, his field, his animals, his livelihood and the frontier of his hopes.

Antoine was afraid of being carried away by the torrent of emotions that had marked the past days, because he surmised that moments lived, like no others, could one day be erased from his memory, remodeled or destroyed forever by the weight of his inheritance.

Antoine was afraid of disappointing Louisa, of leaving her one day on a shore, crying, weeping, sailing alone to other destinations, perhaps also swept away, as Louisa thought, by the winds of history. He discovered the solitude of the new world and its immensity, empty and without reference to anything or anywhere else, as strong as a swaying between two shores of the ocean ; he could feel the fear of never settling down or ending his career spinning around for eternity.

The first cockcrow made him jump. He felt at that moment the full weight of the betrayal that he could already be carrying, temporarily installed in a world so different from his, whose limits he still did not understand.

The first clashes between the men were taking place outside, due to a certain lack of privacy, to unequal relationships and the hangover from the previous day's drinking. Antoine had also got up with a hangover. He did not like this state and he already perceived it as a wasted day.

The climb to the plantations was done, as usual, before the heat slowed the men down. It was the same weather as the day before, the usual weather. The poultry in the backyard called out in a series of strident, chaotic cries. Antoine would have liked to have gone to the ocean and to have immersed himself in it for an American evangelical baptism so that he could evaluate things and convince himself that, nothing being the same as before, he should continue to advance in this world that he did not know.

The thought woke him up. He admitted that it was not possible to change his principles with a simple change in latitude as we change of parallel. They had the same value everywhere ; deviating from them was renouncing them.

Renouncing right now was the surest way to sink, he thought. He would endure whatever it took.

"You're not going far today", called out his neighbor in the line next to him.

"Do you think so ?" Antoine replied.

"I'm sure ! Look at where the others are, you must speed up or you will have problems."

"You may be right," answered Antoine. The man had disappeared just as he had come, hidden among the already tall reeds.

"Where is he ?" Antoine grumbled.

He resumed his work, picking up the pace. His arms were tugging at his back that wasn't as flexible as the previous days. Everything seemed tied up and dry inside.

Antoine had been drinking heavily that day, trying in vain to grease a machine that was stuck. The rows were long and the ends of the planting lines only appeared at the last moment. He didn't have time to breathe because the others had already buried themselves under the tender leaves of the reeds to weed over and over again. Antoine had lost his bearings for the first time. He blamed himself.

The descent took place in a joyous and unusual uproar. They all seemed to have an opinion on the origin of the disorders affecting Antoine, some of which made them laugh stupidly.

The island is small, Antoine thought, like an overcrowded prison. The English must know by now, he observed amusedly to himself.

A man was waiting for him in front of his cabin. Antoine walked towards the entrance of his room without paying attention. When he was about to cross the threshold, the man called him, provoking laughter from his neighbors.

"Pintard ! You are Antoine Pintard."

"Yes sir !" Antoine replied, embarrassed. His neighbors laughed even more.

"Tomorrow you will not go to work ; the master wants to see you."

"What's happening ?" Antoine dared to ask.

"I don't know, the man wants to see you. See you tomorrow !"

"See you tomorrow, sir."

The others had resumed their disorderly laughter, sometimes interrupting their outbursts with silences that spoke volumes about the exchanges that were taking place, resuming their racket and ending in a lot of rambling talk. Antoine ended by also laughing, finding in this delayed hiccup the remedy for the ills that had bothered him all day.

He retained a certain affection for his companions in misfortune, not because they weren't bad, sometimes they were, but because the manifestation of their temperament was infectious and provoked in him as in others a healthy reaction. He thus kept his feet on the ground. As for them, it was their way of paying attention to him.

Antoine fell asleep that night, amid the reassuring image of Louisa, which the affectionate teasing of his companions made him remember incessantly, and the questions raised by the meeting the next day.

37

The next day, Antoine got up very early. The others were preparing to leave. Antoine was in a good mood and ready to face his boss.

The building was large, square and tall, in the shape of a warehouse, a cube under which an entrance, in the form of an administration door, was built on one of its corners. The place was flat, the docks deserted, the store empty. Old barrel hoops were placed against one of the walls. Apart from this detail, the place was in good order. Saint-Christophe belonged to the Royal Domain, the crown lands, and everything seemed organized to satisfy the greatness of the king. A few men walked the corridors that led from one compound to another. These were straight and properly maintained without unnecessary or unsightly storage.

The employees' clothing emphasized their different roles, which could be a dazzling white for field workers. The others, busy with less physical and better paid jobs, introduced a touch of style to their outfits which were kept simple and for the most part in lighter tones of blue. Antoine walked to the door and tried to turn the handle, which didn't budge under the pressure of his hand. The door was locked. Antoine was not used to finding a locked door, since he lived in a house open to the four winds. He tried again, but the latch just didn't move. He turned around in a full circle. Nobody.

"Who are you looking for ?" shouted a man staring at him with a hard, fixed gaze.

"I have an appointment with my master !"

"Who's your master ?"

"Monsieur d'Angennes ! "

"What makes you think Monsieur d'Angennes is going to see you ? He has other things to do, if he happens to be in Saint-Christophe !

Are you Antoine Pintard ?"

"Yes sir," answered Antoine.

"Then I will see you." Antoine entered the simple and clean office. Several documents were stacked on one corner of the table. The rest of the room was empty except for a crucifix in a place of honor on the wall, clearly visible. The two men took their places around the table, on plain wooden chairs. The office appeared to have been abandoned for several weeks, as the man had to forcefully push the espagnolette lock to open the blind that protected the only window.

"Good !" the man said as an introduction. "I need a man like you. Since your arrival, I have watched you and you have given me complete satisfaction. One of the planters died last week and we must replace him immediately, otherwise the fruit of his labor will never materialize."

Antoine let the man, whom he did not know but who seemed to know him so well, continue.

"I'll get straight to the point. Are you ready to take over this vacancy ?"

"But isn't there a successor in his family or in his immediate circle ?"

"If there were, you wouldn't be here in front of me. In any case, things are not done that way here in Saint-Christophe. The island belongs to the Royal Dominion. Awarded to important people through a personal connection as a tribute to their king, you should know that."

"Yes, of course."

"The plot of which I speak of, belongs to Monsieur d'Angennes, who has given the use of the farmland to several tenants, including the one who just died. It is now a matter of taking his place. I want you to take on this responsibility."

"But I have not seen the complete growing cycle of the cane," added Antoine.

"You have seen the essentials," replied the man.

There was something communicative about his confidence. And the more respectful attitude that had replaced the initial familiarity now placed the two on an equal footing.

"But harvesting and processing are not easy things ?"

"Indeed, but you will not be alone."

"When should I give you a reply ?"

"Now."

"Can I take some time to think about it ?"

"Do so," said the man with a stern look, "you have today. I won't be far, so let me know how it goes."

"It's interesting," Antoine added, who didn't want to disappoint the man, but….

"I understand, will see you later."

"Could you give me your name ?" asked Antoine.

"Estrangin . . . Fulcrand is my first name."

"Are you from Languedoc ?" Antoine dared to ask.

"My father was from Guyenne. I was born here."

"In Saint-Christophe ?" asked Antoine.

"In Martinique."

"I'll see you soon."

"That's right, I will see you later."

Antoine left the office in confusion, his enthusiasm muffled by a vague sense of entrapment. Several acres, so fast, he thought. Antoine restrained his enthusiasm, telling himself it was a dead man's belonging. These islands were definitely a special place where inheritances, even small ones, could be quickly built or undone. He walked towards the great alley that divided the rows of warehouses. The heat was intense, but Antoine didn't feel it. He was too absorbed in his thoughts. He only retained the positive side of the proposal while at the same time he categorized the entire offer as a trap. But, once the trap was dismissed as an unlikely hypothesis, only the positive aspects of the matter remained vibrant in his mind, and there were plenty of them.

He thus crossed the deserted docks and the small jetty. He was alone ; everyone seemed to have fled from the place which must have been so busy at other times of the year. Louisa was not there, neither was his brother Jean, nor the pastor, nor Monsieur le Baron, he was alone facing the vast Caribbean Sea. The Atlantic and his hopes for France and Europe turned their backs on him. Only Fulcrand Estrangin could tell him more, help him decide, but he wasn't sure the man was willing to do that. His ignorance of the affairs of the kingdom and its subjects made Estrangin a different kind of man, a new man who did not bother with enlightened exchanges. This man was used to making decisions on his own without consulting anyone. He perfectly knew his place in the hierarchy and made the most of his decisions while respecting the rules of the game. He knew full well that breaking them would bring him face-to-face with the power of the organization and he would find himself punished, wandering the Caribbean in search of refuge and unlikely help. Antoine was discovering that freedom had its price.

He stood there for a long time, restless, eager to see more clearly, to know more. He finally realized that this desire was masking his indecision, his inability to change to another level within the organization. The drastic change that was coming would make him lose much of the natural dependence that derived from his current state, together with its advantages. The new advantages would be the consequence of his courage, his intelligence and his successes. But he did not know if he would be able to carry out such a daunting task. This was the chance to find that out while he discovered himself who he was !

Antoine walked over to the cube and the desk. He was surprised to find Estrangin there, who nodded.

"I accept", Antoine said triumphantly.

"So much the better," was the answer. "Tomorrow you will have to get down to work."

"May I know where the plantation is ?"

"In the north of this part of the island, on the edge of the English lands. We will go there tomorrow, be ready an hour before sunrise, I will go with you."

38

Darkness crept through the plantation. The cabins were bathed in a silence gently stirred by the trade winds. This soft light covered the sleeping bodies like a light sheet. The day had been busy. The meeting had gone smoothly. Estrangin, in a very good mood, had led Antoine to the limits of the southern French part of the island, covering the distance of a mile-and-a-half rapidly. Contact with the plantation men was made quickly.

Estrangin had introduced them to the new manager, adding that it wouldn't change much, which didn't seem to surprise them. They had walked the property together, its boundaries, its fields. All the plantations were the same, nothing ever changed. He had accepted his new duties. There was no need for him to return to the south of the island as his small bundle represented all of his possessions. The distancing from Louisa hurt him ; he had nevertheless fallen asleep.

The next day, Antoine went to work, trying not to disturb the organization set up before his arrival. He didn't feel at home as yet. He knew it would take time. Still, he didn't feel like he was taking someone else's place. He had not forced the transfer of authority. It was the result of a sudden death and he did not feel guilty about that. His new role was based entirely on the authority delegated by Estrangin on behalf of the interests of the Angennes family.

At that time, Saint-Christophe was like a ship anchored in the open sea, whose crew would change every three years, at the end of their employment contracts. Antoine also had three workers under him, three "thirty-six month" hires. Two of them were from La Rochelle. Their easy and adaptable demeanor pleased Antoine. The third, a restless-eyed man from Normandy, worked better as part of the team than alone.

They were all three at the end of their contracts. They would soon be free to return to France, but they would probably stay here for a time as free workers. The team was completed by three male slaves : three women accompanied the men but he was unable to figure out how they were related to one another. He did not ask the two men from La Rochelle who seemed distant from the group. The slaves had the fixed gaze of those who do not understand what more is being asked of them, because they have already given everything. They knew that their return home was impossible. They couldn't even pinpoint where they originally came from, especially since most of them had been born on the island. Their only hope lay in the eventuality of liberation, a change of status, which in the end could only be an appearance of change, as they would continue to live and work in Saint-Christophe.

As none had really come there of his own free will, each one would end their days dependent on a powerful master who would give them subsistence and security in exchange for their hard work. None of them had the courage to face the unknown alone, and they had no other choice than to suffer rules and restrictions. Transfer to another island was rare. Movements between the two ends of the island were by boat because of the division between French and English territories. The Atlantic coast was not accessible by sea. Any journey on foot forced one or the other to cross the open-air plantations arranged in strips up to the top of the island. With no escape, no hiding spots, it was virtually a prison. Only the struggle between the European powers could bring about change.

The capture of Saint-Christophe by the English might have hinted at some glimpses of change for its inhabitants, but the treaty between France and England had been honored until now, even going so far as to regulate trade with the Dutch : a free-trade agreement based on mutual respect for the benefit and influence of the signatories, without the brutal boarding and seizure of merchant ships as was practiced elsewhere.

Saint-Christophe had gone a step further by asserting the pre-eminence of sugar diplomacy. The island was ahead of its time.

Antoine walked up and down the acres of land that made up his new home. The property cut out in the shape of a rectangle had long sides. He now possessed a piece of Saint-Christophe and spent the following days convincing himself of it. You cannot take care of or dedicate yourself to the maintenance of land, beyond what is reasonable, he thought, if you have not made it first your own. Antoine, after a few days, no longer wanted to be reasonable. His work absorbed him completely and it was better that way. He kneaded the soil and reveled in the brown spots on his palms and between his fingers. Hard work did not scare him and he was eager for the next day, to work again and become one with the plot facing the ocean. Antoine was beginning to love the island.

Discovering his territory, a little deeper every day, he took notes, anticipating his approach to a slope he knew, or taking a breath at the foot of a hill before climbing. He now listened to the wind and the rain in a different way. Each sign now had a different meaning. They were intended to link growth with fertility. The higher the stalks rose in the sky and the more they resisted the wind, the greater would be the profits, thus predicting investment and improvement projects. Antoine was being won over by the rules of the game in Saint-Christophe to the point of forgetting everything else. He was content and felt fulfilled.

39

Louisa arrived early. The sun had barely risen. She had set out before dawn to keep her visit discreet. The dogs had barked as she crossed the plantations, sending their calls back to the small inlets and backyards. A few disturbed roosters had crowed an early alarm causing some people to roll over on their straw mattresses. The deserted shores of the beach had not welcomed the strident noises in the ruined huts, abandoned some years ago by the Indians, letting the screams fade in contact with the first waves of the sea. There was the entire settlement, reduced in her eyes to a set of wooden houses whose occupants shared the same destiny. Louisa carried a basket full of fruits and roots, vegetables, and a bouquet of flowers. Her bare feet, although accustomed to walking on uncomfortable roads, made her suffer under the weight of the burden. She was happy but also worried. She found her demeanor bold, but she trusted the surprise she would provoke. She waited eagerly for dawn but, as the darkness of the night still enveloped her apprehensions, she told herself that she still had time to turn around without anyone ever finding out about her attempt.

As she approached Antoine's house, she slowed down. The place was deserted. She would have liked to have shared the dawn with him, when the dim light does not yet smother the depth of words and gives them the time it takes to bloom. She knew that this moment would not last forever. There were no dogs or chickens. The place that she had been told about corresponded with what she found, situated there on a hill. The master's cabin was separated from the other barracks by a wooden closure around an abandoned garden. Everything seemed so simple. Louisa walked to the entrance. She placed her basket in front of the rickety door. Antoine was there, behind the thin planks with scattered holes that let her sense his breathing. She did not however have the courage to enter. Louisa left the house as silently as she had come. She took the way home satisfied with her offering, blaming herself nevertheless. On the way back, she felt that her venture had been dangerous. The sun was now rising in the east. It would soon let its rays slide down the back of the island.

If that was his house, she thought, her present would have its little effect. Louisa spent the day waiting for a signal that never came. The sun's rays disappeared towards sunset. Night fell everywhere and the roosters fell silent. The small inlets and the ruined huts were once again covered in silence and so were the surrounding cabins. Louisa could see the scattered holes in her door from her bed. The moon lit up the outside, transforming the shadows of the trees blown by the trade wind into the shape of Antoine. This shivering sounded like the footsteps of a man coming home late. Louisa thought of her little basket.

The next day, she remained busy so as not to get caught up in her thoughts. She took the road to the cane plantation with the others and with her mother. Their presence was comforting to her, although she didn't speak for a long time. She liked their company. Either way, she had no choice. Her mother enjoyed a privileged status in Louisa's father's household, but she could not avoid farm jobs. Both knew the limits of the benefits granted by their employer and did not abuse them. Louisa was looking in the direction of the mountains when she asked her mother what the tallest mountain was called.

"*Pointe de Sable*", [53] her mother replied.

"Are you sure ? That's a funny name !"

"For sure, my daughter, *Pointe de Sable*, it looks like all of us. Made of sand, there is not much to take root on. It is reassuring for those who want to leave. As for the others, you have to know how to be content with what you have."

"But I will never be satisfied with what I have !" Louisa exclaimed.

"Oh ! But what's wrong with you ?" her mother retorted.

"Nothing."

"So go ahead, you naughty girl !"

The two women began to weed their rows again. Louisa stayed close to her mother as she did not want to be left behind. After all, her mother was all she had.

---

(53) N of T : *Pointe de Sable* : Sandy Point

Louisa waited until the end of the day to go to bed, peering out through the holes on the door. Antoine wasn't the kind to come in the middle of the night. Therefore, Louisa decided that she would meet him soon and in broad daylight. Her self-confidence pleased her and she finally fell asleep thinking about Pointe de Sable.

"Louisa's Mountain" is a better name, she thought.

40

The wind began to pick up in the middle of the night. An Atlantic wind, dense and compact, loud and regular, passing over the shacks until it blew them down and then slowing its course, giving a little respite to the wooden planks that groaned and creaked under the slow gusts. The wind grew stronger every quarter of an hour, throwing all kinds of branches and plants against the partitions of the cabins as if stripping bared the entire island of its vegetation. Outside, the screams of the workers pierced the storm at times and disappeared again like drowning men. The sand lashed the walls in a fine rain that penetrated on all sides, immediately mixing with water on the ground and turning into a thick, muddy deposit.

Louisa, terrified, was curled up under her mattress, her arms encircling her knees. The temperature had dropped rapidly, adding an unusual element to this end-of-world rampage. Louisa stared at the door, her head now resting on her knees, listening for the creaks that would announce the collapse of the ceiling. The cabin was moving. It seemed like the walls were closing in a deadly kiss. Disorder seemed to reign everywhere. She suddenly heard a thud like a bucket full of water thrown against a wall, a hoarse scream and then nothing. Louisa stared at the wall where the noise seemed to be coming from. The planks vibrated spasmodically, as if by a force unrelated to all this but with a mechanical regularity. She called in that direction asking if anyone was in trouble. No one answered, but the ghostly vibration continued for a moment more accompanied by a dull rattle of convulsion and outflow of life. Then, nothing. Louisa, seized with terror, closed her eyes, not knowing what to do, paralyzed by fear. The storm was not calming down, it had yet to release its accumulated force on the warm waters of the ocean. The island moved now as if it were separated from the seabed to which it had been anchored. This terrifying hesitation often led people to wonder what to expect. Had they been transported to an abyss where they would sink for eternity, bleating like calves on the way to slaughter?

The blood had at first appeared fluid at dawn, a red and bright color from the water that carried it with the sand blown by the wind. The initially narrow stream had turned into a wider and denser flow despite the rain beating down outside. Louisa noticed the red trail that was widening and turning into a black pool like pig's blood. Louisa realized there was something behind the storm-washed wall. But she just stood there, paralyzed with fear, just continuously screaming. Her screams were muffled by the hideous cracks coming from outside. She tried, in a moment of respite, to take matters into her own hands, but the gusts of wind were pushing her back inside. She had the courage to open the door a little to discover that the patio was empty. Her mother had not returned. She had undoubtedly taken refuge in another hut. Louisa didn't know what to do. The storm lasted well into the night. It was late when the last gusts ceased, carrying their desolation toward the northern islands. The men emerged one after another, illuminating the surroundings of the huts with their torches. Louisa did the same, trying to find her mother. She walked around the house assessing the damage. She had no lantern and the night was dark. She detected a straight shape leaning against the wall of the hut. It was her mother, mouth opened in a grimace, feet in the water, fatally impaled on a metal hook to hang bags. The iron had pierced her liver.

Antoine arrived at the last moment before the earth completely covered the coffin of poor Louisa's mother. He kept his distance. Slaves and indentured workers stood side-by-side. The planters were there too. Louisa was not alone. Women surrounded her. The ceremony had come to an end. With the farewell words spoken, only words of comfort remained. Antoine participated from afar in a show of affection and support. They had all been afraid. The shock was still visible and, from the promontory where he stood, Antoine observed the movement of each group, together and in an orderly way, so as not to get lost or make a mistake.

The ancient inhabitants, those of 1627, the year of the treaty, and those from an earlier time were a small and compact group.

The new planters[54] advanced in groups but their community was less tightly bound, not yet consolidated by common memories or marriages within the group. The workers, both black and white, were gathered according to their origin, whether African or European, nevertheless sharing the same job and the same deprivations. The groups were also distinguished by their mourning clothing ; the dark of the white workers contrasted with the white of the black workers. The imagination of the ancient inhabitants was expressed through the rags often collected in the raids of the old buccaneers, in contrast to the grave simplicity of the newcomers.

The dead woman had been buried, still beautiful, in a blue organdy dress, secretly dressed by Louisa's father, as a testimony to the bond between the groups, the announcement, perhaps, in the islands, of the crossbreeding of an entire continent.

---

(54) Planters were called *habitants* in French and *habitation* still means a plantation in the French West Indies.

41

Antoine woke up early the next Sunday. He quicky walked the mile-and-a-half that separated him from Louisa.

He carried with him the basket that he had re-filled for her in re-turn. The storm damage had not affected all parcels equally. The massive weeding that the weather had brought to the vegetable plots wouldn't cause a prolonged disruption of supply, Antoine thought. All of this would grow back very quickly thanks to the climate. He could give part of his small crop to Louisa. The sugarcane had suffered, although everyone agreed that the damage had not been as great it could have been. The elders confirmed this was often the case. However, there was a lot of work to do to get back on track, for the people to recover their plots of land, farmers armed with their tools, like seamstresses with scissors and needles. They would have to toil over their narrow bands of land for a long time, plugging the holes and redrawing their outlines. Roads were in very poor condition too and would require hours of work after recovery of the plots. The women and children were already clearing the branches that were in the way in some places. The elderly also worked. Everywhere fires were lit, covering Saint-Christophe with the color of mourning. Antoine approached Louisa's cabin, comforted in his decision by the basket that he held tightly against him, overflowing with products from his garden. She was not there so he had to wait. He discreetly walked around the house to observe the enclosure and evaluate the storm's damage to the vegetables. Everything had been destroyed. The large leafy vegetables were scattered, weeping underground, as if crushed by an incredible giant force. The others, with sparse, straight and pointed leaves, were broken, sometimes finely chopped as if they were tobacco leaf waste.

"Antoine !" Antoine spun around.

Louisa was there, beautiful and dignified, dressed in white, her hair up as if for a ceremony.

"Good morning, Louisa. Here, I brought you this." He handed her the basket, which she took, brushing against his hands.

"Wait, I'm stupid, where do you want me to put it ?"

Louisa pointed to the table under the awning at the front.

"You can sit. I'm glad to see you."

"Me too," answered Antoine. "I was not sure if I would find you".

"I was about to go to Mass."

Both of them cast their eyes in all directions, nervously wondering what might be said about the encounter so early in the day between a mulatto and a white inhabitant.

"I can go with you !" Antoine dared to suggest.

"But I thought you …"

"I didn't say I would go into church !" he exclaimed, smiling.

"Ah," she replied", with a bit of disappointment. "So, let's go !" she said cheerfully.

They walked, a good distance apart from each other, in the direction of Basseterre, where the Catholic Church was located. Along the way they were unable to keep their relationship secret. They encountered all kinds of pilgrims whispering among themselves. This slow procession, however, turned out to be endearing like a Sunday communion of the whole island heading towards the priest ; like the shepherds had approached, timid and awkward, the baby Jesus. The outlines of the trails dug by the storm disappeared under the procession, and the joyful women created a bond between the groups through their frankness and, at times, impudence. Louisa and Antoine walked among them in silence. As they approached the church, the crowd became more compact and Antoine's fingers brushed against Louisa's. The parishioners had turned up in greater numbers than usual : everyone wanted to thank the Lord for being saved. Louisa didn't seem sad.

"You did not want to enter the church, and you have succeeded, we are not all going to fit in."

The priests had opened the doors wide to allow people outside to follow fragments of the Mass and bring some air to the suffocating parishioners inside.

"Let us thank God," said the priest ! "Praise to the Lord !"

The groups had not been able to reconstitute themselves outside ;

great disorder reigned. The Capesterre church esplanade looked like a vast and colorful community where different groups breathed and chanted the Credo in their common Catholic faith.

Louisa had caught Antoine's gaze, impressed despite himself.

"It's beautiful !" she exclaimed, waiting for an answer.

Antoine had not wanted to answer but he said yes to Louisa. "The priest told me that "catholic" means "universal" !" Louisa added. Antoine didn't reply. However, he was moved by the belief manifested, by this immense communion, indeed, by the liturgy. Antoine would keep all of this as an intact memory for his entire life. He had felt the faith in the midst of it all, vibrant under the sun. He would preserve all his life a respect for the religion of others and avoid, forever, sinking into a narrow militancy.

The end of the celebration transformed the esplanade into a joyous fairground where the exchange of words and news had replaced the usual exchange of goods. All exclaimed and outpoured their fear but also their joy at being alive among their own people. The church continued to empty, bringing newcomers to the esplanade, new intonations, and additional confusion. The conversations continued for a long time, an immense exchange of feelings, questions and consolation. People did not want to leave each other, to convince themselves that it was time to start on their way back, arm-in-arm, hugging ; a beautiful humanity entrenched on its island, happy and proud, for a time, of their destiny, oblivious to the days to come, peaceful and joyous as a wedding party. Louisa and Antoine in turn forgot themselves, holding hands to better navigate the crowd. They were pleased by this physical closeness, delicately elbowing people, brushing against shoulders and plump or lean bellies unable to avoid their hands joined closely together in a knot that could no longer be untied. Louisa, thus attentive to her guests, walked radiantly, like a happy bride.

42

The shot rang out loud. The workers turned as if they were a single person in the direction of the beach from where the discharge seemed to come. A small cloud of dust marked the location of the shot. Antoine called out to his men to resume work. A second shot came from the same place. Antoine straightened up and looked towards the shore more closely. Two men were shouting in the direction of a fragile ship that was now lowering its sails. Faced with this sign of submission, the shooting stopped. The ship was loaded with silhouettes poorly outlined against the sun that, reflecting in the sea, made it difficult to distinguish its content.

The skiff approached the shore at the outer extremity of the inlet. Its approach took a long time as it was being rowed. Other armed men had arrived on the beach and appeared to be discussing among themselves, standing close to each other. The sea was calm, with no ships on the horizon.

The access to Nevis, the sister island too distant to distinguish any current navigation, nevertheless seemed deserted.

Antoine asked his men to resume their tasks, each keeping a close eye on what was happening below. The sugar cane shoots were broken in places, revealing through gaps a narrow view of the bottom of the plantations. Frightened oxen were bellowing on the ridge.

"What do we do ?" asked one of the indentured workers from La Rochelle.

"Nothing, let the armed planters do what is needed, we wouldn't be of much use," replied Antoine.

"But what if they were English !"

"What would they come to do here on a single ship while having a whole navy ?" answered Antoine.

"It seems they suffered a lot with the storm," continued the thirty-six-month man. (55)

"They just have to ask for help," answered Antoine.

"Perhaps that is what they *are* doing," added the man from La Rochelle.

"I'd be surprised . . . it's not their style. No, it must be something else."

"Well," the indentured worker replied, "we'll see."

"Yes, we'll see," concluded Antoine, who was eager to finish with the task for the day.

The two men went back to work, encouraging the other teams to do the same. The sun was now sinking below the horizon. The night would soon envelop the inlets and the hills. The sweet twittering of the birds was fading like the end of a great excitement. Now everything was at peace. The frogs' croaking would soon take over as if to mark an ever-reborn life in these latitudes on an island that never slept.

The end of the evening brought the beat of the drums of the maroons, runaway slaves who, unable to escape by sea, lived scattered in the forests, accompanied by Indian women as abandoned as themselves.

The drums were a provocation, reminding their brothers that slavery could be broken, that they were still there, alive, and that the soft night they spent with their wild wives would one day bring offspring full of rebellion and insubordination.

Thus, they were prickling the island, after nightfall, like the itching powder that stings submissive slaves and their powerless persecutors. Antoine loved the drums of the night. They resembled the *Cévennes* mountains at dusk, when family members exchanged forbidden words by candlelight. The sounds of the drums carried farther than the readings of his father, covering with their haunting rhythms their oppressors' desire to sleep.

The night finally became calm and quiet. The maroons, their wives and their children had fallen asleep in the deep forest, in the heart of a wild kingdom that would never be party to the treaty of 1627 between the two nations that shared the dominion of the Island.

Antoine finally fell asleep, accompanied by the drumbeat coming from the peaks, human and terrifying. Seeking only peace and slumber,

---

(55) Indentured servants were also called "36 months" because they had to work without salary for 36 months to pay the crossing to America. Indenture servitude was also common in British America.

he imagined the maroons' eyes rolling like the devils' in the heat of the night.

Lying among their starving children, the maroons' provocation was like a cry for help to the plantations.

Antoine was not dreaming.

Basseterre in Saint Christopher (J. Stephen Conn, CC BY-SA 1.0)

43

The day had started well, each one taking his accustomed place, carrying out his tasks, sowing, weeding, cutting, beautifying the land and the plantations. A second ship had approached late in the afternoon. The men now stationed facing the beach had their weapons within easy reach. The occupants had disembarked from the ship, greeted by the Quartier militia, who helped them run aground the boat and led them to the shore. Antoine could not see what happened next because the view was not clear along the entire coast. Things seemed to go smoothly and everyone seemed calm and happy.

"You know something ?" he asked the man from La Rochelle, pointing toward the beach with his chin.

"Nothing."

"And nobody said anything ?"

"No."

"Then it could not have been important," added Antoine.

"That's not what they say there," said another servant, in a confident tone.

"And how do you know that ?" Antoine interrupted him.

"I know what they told me. It seems that these people come from Saint Martin."

"From Saint Martin, then they are French !" exclaimed Antoine.

"Well, no, . . . they are Irish."

"Irish ! But what are they doing here ?"

"They are asking for refuge. I don't know anything else."

"Shelter ?"

"Yes, help, that we accept them here in Saint-Christophe."

"And why is that ?"

"I don't know, that's all I know."

"And who told you all this ?"

"A woman from down there whom I know, that's all."

"Well, we'll see," Antoine concluded, "but it's very weird ! I have heard of the Irish and usually when they arrive somewhere it is because something has happened where they came from."

"How's that ?" asked the first one from La Rochelle.

"How's that ?" Antoine continued. And he told them what he had heard in La Rochelle.

The men were indifferent to the fate of the Irish. They did not care that they were mistreated on their island. After all, these English had only to work things out among themselves. For them, the main thing was that all this should not create a problem here in Saint-Christophe.

The following days brought with them an avalanche of refugees, tall, massive and red-haired. In fact, they were all Irish. The indentured workers from Brittany understood their language, which suited everyone. The Quartier militia was in charge of welcoming them. They were then transferred to Basseterre where the governor's services took care of them. Antoine knew the true significance of the story. It was a ship with supporters of the Stuart king James II who had just been dethroned and replaced by William of Nassau, with the complicity of a part of the English nobility who did not want a Catholic king. Those unfortunates must have left Ireland, abandoning everything. They had sought refuge in Saint-Martin, where they had been surprised to learn upon their arrival that the French had been expelled from the island. The British had then pirated their ships and left them free to go and be captured elsewhere. That was all, except that the most politically educated correctly pointed out that James II had also left England, and that Louis XIV, his host and his cousin, was likely to do something. Antoine pondered on this knowledge and expected chaos in the area. The Jacobites did their best to integrate quickly into the plantations, waiting for better days to resume their ascent to the heights that best suited their social standing. They assimilated better in Breton plantations and no one heard of them again except on rare occasions.

The governor of Saint-Christophe received orders from France with the next ship. Things were not going so well in Europe. It was preferable to be organized and be able to respond to any warlike attempt by the English who, unsure of the legitimacy of their new Dutch king, tried to have him accepted and recognized by his people and the entire nobility, who spoke of a Dutch conquest of England, by baptizing him

English. France, their ancestral enemy but also the mother of their nation, [56] knew her offspring well. She had to expect a confrontation. This was the official position.

The islanders were still excited about their work, pleased with the reparations made after the storm to the plots, which were now all restored. The edges of the plantation strips that extended towards the summits had been cleared of the fallen and cut cane. The big task of rearranging had been a success and no one would trip on the carpet of cane again.

The people were carefree. Their difficulties had been left behind. For their part, the English party was having a harder time getting over it, but they certainly would, in due course.

Saint Christopher could rest assured that it would be at peace for some time.

---

(56) Guillaume le Conquérant, that is William the Conqueror, is the founder of the kingdom of England after the Norman conquest of Anglo-Saxon England in 1066. Normans and French completed the unification of England attempted by King Alfred in the 9th century. All British monarchs after 1066 claim descent from the Normans.

44

Antoine was summoned early by his neighbor across the gate. The two men met, each with a bundle. Antoine had ordered the employees to take charge while he was gone. Both descended towards Basseterre, the capital, where the recent Irish crisis had made the population nervous. They passed houses, walking along the paths abandoned by the militiamen who had been in charge of their maintenance.

The island was divided into Quartiers with the Treaty of May 13, 1627, to which all had agreed before it came to battle. A commercial agreement had been signed between France and England. It would make Saint-Christophe the "mother island" of the two great nations in their expansion and conquest of the Antilles. An economic community had just been born that required the authorization of the representatives of the two powers to allow Flemish ships to enter.

This prosperity had a price : that of its protection. Initially organized in two parts, each part of the island chose its own organization, and the French part was divided into districts up to the top of the *Pointe de Sable* Mountain. The division of the island had encompassed the salt flats of the southern part of the island. The French were to be the owners of the salt. Antoine and his neighbor had their backs to the volcano-shaped mountain, whose summit some said contained water and whose natural springs were more generous on the English side. The English therefore were the masters of the water.

"We will not meet with anyone to sort this out today. They are all in Basseterre," said his neighbor.

Antoine said nothing, scanning the surrounding countryside. The gardens were full of peas, potatoes, and cassava. The damage, already cleaned up after the storm, was only visible on the fig trees at the bottom of the plantations and along the streams. Their branches had snapped. Their fruits were scattered under the meager foliage that now almost disappeared, revived here and there by a shattered stump that the sun would heal. The banana trees sheltered from the vast storm had resisted. For others, they were starting anew. The plantation workers had returned to their plots to weed again the fertile soil that constantly gave life to all kinds of plants between the rows of cane. Maintenance was immediately beneficial, but it was also suitable for the wild varieties of the island that, brought by the winds and carefully watered, made their bed from this soil.

Antoine and his neighbor duly appreciated the results of the planters' efforts as they walked through the scattered homes and gardens that evidenced the pursuit of individual gain.

Their arrival at the *Place d'Armes* was punctual. The young recruits were separated from the old militia. Both armed and unarmed men gathered around their captains. These showed their noble origin by adhering to the rules and discipline of their social order. The others could fit into a beautiful layout by donning the mask of alleged noble origin, which sometimes allowed repentant pirates or descendants of the first adventurers of the Caribbean to hide. False or not, most presented a fine sight and while they weren't always commendable, they proudly displayed their past. The king needed them. One day they would go to other destinations, without resentment or bitterness, taking life as it came.

The colonel gave his orders to the captains, who in turn transmitted them to the lieutenants. The *Place d'Armes* in a few minutes presented a different formation.

Antoine joined his task force upon hearing his name. He now belonged to the company of Monsieur du Poyet whom the notary of La Rochelle had already told him about. He was assigned, at least temporarily, as an unarmed resident, to the task of maintaining the roads in his neighborhood. If they attacked the island, he would have to defend it. He thought he would be armed if that happened. The day was spent gaining knowledge about the general organization and the places that the militia would occupy under the orders of the captains.

The small army had no barracks or place reserved to drill and prepare itself for the implementation of its objectives. Saint-Christophe was a business enterprise. The militiamen had to know how to operate the system, both from a military and economic point of view, starting from the warehouses in which they registered the part of the crops owed to the sovereign. Religion still dominated everything and set the tone in the chapels of the militia ; nevertheless, a work organization and life in common announced a new economic model whose effectiveness went beyond the artisan guilds and corporations active in Europe. Since all this was put in place, as always, for the common good, the militiamen were not allowed to escape from Catholic worship. Antoine understood this requirement well.

Antoine attended many meetings and discovered the mode of operation that would change his existence and his way of reasoning for weeks, having from now on one more constraint to integrate into the great equation of the New World.

45

Antoine made his return trip alone the next day because his neighbor had to stay in Basseterre on business. He walked back along the path, thus discovering another view of the island. Everything seemed different and the beauty of the place amazed him in the variety of landscapes that he found in such a short distance. The reality of the island was difficult to perceive. Antoine was aware of that. He liked to walk alone like this and he regretted that the return to his house was not a longer way. He kept Louisa's Mountain in sight. The summit they had reached was not the highest point on the island. It was just a bulge compared to the huge mass rising to the north. The reality from here was more complex. They must have inadvertently passed through a small portion of the English side. The violation of British sovereignty amused him. Decidedly, he lived in another world, admittedly a vast one, but so fragmented that men circulated like confetti of all colors through fine borders cut like fancy lace.

Antoine heard the footsteps of a man striding up to him.

"Hey, you walk fast, it took me a while to catch up with you."

"Hello, friend", said Antoine. "Where are you going ?"

"To *Pointe de Sable !*"

"We do not know each other, do we ? Unless you're from Basseterre ? Do you own a home in *Pointe de Sable ?*"

"Yes, indeed", the man replied.

"But you'll have to go through England. And will they let you pass ?"

"Oh, they won't even see us. And when they see us, they don't say anything unless it's their militia. But it always ends up being resolved."

"It must be said that this division is poorly made !" Antoine added.

"They did what they could at that time and since we were at both ends of the island and they were in the middle, the Treaty tried to take that into account. But it is true that we are passing through England. I have done it often during my life. Bear in mind that my father has done the same his entire life and he is still alive." The two men smiled.

"Was it your father who established the plantation ?"

"Yes, in 1639, exactly 50 years ago."

"You have not forgotten. But you were not even born then ?"

"No, I must be a few years older than you, but a date like that cannot be forgotten."

"What happened ?" asked Antoine.

"Everything happened up there", replied the man from the north of the island.

"In the mountain, there, in *Pointe de Sable ?*" asked Antoine.

"At the *Pointe de Sable* as you say, *Pointe de la Misère* yes !"

"Summit of misery ! Why is that ?"

"That's what the slaves have called this mountain ever since."

"Why is that ?" Antoine asked, very interested. The Northerner sat on the side of the road and began to tell the story in a low voice, avoiding meeting Antoine's gaze and contemplating the Summit of Misery obscured by clouds.

"In 1638 everything was going well, my father always told me. Tobacco was still being sold at that time. The plantations in Santo Domingo were not developed as they are today and, although our tobacco was not as good as theirs, we were almost the only ones who produced it in large quantities for the markets of Europe. The treaty was honored by both parties for the welfare and satisfaction of all. The island was covered with buildings necessary for our businesses. The only problem was manpower. The Indians weren't good at heavy work. They were easily exhausted and didn't have the stamina. We tried to bring in more whites but it was not easy, even the *thirty-six months* were scarce, these whites that we sold amongst us. Workers were still needed. Some planters already had slaves that had been stolen from the Spanish when the landowners were also privateers, but it was not very common. And then slaves were expensive because it must be said that African merchants did not give them away for free. In any case, that is what the Spanish said when the pirates stripped them of their cargoes, always asking that they leave their slaves. Lastly, the situation was good except for the workforce. The slaves knew it. They were increasingly numerous because they were born in the plantations but not sufficient in number to cover all eventualities. Discontent was brewing. Some days men were reluctant to follow orders or grumbled as their master passed by, and all this was taking on worrying proportions. The planters knew that a slave revolt could happen at any moment sparked by a careless expression or gesture. So, they were cautious and treated all men well, favoring some over others, especially the smartest and strongest. But news travels fast here and every event that takes place on an island spreads like wildfire.

In fact, each ship, when there is trouble, becomes a fuse that spreads the explosion. So, when the riots in the southern islands became known to all, we felt - well I say "we" even when I was not born yet - we felt that the situation had changed, that this bad mood persisted and that something could happen. All of this lasted for several months and everyone remained vigilant."

The man, who was decidedly eager to speak, paused for breath and continued in the same passionate tone.

"One day in 1639 about fifty male slaves left their homes together and no one heard from them for a while. The owners were worried, work was delayed, and the pain, which was already intense, was shifted on to the shoulders of the remaining slaves. All of this increased the risk of a general revolt that would bring nothing but desolation. The landowners affected by the escape decided to find the fugitives. But it was not easy. The mountain is large and high. So, searching for fifty black men in the forest took time, especially since the slaves, no doubt assisted by the Kalinago Indians, the Caribs, lacked for nothing. At night, they mocked their pursuers by beating their drums. The situation could not continue. The island authorities were ridiculed, as were the militia and also the residents. The entire organization of Saint Christophe could have collapsed. Someone had to react. The militiamen were summoned in great numbers and a sweep of the mountain was carried out. After days of searching in difficult conditions, the rebellious slaves were finally discovered. The colonel ordered the militia to show no mercy. It was about the future of the island and the credibility of the governor's authority over the slaves, they argued."

The man didn't give Antoine time to reply.

"The governor, who was accountable to his superiors in France, added his touch to all this violence by burning the leaders alive. Survivors in poor health were taken to *Pointe de Sable* where they were dismembered as a lesson."

"How could that happen ?" Antoine dared to ask.

"That day nobody paid any attention to those men. My father, who was not used to this kind of situation, always told me so. We looked only at the general interest on which ours depended. He even told me one day that he should have stayed in France."

"What for ?" asked Antoine.

"When I asked him the same question, he replied : to remain poor. He added that there is always unhappiness in becoming rich, even, he had said, a little richer than poorer and you become different and no better than the ones who are really rich. Only they can resist and return to their lands, while the poor and others sometimes descend to hell if they want to defend the general interest that is above all their own."

"You're right," said Antoine who hadn't expected to find anxious planters.

"But it's difficult !" added the planter.

"Saint-François did it" replied Antoine.

The two men stood up as if to pay tribute to the forgotten dead on the mountain that, cleared of the clouds, now opened to the island, heedless of the past. They took the north road. They soon reached the house where Louisa lived.

Antoine slowed his pace, expecting to see her. She was there, near the road, busy with her work. The northern landowner stopped, decidedly in a good mood.

"You see that girl over there, well, her grandfather was one of the mutineers. He was one of the leaders."

"Are you sure ?" Antoine asked him.

"Sure, she also knows that my father was involved in all of this and she hates me for that. I will leave you here, each one to his own, it is better for you." The man immediately left Antoine without adding a word. Louisa had heard the two men talking.

"Good day Antoine."

"Louisa !"

"Do you know this man ?"

"No, I met him on the way. I just got back from Basseterre."

"Yes, I knew that. But what was he saying to you ?"

"Old stories, of older people."

"He knows a lot of stories."

"That's my feeling too !" Antoine added with a smile.

"And what did he tell you ?"

"Louisa, did you know the name of this mountain, the real name of "Louisa's Mountain" ?"

"No, I only know the "Mountain of Louisa"."

"Louisa, why don't you tell me the truth ?"

""Louisa's mountain" !" she repeated.

"Antoine insisted, "It is said to be *Pointe de Sable* Mountain. "

"So, if they say so ..."

"Louisa ! Why don't you tell me the truth ?"

"The truth ! Its real name is the one the slaves gave it ! It's *Mont Misère* !"

"What happened up there ?"

"Why do you ask me if you already know ?"

Antoine, disconcerted at first, recovered and added that he preferred to hear it from her.

"I do not have time now. You just have to come and see me tonight."

"You know it's impossible, people would talk".

"So, we have to meet halfway like the English and the French when they shared the island," Louisa smiled.

"All right, I'll see you tonight !" Antoine agreed.

In the evening, they met as planned, halfway between the Pintard plantation, as Louisa called it for fun, and Louisa's cabin located on her father's lot. The latter watched his daughter from afar because she, although a bastard, was still his daughter. Louisa was loved by her father. She knew it and that strengthened her decisions.

"What is all this about meeting halfway that you told me this morning ?" Antoine asked curiously.

"You like all this," Louisa said, pinching his forearm.

"I must know this island if I want to stay here."

Louisa didn't raise her voice. She told him her story.

"When the French arrived, a long time ago, the English were here, few in number, not far from here. The entire island was occupied by the Kalinago Indians. Our neighbors had started a small colony that was visible from afar because a huge tamarind tree marked the entrance. The place was pleasant and above all the anchorage was in quiet waters. The French were under the command of Monsieur d'Esnambuc, the English were simply poor settlers. They knew they would have no advantage ; so, they told the French that they were not against their settling in the bay as long as they respected the tamarind boundary. The Frenchmen agreed." Louisa spoke well, adding graceful gestures to her story. Antoine was captivated. She continued.

"The French settled in and everything went well for months. More than a year after this agreement, the English, who had strengthened their colony, came to see the French, politely asking them to withdraw. The French thought that it was a joke at first, but the English were being very serious. They claimed that the roots of the tree had grown and that they should withdraw beyond the roots."[57]

"No !" Antoine protested.

"Yes indeed", Louisa added.

"That's not fair !"

"Justice in all this", Louisa replied.

"But admit ..."

"Well then, decide it among yourselves !" Louisa exclaimed, pushing Antoine and rolling him across the grass.

Antoine, who was holding her closely, took the opportunity to kiss her lips while still laughing.

Louisa, relaxed and happy, looked at Antoine smiling.

"Perhaps it has been since then that the island has been so stupidly divided with the English part between two French parts," Antoine added.

"That's what people say," Louisa replied.

"But then, if I understood correctly, if this tamarind tree becomes gigantic, the French will have to go as the roots will reach both ends of the island. The English part will have covered it all, thanks to the roots. This is completely idiotic !"

"Maybe, but you should have thought of that !"

"Only the English can invent such things."

"You shouldn't have signed," Louisa answered seriously.

"But do you think it's in the Treaty ?"

"I don't know, I've never read it."

"Chased away by the roots of a tree, my God !" Antoine was getting angry.

"Antoine, it hasn't happened yet !"

"But there are other similar agreements in the Treaty."

"Sure ! But I don't know about them. It's a treaty, my father says, everyone can read it in his own way."

"Roots ! I hope that's not in the Treaty".

"Antoine ! Time is running out and the roots may part us soon," Louisa stretched out delicately on the grass.

"Kiss me," she whispered. The drums were silent. The night was dark and thick and warm.

---

(57) It is the legend of Saint-Christophe, nowadays Saint-Kitts.

46

Antoine was looking at Louisa who in turn was looking at *Mont Misère*. When he asked her what she was looking at, she didn't answer. When she asked him when they would marry, he replied : "When there is a Protestant Church in Saint-Christophe." Louisa had insisted on the possibility of marrying in the English sector even if it involved great risks. These were more than great risks according to Antoine, since it would amount to breaking the religion of the king to embrace the rites of the enemy. In other words, a betrayal. But we are at peace with our neighbors, Louisa had added. Antoine had nodded, noting however that the two nations were at war in Europe.

"What religion was your grandfather, Louisa ?"
"Why are you asking me about my grandfather ?"
"And why don't you want to talk about it ?" Antoine asked her.
"It's not very glorious to end up like him."
"No, but like the people of my mountains, he died for his ideas."
"What does that change ?" Louisa replied.
"It changes everything !"

Antoine explained that, for a long time, men had died gloriously fighting for someone else or for something else.

"Today men can die for ideas. The difference is the silence that surrounds the death of some and not of others. There is no reason to be silent about your grandfather's death. When one dies for a king, one does not die alone. One is surrounded by friends like a soldier on a battlefield. Whereas when one dies for one's ideas or for one's honor, one is often alone in a clearing at dawn or at dusk in front of a firing squad. Such men will certainly not speak. They are not proud of their crime. But if everyone remains silent, the sacrifice will be in vain. If you believe in the ideas that your grandfather defended, you must talk about them, you must continue to keep them alive. Talking about him is building a bridge between you and him. It's about loyalty, Louisa."

"You're right." she whispered.

They sat there looking at the *Mount of Misery*. Louisa began to speak when the gloom invaded the brushwood.

Antoine listened to her in silence. It all sounded like what he had experienced personally. Force, coercion, violence : the inability to speak ; the confidence of some confronting the arrogance of others, resulting in a fight where one of the two antagonists ceases to exist, hindering any negotiation and condemning the weakest.

The revolt sounded like a cry for help, eliminating the hope of the men who were going to die. The revolt was plowing its furrow, pushing aside the despair from which perhaps the energy necessary for new revolts would spring. Antoine understood when listening to Louisa that despair is the result of disorder, that it is nothing more than the inability to build a form of coexistence based on clearly established principles and rules.

Antoine compared the situation of the Protestants with that of the slaves. He envisioned that the latter would still suffer when the former would no longer suffer, because the Calvinists now had in their hands the tools of religious freedom to combat the afflictions that overtook them. As Reformed Protestants, they were testing them in many places in the Christian world and beyond. The slaves did not have these tools at their disposal because they had been forcibly transported as a commodity, as a result of a transaction between a seller and a buyer. Their tools had remained in West Africa, in the hands of their sellers, warlords and merchants, who did not pass anything on to them.

Saint-Christophe was not conducive to the flourishing of any structured thinking or doctrine, because there was no elite. It was a hierarchical organization in which each one had his place depending on the task that he had been entrusted with. It had nothing to do with human society. There was only room for obedience or confrontation.

Antoine knew that the Protestants would one day build their society, but not here in Saint-Christophe nor in the West Indies because commerce absorbed all their energies. He perceived that the winner always grew in arrogance and confidence because his emancipation led him to think that his means and his tools were superior.

The oppressed becomes the oppressor. In turn, almost naturally, he denies the right of entry to another because his victory is his identity.

He cannot welcome those who do not share his ideas or his tools. He also cannot admit anyone who challenges the thought process that has led to his liberation. Never before has a victorious nation been seen destroying its own cannons, sinking its own ships, and shooting its own generals.

Antoine listened to Louisa with great interest. She who had not been willing to talk was proving to be passionate. That night, she was talking of rebellion, letting out the flow of emotions that animated her. This overflow spilled over onto Antoine. Her emotions devoured her like hatred did others.

Louisa spoke again. Antoine, sadly, understood where all this could lead. He realized how different his ambitions were. He was young and wanted to build a new world based on the principles he believed in. He knew his world would be a better place, but also that it could breed injustice. He preferred injustice to the hatred that destroys bodies from within, that shreds souls and scatters them to the four winds. Perhaps the remains of clothing they had discovered clinging to the thorn bushes of the hills, abandoned by tireless fugitives, were only there to remind both of them of this strange truth. The island was a closed space from which one could not escape like the Protestants could not escape from the kingdom of France. Antoine remembered this while he listened to Louisa.

This island, built in part on injustice, would only find its salvation by questioning the causes that had favored its development. The island was a business, a mercantile company that, after numerous bankruptcies, had been attached to the Royal Domain, nationalized. Therefore, Saint- Christophe was not a society in which people fought against the laws. It was a business model whose evolution was linked to the method of its operation.

When Antoine had arrived in the colony, he had witnessed the birth of the massive cultivation of sugar cane. He understood that from now on, the workforce would be made up exclusively of slaves. Small farmers would eventually disappear, as well as indentured servants. The island was turned totally towards production and trade. Saint-Christophe depended on the rest of the world. It was in the process of inventing a new model that would later be exported across the Antilles to Santo Domingo. Saint-Christophe focused solely on profit. All means were acceptable in the pursuit of profit and one emotion responded to another emotion ; between the two there was no right or wrong, only strength.

Antoine realized that night that Saint-Christophe was at an impasse; for it was here, also, that the bodies of the most recalcitrant people had been burned and the limbs of other unfortunates had been exposed on stakes after they had been dismembered.

Louisa had finished telling the story.

"How about leaving now ?" he asked.

"No, I'm staying."

The night had invaded the thicket for a long time, but Antoine and Louisa had not noticed it, or perhaps they had pretended not to notice it so as not to break the spell.

Mont Misère disappeared into the distance like a *Mont du grand brûlement*,[58] which would devastate the *Hautes Cévennes* a few years later.

---

(58) The *Grand brûlement* is the king's devastation by fire of the *Cévennes* Heights in 1703.

47

February 1690 : time has passed. The Augsburg League war so far has neither clear victories nor decisive defeats. [59]

William of Orange was proclaimed King of England, Scotland, and Ireland in April 1689 after the desertion of John Churchill, the first Duke of Marlborough, who allowed him to land in Devon in November 1688.

The French colony of the Antilles cannot rest easy. It sees a threat in the return to London of a Protestant king. Some nights its English neighbors are emboldened to take turns to grimace and hurl abuses. The French also grimace at times, but for other reasons, notably because their navy has returned to Europe, where the war of English Succession is on. The privateers could have alleviated the navy's absence, but the French pirate ships had been disarmed for the sake of good order by Charles François d'Angennes, himself a former buccaneer.

The war is also unfolding at sea and the Anglo-Dutch coalition is firmly anchored by the Stadtholder of the United Provinces. It is the Glorious Revolution of England and many in French Saint-Christophe think only about winning, without taking risks. But the general government of the Islands, transferred in 1667 to Martinique by Charles de Baatz de Castelmore, a relative of D'Artagnan the famous musketeer, is taking measures to organize its defense if necessary.

---

[59] The war of the Augsburg League (1688-1697) sometimes called the War of English Succession had three causes. The invasion of the right bank of the Rhine River by Louis XIV, the Revocation of the Edict of Nantes and the invasion of England by William of Orange with 14000 Dutch, French Huguenots, Brandenburger, Swedish, Finnish (and the help of part of the English nobility). France fought along with the Jacobites against a western Europe coalition in order to put James II, the Catholic King and cousin of Louis XIV, back on the throne of England. It ended with the treaty of Ryswick after it had cause 680 000 deaths. William of Orange was recognized as king of England, and Alsace became French as well as the western part of Hispaniola (Santo Domingo nowadays Haiti).

Censuses of indentured servants were carried out on April 20, 1689, at Basseterre and on May 6, 1689, at *Pointe de Sable*.

Nobody knows how things could turn out here, so far from France, amid the coalition members who want also to halt Louis XIV's ambitions for the Spanish succession. France is all alone.

Saint-Christophe, which produces half the sugar consumed in France, is a coveted prize. It is a great company that would make many shareholders very happy. All men must be counted in order to draw up a list of its defenders. That year, the planters in turn will be meticulously counted to become members of the militia under the command of their captain. Antoine Pintard appears on the list of unarmed planters, drawn up at the request of the Governor-General of the islands, Charles de la Roche-Courbon. He appears in the militia company whose captain is none other than Pierre Girauld, Sieur du Poyet, father-in-law of Charles d'Angennes, former Marquis of Maintenon.

D'Angennes had arrived in the Antilles after having sold his castle and his noble title to Françoise d'Aubigné, a native of Martinique, who would become the mistress of Louis XIV and his "openly secret" bride[60]. After living as a buccaneer, d'Angennes became the richest planter in Martinique, where he died in 1691. Separatism was under way and some nobles were ready to abandon their noble rank to do business and get rich.

Antoine is there. He submits to the census and prepares to defend the island. He is part of the organization. He molds himself into the hierarchy like sugar in a dry barrel.

Sugar, there is plenty this year. The harvest is satisfactory and the processing is well advanced in the early spring of 1690. Saint-Christophe is covered with smoke fumes that, emanating from Basseterre, rise in white, vaporous clouds some afternoons, towards the summits of the mountains and the folds of the hills, filling the valleys with their sour scent. All the men are at their posts. The flames feed on the debris from the leaves and the tips of the reeds, the plants having been carefully thinned during their eighteen months of growth.

When ripe, about five months after flowering, the cut cane is transported to the mill where the bagasse, a mixture of gum and green starch, fibrous material, and saline material, is compressed and processed.

---

(60) Morganatic marriage was not recognized by French law but the marriage of a king with a bride of a lower rank was possible under conditions : the bride was past child-bearing or the prince already had dynastic heirs with another spouse of royal descent.

This agglomerate ferments so fast that it needs to be boiled. But before recovering the syrup, it is necessary to continue with a dilution process with lime in five boilers which requires a skillful balance during boiling, to recover the greatest amount of crystallized sugar at the end.

During each step in the cauldrons, the liquid is skimmed to remove impurities.

If it boils too quickly, the contents of the boilers will turn to molasses too soon and the amount of sugar will be less. The teams feed the boiler which they are in charge of, and the bagasse thus goes from the "largest" to the "clean", then to the "torch" and finally to the "syrup". This set is called a "battery" and the planter is responsible for everything. This is how an organization is set up for the development of a complex product. Each one must be in his right place, understand what he is doing, and master the technique.

From this point of view, Saint-Christophe is also ahead of its time, selecting men and keeping them in their role according to their ability and responsibility. Sugar, like wine, is one of the first elaborate products. It requires knowledge. Besides being a product of agriculture, it is also a product of industry. The human hand controls the result, the quality, as with wine and beer, but also the quantity of the harvest. A good but badly processed and refined harvest is a disaster. The peasant becomes a worker and Antoine likes this.

He watches, listens, talks, and learns. Those who teach him appreciate him. Antoine is docile and accepts being reprimanded and reproached ; he is a novice manager. He knows it. But Antoine loves humanity and relates easily to them, always eager to learn and looking for novelties. He has changed. It is a learning process without any books, which he does not dislike. The transmission of the experience is smooth and painless. Antoine is far from his mountain in the *Cevennes* and from a peasant world steeped in a fatalism common to all of Europe. Here, there is no opportunity to blame the weather. Tropical latitudes carry with them a rhythmic rigor that excludes climatic accidents and concentrates energy on the result : the amount of sugar that will be obtained from boiling. The greater it is, the more satisfied the men and the teams will be, even the slaves and the white indentured servants.

The objective will have been reached, as the promise of a change, of an emerging dawn over Saint-Christophe, cleansed of its vapors and its defects thanks to sugar, a source of double-digit profit. The locals rejoice in the great packing of panela, the brown sugar that will be made at Charles d'Angennes's refineries in Martinique or those of the Walsh family, the Jacobites who had settled in Nantes with the blessing of the King of France. The juice only turns to sugar after a good boiling, while the drop squeezed between thumb and forefinger turns into a hook-shaped fiber from forefinger to thumb, when the fingers are spread to remind men that its sweetness also masks roughness. Skill and know-how are needed. So, sugar and industry walk hand in hand. Sugar makes them forget past alliances like Stapleton, Irish governor of the island of Nevis, whose sugar investments will prevail over his Jacobite commitments. Saint-Christophe is like that too. A revolution was born in Saint-Christophe and Antoine has moved to a new world.[61]

The boiling ends when you can no longer extract sugar from the syrup in the last pot, the "boiler". But there, again, Antoine discovers that this waste is exploitable, recoverable. The molasses has a sweet taste that allows it to be included in other products. In the British colonies in America, they appreciate it and Antoine discovers it the day he sees the first ships.

"Look, Antoine, these people come to fetch the molasses that would overburden us if they weren't there and that's good," said one of the boilermen.

"I see that", answered Antoine. "And what do they do with it ?"

"Whatever they want, but it is also an inflow of money for us that is not negligible."

"But they must do something with it ?"

"Ah ! Sure, putting it in the wine is what they say they do."

"Ah right !"

"You see, Antoine, sugar has a secret : it crystallizes. That is its property, while other bodies do not crystallize. But once crystallized, it is soluble in all liquids, you transport it in loaves and when you arrive at your destination you dissolve it in water or wine, that's wonderful !"

"You're right," Antoine answered, "and I think those who know the sugaring technique will always succeed because its taste pleases everyone."

"Even the horses !" added the boilerman, laughing. "Look how they devour the canes !"

---

(61) According to James Pritchard, Saint-Christophe produced 40 % of the French output of sugar in 1674 : *In Search of Empire : the French in the Americas, 1670-1730*, Cambridge University Press 2004, p.484.

48

On July 10, 1690, James II and the Duke of Lauzun [62] were defeated at the Battle of the River Boyne, near Drogheda in Ireland, by the Anglo-Dutch army supported by Huguenots and Danish soldiers. [63] Gone were the hopes for the return of a Catholic king to the throne of England. James II returned to Saint-Germain-en-Laye.[64] The Glorious Revolution ended in October 1691 with the surrender of the last Jacobite troops in Ireland, near Limerick, expelling groups of people into exile in the West Indies, after their lands were expropriated. They were deported to the Windward Islands in virtual slavery.

The English took over Ireland. Led by Christopher Codrington, they anticipated events by attacking Saint-Christophe on June 30, 1690.

This was the end of the Treaty of Peace and Commerce that had governed the relations between the two countries in Saint-Christophe since 1624. European affairs had an impact even in the Caribbean Islands where large sugar companies such as Codrington's, the sole owner of Barbuda, invoked popish threats to justify their wrongdoing. As is often the case in complex conflicts, the causes were a tangle of multiple interests.

---

(62) Before that defeat, Lauzun was imprisoned for nine years (1671-1681) in the Pignerol fortress together with "The Iron Mask", which is now part of history.

(63) More than a half were English soldiers. About 46 % were Dutch, Huguenot, Swiss and Danish soldiers. Michael McNally, *Battle of the Boyne 1690, the Irish Campaign for the English Crown* ; Oxford, collection Campaign, 2005. The Battle of the Boyne is at the origin of a conquering Protestantism. Catholics have been discriminated in Great Britain for not being Protestant by the Penal Laws until the beginning of the 19th century.

(64) Saint-Germain-en-Laye is a town near Paris where Louis XIV was born. The castle can be visited nowadays by the public.

The Antilles were weakened by their ill-established foundations, with their economy based on the forced labor of blacks and whites who carried with them resentment and its consequent environment of rumors, suspicions, and the ruin of souls. Trust no longer existed and how could it have been otherwise ?

Exiled French Protestants, mistreated by their Catholic king, found themselves alongside English Protestants who were their enemies despite professing the same religion.

The latter mistreated Irish Catholics who regarded the French islands as a haven of peace, while battered English Catholics regarded France as their enemy. In the months that followed, confusion reigned. The attacks led to raids on the slaves, demonstrating the inability of a nascent sugar industry to create real conditions for managing labor. Planters kidnapped people while kings tore apart foreign colonial empires. Attempts at conquest could be real successes. Treaties cemented international recognition a few years later even if they had lacked a legal basis before. Meanwhile, it was chaos and each looked after his own interests becoming in turn diplomat, warlord, adventurer, or prophet.

The Antilles were teeming with visionaries and generous men whose sole purpose was to satisfy the metropolis and to help themselves in the process. This part of the world resembled the dawns of all history where violence creates acquired rights and gains, turning a seizure by force into a heritage marked one day in the future by the formal stamp of heredity.

Antoine noticed the deterioration of the Antillean arch through news from unknown islands or the sight of amputees. The sea was now spilling out its share of fugitives landed by the merchant ships that had collected and disposed of them near Saint-Christophe. Whatever they had lost, an arm or a leg, their mind, they had all lost their homes ; and would have to re-learn everything, except the cultivation of sugarcane which they could never forget.

The religious conflict raging across Europe underscored the fragility of island settlements based solely on trade and profit. Antoine was convinced that in this world with no restrictions or constraints, and with the interests of nations mixed with private interests in a new and unstable alliance, only the rule of law would finally bring order and define the place and actions of each party, redirecting this whole chaos into everyone's legitimate interest. But neither men nor nations undertook this path.

The attack on Saint-Christophe took place without a specific order from any admiralty or command. It seemed like an uprising, a crisis, an excess of anger. The upper hand was for the English who, taking advantage of the senseless separation of the two French sectors, did not allow the latter to develop their military power. The counterattack could only be carried out without order, motivated only by the desire not to die without a fight. Codrington meanwhile, had his own troops.

The Sovereign Council of Saint-Christophe had its militia, often made up of unarmed men, inhabitants with no experience of handling weapons, simple cane cutters, and loyal but empty-handed slaves. The English side was in no better shape, but they had Codrington.

The fighting was long, and spread wide, as the plantations were scattered. Those located near the coast quickly ceased the uneven fight. In front of them was a navy that landed its troops, imposing itself almost without fighting. The residents hiding in the hills might have believed that their isolation would provide security and that fear of possible skirmishes would restrain the attackers, but the opposite took place. The penetration of the island occurred at a rapid pace, and the English brutalized the blacks and whites entrenched in their huts so that the echoes of their exactions would penetrate the mountains and suppress any attempt at resistance among the populations they terrorized.

As they advanced, the men were classified according to the color of their skin, the blacks being the human loot. The whites were the abscess that poisoned them, the cause of their anger, drunkenness, and extravagance.

A huge rake went through Saint-Christophe. Its clenched teeth carved thousands of furrows right to the bottom of the valleys, excavating, sweeping, and exposing the bodies that ended up bruised and gathered in a procession full of spasms and fury.

The French, taken by surprise, became paralyzed under a shower of blows that their unarmed bodies tried in vain to dodge. But the brutality of the soldiers shattered the unprotected bodies and ripped out piercing screams.

The slaves weren't in a better situation, hugging their newborns against them, begging that the disorganized band of soldiers spare them. Antoine watched the massacre helplessly. The proximity of the English troops that should have put them in imminent danger, curiously protected them.

The English settlers had preferred to direct their anger towards *Pointe de Sable*, leaving Basseterre in the care of Codrington. The raid lasted several days, each losing a wife, a child, a neighbor, a slave ; all victims of the barbarism that deeply divided them in a secret self-serving quest of each man for himself. The gangs, drunk with blows and wild screams, ended the day in a sordid face-to-face with themselves, and everyone else, with eyes reddened with exhaustion, mouths with prominent, uneven teeth, wide open as if to breathe easier. Everyone was afraid, settlers, slaves and soldiers alike. This unstable world was falling apart. It was the beginning of a long process of decline that would last a long time but that would inevitably end with a settlement between the European powers. In the immediate future, only the use of force could achieve a result.

Antoine and his men stayed in their shelter, isolated in the border area. Codrington's troops no doubt thought that the English of the central zone of the island had taken care of them whereas the latter were busy fighting a war in what they already called Sandy Point.

Other residents of the border zone were surprised at how little attention was paid to their plight. This caused concern among some who saw no good in this unequal treatment as if it were a foretaste of an unenviable fate. The men were uneasy and the women still preferred it to the treatment that would be given to them down on the beach.

Antoine was thinking of Louisa.

Antoine and his men were arrested by their English neighbors a few days later. Night had fallen and they were all hungry. Other inhabitants of the zone had violated the instructions for secrecy that circulated among the plantations. Their hunger was too great. They had lit a fire which aroused the curiosity of the English.

No one was angry when the culprits were found. They could not remain hidden indefinitely in hollows covered with cane debris during the day, going out at night in search of the previous day's sun-warmed traps, along with fruit gathered by groping in the dark. It was fine this way and whatever had to happen would happen, they were secretly thinking.

The English, who knew them, gave them an embarrassed welcome, informing them that it was better to be reasonable.

That night, the slaves' drums hidden in the forest greeted the end of the French presence in Saint-Christophe.

Antoine and his men were taken the next day to the beach, which was almost deserted. At the end of the small cove, there was a group of unarmed men surrounded by other men who were armed. They all stood together, as if engaged in a friendly conversation. From a distance it was difficult to guess to which group the unarmed men belonged, whether they were slaves or planters or indentured hands, except that the slaves were seated in a separate group.

No agitation was noticeable, a peaceful discussion among men pacified after a tough physical exercise, their standing position emphasizing a mutual respect. The scene seemed to indicate that there would be other encounters and there would be no hard feelings. [65] Tranquility had returned very quickly. The victors accompanied the defeated until the last boat left, secretly promising to meet again in other places of confrontation, in other cane fields. Antoine saw a fragile skiff approaching that quickly filled up and headed for the vessel that was anchored a stone's throw away. Antoine and his men were now alone on the beach. The men from the end of the cove finally approached them. They spoke to Antoine in crude but understandable French. There was talk of leaving for Martinique without further explanation. The slaves would remain in Saint-Christophe. There was nothing to negotiate, nothing to discuss. That's how it was. The English had won this time. They treated the French like gentlemen, no doubt in the hope that this would be remembered. They thus hoped to conclude in favorable terms an episode which they themselves perceived to be disastrous. The civility after this chase seemed like installing a set of rules at the end of an attack that did not have any. The French were not fooled.

This last-minute equity of treatment was only there to avoid problems when the balance of power switched sides. The French did not need to be forced to adopt a similar attitude if events were to turn in their favor in the future. They had acted this way before in 1664 and they remembered it. They did not respond because they did not need to take any lessons in chivalry.

They ended up being loaded onto the rowboat when it returned empty from the larger vessel. Antoine greeted the slaves who looked him in the eye. Their fate was not enviable. Antoine was losing the fruit of his labor and had to go into the unknown. The slaves stayed and would

---

(65) The French re-captured Saint Kitts in 1782 and gave it back to Great Britain in the Treaty of Paris of 1783.

have to work for their new masters. A change was taking place. Louisa had disappeared. Antoine had gained nothing at Saint-Christophe, at least that is what he thought when the ship passed the summit of Basseterre, sailing towards Martinique. The roots of the tamarind tree had reached his plantation as they had reached the entire island, chasing thousands of people. Antoine watched Saint-Christophe as he sailed away. He was not really attached to the plantation assigned to him. He had never felt like the owner of the place. He had prospered working and learning the sugar trade. It was what he had earned and he carried it with him. Deep down, he had lost nothing. He knew enough to continue his journey through the Caribbean Sea. The conflicts between the European powers hardly worried him. Antoine was tired of being buffeted by his king or the kings of others. He had lost his family ties ; and he did not care about current events in Europe. The king was working on the geography of his kingdom, it was time for him to draw up the new perimeter of his assets. The roots of the tamarind tree had driven him out of Saint-Christophe. He had to put down roots somewhere else.

Antoine was then 32 years old.

He secluded himself on the deck. The rising heat invaded the tiniest recesses of the ship. He preferred to stay there, thinking of Louisa, who now filled his thoughts. The ship headed south. He understood the final destination would be Martinique.

He found himself grouped with the indentured men from his plantation, released before their time, who did not appreciate their emancipation too much, and who from time-to-time approached him in search of a reassuring word. The freemen, more experienced, saw it as one more test that they would certainly overcome with God's help. The group of men who had been led to the boat first from the end of the cove were together at the stern, showing some solidarity. Antoine knew that the solution to all his problems lay in patience. He would once again have to allow for the pitfalls, accept the disappointments, silence the sufferings, suffer the regrets. The little world that he had created was now gone. The "Mountain of Louisa" would soon be no more than an extinct volcano drawn on the horizon. If Louisa was gone, he would have to start all over again.

"Antoine, do you think we'll all see each other in Martinique ?" asked the employee from La Rochelle.

"I hope so", answered Antoine.

"The others there say no."

"What do they know ?" Antoine replied harshly.

"They were arrested a few hours before us and had time to talk with the English."

- "And then !" Antoine cried impatiently.

"So, they separated families".

"How so ?"

"They separated the wives from their husbands and children and even the children of the same family were sent in different directions. They called it a sorting out."

"What for ?" Antoine asked worriedly.

"So that they don't come back. Who would return to Saint-Christophe, to the place where you lived with your family that was now scattered all over the islands ?"

"Nobody !" Antoine replied. "Maybe Louisa won't be in Martinique."

"Nothing is certain," added the man from La Rochelle.

As they spoke, Antoine had taken his eyes off the horizon. When he looked back at Saint-Christophe, the *Pointe de Sable* had disappeared. Antoine suddenly felt very alone when he passed in front of Montserrat. Another volcano loomed in the middle of the island, with no history to share with anyone, no connection to link it to anyone, just a volcano. Antoine forgot the beauty of the place that disappeared behind his veiled eyes.

The captain of the ship was French. He was a former filibuster who had succumbed to threats from Angennes, a repentant filibuster commissioned by the king to liquidate these sea wolves. He knew the English well and had often shared the acts of piracy and their spoils on Tortuga Island. A passing English ship had informed him of the hunt in progress at Saint-Christophe, and he had not hesitated to take charge of the last persecuted persons on the island. The largest landowner in Martinique was the Sieur d'Angennes. The captain had found the destination perfectly acceptable for his business and on arrival would seek a compensation for the delivery of skilled manpower.

Antoine thought that perhaps the Sieur d'Angennes when losing his lands in Saint-Christophe, was thus unintentionally consolidating his immense sugar estates in Martinique where they lacked workers. Antoine momentarily lost confidence. Each pursued his own interests.

The king had lost an island.

The descent towards Martinique unfolded a chain of tropical beauties. Antoine crossed islands whose poorly established owners made any settlement precarious and the results of investments also uncertain. Sugar had disrupted the archipelago, and the efforts of some were echoed in the temptations of others. Mass sugarcane cultivation was difficult in Guadeloupe, the captain had told him, while things were going better in Martinique under the Angennes family. Therefore, the whole future lay in the defense that the two large islands could raise against the Royal Navy. Every great European power wanted its share of the cake and conflicts would not end with the wave of a magic wand. Access to land, to the largest amount of land, conditioned the behavior of all. When the cards had been dealt, France had not been so badly served, nor had the English or the Dutch.

Finally, all had been assiduously for decades, helping themselves to the immense and badly defended Spanish possessions. Now it was a matter of redistributing the cards among the three nations.

It would all end in a peace treaty, the captain had suggested, and signing it would bring prosperity. He knew the situation well. According to him, the sugar industry would see a formidable development that was already apparent by the large number of merchant ships that came from Europe as well as from the English colonies in America. He knew the sea and the ports between Saint Pierre de la Martinique and Saint Dominique, Grenade[66] and Tobago, Barbados[67] and Anguilla ; so many sugar islands, so many shipping docks, so many well-filled purses. This part of the world was on the cusp of enrichment like no other in the past. The Dutch West India Company had been turning all its efforts to supplying slaves to the islands after it had abandoned New Amsterdam to the English and the fur trading posts that were devouring all its profits. It was not all by chance. There was a plan, designs built by the great commercial strategists of the United Provinces, sitting behind their chart tables, surrounded by their Rembrandts and their treasures. At that time, the Dutch were everywhere, even in Japan. They knew the world through its suppliers and markets. The Dutch produced goods, but the small size of their country and the annoying crown of Spain forced them to surpass themselves if they did not want to disappear, a victim of the Catholic power that wanted to erase them with a stroke of the pen. The Dutch did not have the patience to suffer

---

(66) A French island until 1763.

(67) A republic since 2021.

forever. They were sure of their genius, their entrepreneurial spirit, and the small size of their territory. What they could not achieve at home, they would achieve abroad. Their adventures would not necessarily end with a systematic return to the Netherlands.

The Dutch went around the world, buying in the Moluccas what they would sell in Madagascar, refilling their holds on this island to empty them in Senegal, from where their ships, loaded with other merchandise destined for the Caribbean Islands, would depart. They needed a lot of wind to satisfy their insatiable appetite for trade and exchange. They knew all their clients. The wind had swept these domesticated people whose emblem is a broom towards their destiny of opportunism, adventure, and amazing success. The captain spoke of them with respect although he admitted that in his life, he had had to push aside a few of them who had got in his way. Antoine listened to the captain with all the attention owed to those who knew. Thus, he heard for the first time about New York, formerly New Amsterdam, this port inhabited by the spirit of Calvin whose owner was now the King of England.

"The world is complex," added finally the captain by way of conclusion.

"I also have that impression," answered Antoine calmly.

"One more thing sir !" added the captain. "Don't waste your time in Martinique, there is no future there for people like you. Large sugar cane plantations will go hand-in-hand with African manpower. Saint-Christophe was out of date anyway, you have not lost anything. Think about what I said to you : It's trade sir, trade !"

Antoine arrived in Martinique the next day. The men of Angennes were already busy with a new sorting out, based on each man's abilities. Antoine submitted to the inventory, having no choice. As night fell, a quick shadow crossed the other end of the camp. Louisa ! he suddenly cried, jumping off his bed. The shadow had disappeared, deaf when hearing that name, distracted without a doubt, unexpected perhaps. Antoine had surely been wrong.

Antoine owed nothing to anyone. The agreements made with the managers of the Angennes family gave him complete freedom as a free worker. He knew these people were eager to hire him into their organization, but he was feeling tired. Antoine was thinking about Louisa and his search having been in vain, it was time to go. Martinique was large but the cleared and inhabited area was small.

In a few days, he had covered it. Louisa must be somewhere else. That was his conclusion. He was now considering returning to Saint-Christophe. It was impossible to get there directly. Thus, Antoine spent entire days waiting for an event that he could use for his plans. It all reminded him of La Rochelle. Patience was a virtue that he knew how to use to his advantage during the long afternoons while he watched, alone, the sunset on the horizon.

The newcomers, in turn, laid wreaths of campfires lined like candles along the beaches. They marked at night a sign of loneliness; the absence of those who would not return. They would wander for a long time through the Caribbean Sea, prisoners of the giant cove drawn by the Mexican contours, souls scattered by the tragedy of Saint-Christophe. Today there are black Pintards in the islands of the Antillean rim . . .

Antoine would never see Louisa again despite his investigation and his return to Basseterre in hopes of finding her. In time Saint-Christophe became Saint-Kitts. Kitts being a short English version of Christopher.

Book III

SHELTER IN NEW YORK

49

The arrival in New York was via Sandy Hook, the natural jetty that partially closes off the lower bay where Verrazano once docked, armed by François I, King of France, and later Captain Hudson. More than eighty years had passed since the last landfall that would mark the beginning of the Dutch presence on the Atlantic coast of North America.

The sloop that carried Antoine to what had been, not long ago, New Amsterdam, now crossed the sandy entrance where the English captain had docked, a few days before taking possession of the entire region on behalf of the Dutch East India Company, in 1609.

The place was deserted and bare as a dune, whipped by the sea breeze, strewn with fragile reeds that silently bent like priests in procession, traversed by equally silent muskrats. The whole formed a desolate strip of sand, bathed in foul-smelling gray silt at low tide, from which salt-petrified logs sometimes sprouted, brandishing their ominous stumps skyward. The western face of the headland offered mooring opportunities sheltered from the surf, which the first sailors continuously exploited before venturing into New York Bay, as a welcome stopover before the big leap. The bay was closed to the north in the same way by the Rockaway cordon. The two projections created the claws of a giant crab ready to engulf the visitor attracted to the Straits of Staten Island and Brooklyn[68] by the beauty of the place.

Antoine knew nothing of the place. He came from the Antilles. His return to Saint Christophe had been accomplished by complicated and expensive means. Since the traffickers refused to take any risk of

---

(68) Giovanni Verrazzano, an Italian naval captain in the service of the king of France, Count of Angoulême, was the first to explore the East Coast of North America and discovered the New York Bay in 1524 naming it New Angoulême. The Verrazzano suspension bridge which today connects Staten Island with Brooklyn is named after him.

disrupting relations with the English, Antoine had had to submit to their will, but to no avail. On the nearby island of Nevis, which had partly served as a refuge for displaced populations from the French colony, he had been allowed, as a favor granted to a fellow Huguenot, to rapidly scout the island in search of Louisa and then leave the colony as quickly as possible.

Nevis was beautiful and well cared for. The plantations were large and the terrain, less rugged than in Saint-Christophe, presaged much better yields. Proper roads were already running between the plantations, suggesting quality organization. Louisa was nowhere to be found.

"You should go home !" an Englishman had snapped at him.

"I don't have a home anymore !" Antoine had answered him, anxious not to provoke his interlocutor.

"Then the world is yours !" the mocking Englishman had added.

"You are right !" Antoine had finished speaking, leaving the man with his philosophy. He had returned to the port. A ship was docked. It didn't matter where she went. He couldn't stay. Antoine had approached the ship. He had money in his pocket. Therefore, he could negotiate his departure. The captain accepted him on board. He sailed the next day for New York. Interestingly, he had no cargo. Antoine didn't ask why. He just couldn't stay on Nevis any longer.

The captain informed him of the presence of French Protestants in New York, where he would surely find help. He told him that as far as he knew there were already all kinds of nationalities there. He added that he had heard of the founding of a Huguenot community in the province of New York called New Rochelle. Antoine welcomed this information with hope. On the other hand, as far as Louisa was concerned, he was able to tell him that a group of Brazilian Jews were in New York, where they formed a community. It was possible that Louisa had joined these unfortunate displaced persons.

The captain had told him the essentials. He seemed preoccupied and did not speak to him again. Antoine sailed the next day and after several weeks of sailing reached Sandy Hook.

Once passed the straits, the bay was immense but inviting because you could guess its contours. The islands, crowned by dense and fragrant forests, formed a protective wall that interrupted Atlantic influences. A multitude of delicately cut inlets offered as many havens as possible on this unknown shore. The captain, who seemed unfamiliar with the place, was amazed at such beauty. Thousands of birds crossed the bay. The proximity of certain islands hinted at the diversity of tree species, the abundance of game, the schools of fish glistening in the sun, the depth of the land beyond. Dolphins and killer whales accompanied the ship in a joyous parade. A scent of wild roses perfumed the air.

Antoine was impressed, and he wasn't the only one. The generally silent crew were ecstatic in the face of so many wonders, such beautiful waters, such wide and regular currents, such a gentle breeze. Everything seemed crafted to perfection, fashioned with order and purity. The first Dutch to discover the bay had taken it upon themselves, before praising its charms, to remind their prince in Holland that the Netherlands were also a paradise. English sailors had dared to compare the fragrances of New York with the perfumed air of France ! Antoine, the captain and his men fell silent before a spectacle that invaded the smallest corners of the most hardened souls. New York and its bay filled their hearts as with a spontaneous affection that does not require acclimatization, a love at first sight, a hallelujah which in the future would be shared by most voyagers at the end of a difficult crossing of breathtaking individual journeys, at the start of a rebirth of souls and minds after years of slow decline.

50

When Antoine lands on the shores of America, New York is just a small port with terraced Dutch houses, their roofs pointing skyward. The two-story houses still mark the architecture of the place with their glass panel windows at the ends of the facades and their red or yellow tiles. Peter Stuyvesant's contested administration has left its mark, pushing the malodorous activities of butchers to the periphery, laying out canals to collect effluents, naming the streets, filling ditches to form docks, and giving this city its initial statutes. Cleaning, ordering, building and punishing were the hallmarks of this governor whom New Yorkers ended up ejecting. For this they allied themselves with the English, in opportunism and in bad faith, exploiting the internal dissensions of a community lacking in unity and clearly established perspectives.

The inhabitants had already forgotten that Peter Stuyvesant was sent by the Dutch Company, eager above all to retain a foothold on the American continent if Brazil were to be lost to the Portuguese, as the last chance to save the colony which at that time was in a very poor state after the disastrous management of William Kieft, his predecessor. In defense of the latter, we can say that he had inherited debts from Pierre Minuit, the Walloon buyer of Manhattan to the Lenape Indians. Furthermore, Kieft had built the perimeter wall that would become Wall Street. New Amsterdam had four hundred inhabitants then. Failure to build the protection would have led everyone to be sent back to the cottages of the low countries we see in Brueghel's paintings. It had required a capable man to take over. But now in 1664, the colony had become English. The declared desire of Peter, the founder of New York, to recognize only one company, one church, one leader, was followed by the greed of the Stuart King's brother, the Duke of York, eager above all to earn a substantial amount of money very quickly as the owner Lord by avoiding any trouble.

At the time, the Dutch were still in the majority, and the community became quickly divided as soon as the Duke of York took possession of the colony. In fact, the absence of harsh measures taken by the English against the former Dutch citizens of the colony, in order not to harm the economic development of the city and its province, led to the emergence of a class of Dutch and Huguenot businessmen and merchants who quickly adopted the customs and language of the new masters. The others, partly locked in their national cultures, stayed away from trade organized by the newcomers from England and ended up impoverishing themselves.

The English, or rather the Duke of York, who in his turn nearly lost his colony to the Dutch, during the short-lived restoration of New Orange,[69] had learned his lesson and left the bridle free on the necks of his subjects. But the elective functions, established by Governor Dougan[70] through his Statute of Freedoms, as well as the privileges were disputed between the merchant class and the gentry. Between the Atlanticists, a rural nobility whose concerns were turned to the American continent and to England, and a merchant class turned to the rest of the world, interests began to diverge, particularly with regard to freedom of trade and municipal freedoms. Especially since the merchant class supported free trade on the condition that they be granted a monopoly on goods entering and exiting America through the port of New York. A free trade ideal combined with exemptions ; distant losses compensated by domestic profits.

These arrangements between people of the same milieu did not satisfy the peasants of Long Island and other surrounding areas who were forced to come to New York to send their potatoes to the West Indies. The only response they got to their complaints was that they

---

(69) The Dutch took over New York in 1673 and renamed it New Orange in honor of the Orange-Nassau family who were Prince of Orange for 180 years. Orange is the main town of a principality the Nassau family had inherited in the South of France. It is located near the city of Avignon. It gave its name to many counties in the US. It returned to France in 1713.

(70) Governor Dougan's *Charter of Liberties and Privileges* "defined the form of government for the colony (governor, governor's council, assembly), recognized basic political and personal rights (trial by jury, no taxation without representation) and affirmed religious liberty (for Christians)". He was an Irish and a Catholic. Edwin G. Burrows and Mike Wallace : Gotham, a history of New York city to 1898 ; Oxford University Press, 1999, p. 91.

were free to look elsewhere. In short, the merchants of the colonies were inventing pragmatism. To this must be added the recent animosities between the English and Dutch communities over the follies committed by the Duke of York, who distributed thousands of acres to New York suburban counts under the noses of Batavians in search of farmland. The latter resisted because they had rarely had the historical experience of feudal pressure. Idealism, in its turn, transformed the great beer-drinking city into an explosive cocktail.

The duke, tempted by an opportune escape, was finally persuaded to stay. The colony would continue to wear down its governors who would fail to impose an authority acceptable to all. Communitarianism was an obstacle and how could it be resolved through statutes whose balance could not be achieved before being signed by all ? This was giving too much power to documents that only confirmed a situation that was disastrous from the start. The same causes produced the same effects, and while nobody was expected to do the impossible, resentments could not help but arise. New Yorkers would have to change if they wanted to overcome this issue, especially since social demands were reaching a point that was not yet called a strike, such as that of the carters, who threatened to interrupt their work. Thus, the class struggle was grafted to a communitarian disagreement, not as a higher level of dissension but as an additional obstacle to a good understanding between the English, the Dutch and the Huguenots.

Thus, Antoine arrives in New York which is facing an insurrectionary atmosphere that contrasts with the plenitude of nature that surrounds the small city of only three thousand souls. It is too much stress for so few people.

The docks are a vibrant place. Several dozen ships fly the New York flag, just as the packaging of agricultural produce shipped to the sugar islands bear the "NY" symbol attesting to the origin of the goods. There is a whole population of sailors and artisans who make their living from port activity. New York, by obtaining the monopoly of the transit of agricultural products, is wrecking New England's trade with the West Indies, benefiting from the advantage of its greater proximity than Boston to the center of wealth that constitutes the Antillean arch : just a week away of navigation.

The Duke of York seeks success in his business. He doesn't care about the investments of the Pilgrim Fathers, those hideous fundamentalists and separatists, when he is openly flirting with Catholics. He does not care either about the English peasants on Long Island who have considered themselves as New Englanders for years, or about the Dutch who refused to swear allegiance to the crown.

They are his subjects now, and he expects a modicum of deference as the landowner, similar to the expressions of affection shown to him by his newly installed American vassals. The last enemies lurk in the deep forests of the New World. The Iroquois, united in five nations, more or less call the shots in the region stretching from the Gulf of Mexico to French Canada. Louis XIV's alliance with the Hurons against the rest of the world attracts the attention of the duke who is already forging diplomatic ties with some of the Iroquois, dividing up their respective spheres of influence, while not forgetting to present the situation as one of mutual interest.

The Duke of York makes progress, but with the reins too slack around their necks, the horses have the impression that there is no driver, or at least that the rider is not up to the task, making it possible to take liberties with him.

Peter Stuyvesant, now dead for nearly twenty years, can only turn in his grave in New York where his fellow citizens, after having expelled him, have in the end allowed him to make Manhattan his final resting place ; a belated recognition. A strange small port that reinvents the world. But what happens in London will have repercussions in America, and while this small port may be anxious for the open sea, it is caught nevertheless in the conflicts between parliamentarians in London and sometimes falls into the traps that these gentlemen set for it.

As soon as he disembarks, Antoine walks across the city. He wants to travel to New Rochelle as soon as possible to find his community. Along the way, Antoine only sees a small town on the edge of a pretty port. He does not see the disputes or debates that are ongoing. Each is busy with his own work, absorbed in his own affairs, carrying, pulling, hurling abuse, calling out to each other, closing deals, counting their pennies : thus, a familiar atmosphere.

Antoine feels at home. He doesn't feel like a stranger to the commotion and tangle of goods and carts coming and going. What amazes him is what America looks like, outside the city. Manhattan has already been subjected to the vigor of the hand of man. No doubt it took energy to clear the pastures which spread out outside the town. The tall trees, which still surround them, suggest that the task must have been immense given their thickness. It must be said that there are also many large trees cut down, gathered in a protective copse that the English call *The Wall*. Everyone has helped himself and is still helping himself, when possible, especially in the northern half of Manhattan. Nature, being very generous, has whetted appetites and it is of little importance if everything changes, as New York governors now find that things are not advancing fast enough.

Peter Stuyvesant would have liked to have kept the newcomers away, but this is no longer the case now. Antoine realizes this when he sets out on the Indian Trail that will become Broadway. He forks to the right after having traveled a league, taking another indigenous road, by which he traverses the island. The houses are increasingly modest in their architecture. A Dutch population lives there, among the poorest on the island, wearing the national and colorful cap that distinguishes them from the rest of the migrants. The path leads to the end of the island where among the ducks and seagulls you can take the Williamsburg ferry to Long Island. Antoine thus unknowingly goes through the districts of the European rebels against the English authority, who have recently made a political union with those of Long Island, to establish the framework of an ongoing revolt. A group of dispossessed people that has ended up establishing a settlement after having temporarily subsisted by hunting beavers now in the process of extinction, in any case in the process of being reduced to just an unexpected element of the landscape, after being an integral part of it, like the Indians. An American people who do not fear the establishment of a republic, like the English who welcomed Cromwell's. Antoine does not pass through this scene in a romantic way as Chateaubriand[71] will do in his time, when he will depict the great Niagara Falls, but it is undeniable that the whole greatly seduces him.

This is America.

He arrives two days later at New Rochelle after having passed Pelham manor, an aristocratic manor house whose owner proudly claims that he brings to his set of living rooms, the sophisticated but irresponsible conversations of his European cousins. Perhaps worse because the English barons were scared in Cromwell's day. They understood that it was better to come to an agreement if they wanted to keep their leader

---

(71) François-René de Chateaubriand (1768-1848) is a French romantic writer and diplomat who traveled four months in America at the end of the 18th century and wrote *Voyage en Amérique*.

and their feathered hats, like the poor Dutch in New York who keep their hats to emphasize their identity.

That is not the case here. The new aristocrats are not content with a hat. The metropolis is distant and Big Ben has yet to be built, which could, via its chimes carried across the oceans, unravel the ongoing complexities of the burgeoning parliamentary debate in England. No, American aristocrats behave like great feudal lords, razing everything in their path and especially the land, hundreds of thousands of acres. The only advantage lies in the splendor of their properties, which cannot be circled given their immensity.

As for the Indians, they have given up since a long time, in fact, they have nothing left to give up. They have almost disappeared from the scene, carried away by alcohol, already the proof of the end of the social cohesion that united them all behind their leader, their shaman, and the undeniable solidarity that the first Europeans had witnessed.

The survivors have been ravaged by exotic diseases brought by the immigrants, or by killing each other due to the unfortunate tendency to quickly lose patience when armed, at night by the campfire.

The massive migration of Europeans has favored the evolution from one culture to another. Barter with whites and the economic specialization in trapping and fur trade have undermined the foundations of their ancestral society, the men refusing to hunt what their women no longer wanted to cook.

Native Americans continue to be living witnesses to all of this, as when cities advance in all parts of the world. Antoine does not see them when he passes the Siwanoy camps on the north bank of the East River, as he will probably not see them in his lifetime, as he did not see the inlaid foyer of Pelham Manor. Antoine sees nothing except the exuberant nature that overwhelms him and fills him with joy. He is already absorbed in his life plan and this is not nothing because it is a completely new perspective for humanity to be sitting in front of a huge cake when all you have to do is serve it to yourself.

Antoine realizes, as he traverses this piece of America, that his existence has finally found a setting where the values he holds dear can flourish. The forest is immense and appears to be so for hundreds of leagues. This thought is dizzying like eternity or infinity. He walks like an explorer in a wilderness where the possibilities seem extraordinary. Antoine advances like an entrepreneur. He sees all of this when he approaches New Rochelle, facing the Long Island Sound, which is as large as several *Gironde* estuaries.⁽⁷²⁾ Here, everything is still to be done.

The first migrants from Europe are faced, above all, with the immensity and magnitude of the task. The bravest rejoice, others prepare to justify their failures by blaming their bad luck that has always accompanied them, and the rest seek protection because immensity is scary. Very early, the colony had been invaded by idlers. Antoine had seen them in New York Harbor, perhaps reproducing ancestral patterns on the new continent as a survival reflex.

GWC, the Dutch West India Company, mentioned earlier, had reluctantly established a chaplaincy to make a selection before fulfilling their duty of charity. Its stated policy was to make sure it didn't provide benefits to poor men who didn't intend to support themselves. Peter Stuyvesant was a strong supporter of this position. It was not a church but a business enterprise, to each his task. New York City, once chartered, echoed these concerns. When GWC left, New York could not accommodate all the misery in the world without becoming impoverished in its turn, to the great misfortune of all. Sentimentality and irresponsibility had not yet been invented. Thus, lacking in funds, the municipal authorities continued managing the dispossessed population by sorting them out on the basis of the degree of honesty and willingness to work of the applicants.

At the time, New York only produced a few agricultural products and manufactured almost nothing. It was a port through which goods passed. People's jobs often consisted simply of carrying bundles of goods from one point of the city or port to another. New Yorkers therefore, wisely considered that it was difficult to admit as recipients of public funds those people who refused to transport goods. Despite this selection reflecting a sound moral and economic administration, unwelcome people continued to crowd the city, probably thinking that the situation of each was only the consequence of the change of latitude by a few degrees. New Yorkers, wary of overly simplistic reasoning, quickly took steps to restrict entry into the province. The economic development that everyone expected prepared them intellectually to consider the economic effects on the situation of the people. But anticipating events that had not yet occurred, they preferred to deny access to their territory to migrations based solely on geography.

---

(72) Gironde estuary is the estuary of the Garonne River, downstream from the city of Bordeaux, that Antoine walked by on his way to La Rochelle.

Meanwhile, the port was developing like it never had before under Dutch management, because the Company had set other goals for it from the start. New York welcomed useful migrants provided they met the acclimatization requirements established by law. That was Antoine's concern when he entered New York.

Antoine submitted in 1691 to the governors Sloughter and Ingoldsby an application for admission as an inhabitant of the province of New York, under the given name of Anthony. It occurred apparently in spring given the chronology of the records held in Albany, since the exact date was not recorded. These letters of denization or residency did not give him access to full citizenship, but they did allow the applicant to become a homeowner and to practice his profession.

At the same time, four other persons applied for full citizenship. Abraham Tonneau, Alexander Morisset, Peter Tillou and Laurens Cornifleau, all French and Protestant, had also adapted their first names to the local custom, marking as did Antoine their intention to settle permanently in the province. Therefore, Antoine was not alone.

Anthony Pintard will make the written request himself and will sign by his own hand "because of the severity of his king towards the Reformed Church", as ground for an official passport application that generations of persecuted people will reproduce.

Freedom at last.

51

The Dutch had designed New Amsterdam as a trading post dedicated exclusively to the fur trade. Being so few, they had no conquering ambition, only business intentions that naturally led them to transactions rather than confrontation with the Indians, as the later acquisition of Manhattan demonstrates. So much so that the initial sellers were outmatched by the irate real Indian occupants of the island, who challenged the transaction on the grounds that the Indians, party to the contract, had sold usurped property. A few years later, they demanded compensation through a new deed, once the legal notion of property, foreign to the Native American society, was understood. This episode could have marked the foundations of Comparative law in America if the Indians had not assimilated the concept so quickly.

Apart from acquiring Staten Island and other surrounding islands, in exchange for transferring technology in the form of various tools and utensils, the Dutch, fortunately, never actually exploited it because it was not their plan to establish a settlement there. Nor was it part of their project to respond to the desired settlement of dissidents from diverse variations of European Protestantism.

The synod of Dordrecht seemed to have resolved the conflicts between traditionalists and progressives in the Dutch Reformed Church, forbidding the latter from praying in public, even in a moderate form, on the same basis as other Protestants, Jews and Catholics were forbidden. Thus, there were officially no nationals of the United Provinces oppressed by their *Stathouder*, in the same way that the French Protestants were not fully discriminated against by their king as they were still allowed to practice their devotions in their bedroom. French history has only preserved the actual abuses of Louis XIV, no doubt a communication problem on his part and a political reading linked to the violence with which he implemented his rulings, because simply, he belonged to his time.

The church of Holland that Antoine had seen facing the harbor was therefore in part a nationalist flag with which the community identified. The broom, symbol of the nation, had swept away all synodal sensibilities other than orthodoxy.

Peter Stuyvesant had ruled the colony with an iron hand. He had held the handle vigorously, to such an extent that the progressive Calvinists, flexible like the bristles of the emblematic tool, the Swedish or German Lutherans, as well as others, wondered if they had really touched the shores of freedom or whether they had been deceived. Moreover, the lack of piety manifested by the inhabitants from the Netherlands in the colony showed that theological discussions had been closed for a long time since there was nothing more to say. Therefore, the debate was no longer interesting to anyone and ungodliness was on the march. The unwelcome Lutherans went to pray elsewhere, in the many surrounding islands, but Peter Stuyvesant's broom was large enough to bring them back to Manhattan.

The Company was alarmed by such excessive austerity which in the long run was not conducive to trade. But Peter Stuyvesant was far away and was doing just what he wanted. He had to pay very dearly for it. Everything has a price ; he had been told in Amsterdam.

His hostility towards the Jews, and in particular towards the Spanish or Portuguese Sephardim, who had come from Brazil when Louisa's father had taken refuge in Saint Christophe, did not last long before the Company's Board of Directors. The Jews of Holland enjoyed full citizenship. The sweeping of his broom did not weigh much against the Jewish community's shares in the GWC's capital, thus putting everyone in their place.

New York, for its part, was becoming the burgeoning bulwark of religious tolerance, determined by the economy. The city was historically subjected, thanks to the GWC, to profitability requirements that surpassed believers and non-believers. They were all intolerant because they were all human beings, but they were beginning to find in economic returns the appeasement of their former words, as a higher stage that would one day unite them all.

By submitting to the concept of profitability, the city escaped the clutches of ordinary mortals and their beliefs. The little port had now a goal for itself. As for the rest, it was likely that believers and non-believers would end up agreeing on a regulation that would allow them to live together.

New York is a strange case from the beginning in a world steeped in ideals, God, King, nobility. It joins the ranks of cities like Amsterdam or Venice, except that its much later emergence includes it in a world where protesting against the Catholic Church is a lot like protesting against God, or worse, like indifference. New Yorkers have better things to do than gut each other in futile squabbles over saints and angels, especially since there will be no good schools in which to do so for a long time. The little harbor likes crowns and wings, but they must be golden crowns, and the wings must be good for the economy to take off. The newcomers, mostly religious, prefer sects to churches, it is a question of hegemony. While they reject any political or religious authority, they are instead more open to the most eccentric reasoning. This is, of course, sometimes the fate reserved for the self-taught, but Peter Stuyvesant has reached the limits of his tolerance, especially with regard to the Quakers who are arriving in a continuous stream to the colony. The Quakers make him crack up. The simplicity of their customs prevents him from sweeping them under the carpet with his broom, since there are none in their homes. When thrown out the door, they return through the window, refusing to take their hat off when spoken to, and other unpleasant things.

Peter Stuyvesant is alone, an absolute monarch on the verge of a nervous breakdown. The small port advocates religious tolerance since after all, it does not matter so much, and the most fragile change their religion as if they are changing their shirts. The GWC wants to stay out of trouble and business continues. But since all good things have to come to an end, New Yorkers ended up getting bored with Peter the Fundamentalist and threw him out.

The general public didn't really remember this aspect of his personality, nor the fact that he had saved the colony. Peter Stuyvesant went down in history as the man who founded New York, and that's the way it should be. Mercy, to every sinner.

Antoine belongs to the Reformed Church of France. As a Calvinist, he is the same as a good part of the nationals of the small port. Anglicization is underway, of course, but the descendants of the Dutch are still in the game ; all the more so since the English have intelligently relied on the most enterprising members of their community. The claim that he belonged to the spirit of Calvin when he applied for his citizenship reflects this truth well but may have been whispered to him by people well informed about the parties involved, as a way of facilitating his application. Peter probably would have liked it, but he had been dead for a few years when the petition came up. In any case, Antoine enters New Rochelle as a member of the Calvinist community in terms of religion and French in terms of culture, providing him a good base for integration.

The welcome reserved for him is fraternal and material first aid soon follows as always in such a case. Beyond food and lodging, Antoine finds his way to the church, for the first time as free and light as the fragrant air of the land that borders the Atlantic. Antoine thinks first of his family at home. He would like to have news from France and more particularly from the *Cévennes*, frank and free news of even the worst of events, those which we keep silent because they are too unpleasant to tell, news, whether fresh or not, in any case free of fear and even threats that only lead to falsifying the truth, objective news exempt from all militancy, from all subjectivisms.

Antoine just wants information. He finds something, but so far it is general news about the situation of the Protestants in France. Many of them have left the kingdom. They have taken all kinds of risks in the face of prohibitions enacted, not to prevent them from going elsewhere to pray to God in their own way, but to prevent their skills from going abroad and their money from feeding the nascent hosiery industries of the German principalities or Swiss watchmaking in Geneva or Lausanne.

Authoritarian regimes are learning in both France and England that targeting this or that category of the population will inevitably affect the elite and that at some point they will be missed. English and Irish Catholics have enriched France. French Protestants have enriched the rest of Europe. The balance is not in favor of either of the two great nations, to whom persecuted Catholic or Protestant communities have often paid back in kind. Brazilian Jews and many others have enriched New York City. As for the political balance, it depends on the events that occur at that time, when historical events are analyzed.

Antoine understands that the finances of the kingdom of France are not good and that the wars fought by Louis XIV are a burden to those who stay. For the king, unable to assign large troops to carry out his laws, recruits indiscriminately, sometimes including men whose brutality make up for their small number. In fact, he will later recruit

Irish Catholics to fight in the *Cévennes*. It must also be admitted that the Protestants of France, deprived of their leaders, overwhelmed by injustice, have gone into hiding like snails in their shells.

The number of arrests is less than at the time of the Revocation and the rowers are less numerous on the galley benches because there are no more confrontations. Across the Atlantic, Antoine is informed that silence is golden and that the *Cévennes*, like Protestant France, are in mourning. The new generation is only ten or twelve years old. Nobody knows yet that when it will react a few years later, it would not be to burst into tears.

Those who have stayed in the country are not the elite. They are carders, butchers, pig castrators. They will not have the apprehensions of their elders and the sight of blood will not bother them during the Great Uprising in 1702. They will know how to be attuned to their torturers. For now, the news only speaks of an immense and white shroud that momentarily covers the Protestant countries of France, under which civilly dead men still move and reproduce. If the idea of returning could have germinated in Antoine's mind for a time, the sad news of a people buried under a blanket of mourning confirms Antoine's desire to stay away and settle permanently here.

At New Rochelle, the community is active beyond denominational aspirations. The Huguenots of France are thus gathered on the banks of the East River, so vast that that they resemble a seashore where a second wave of refugees could be welcomed. The first wave came through another starting point, that of Breda in Holland, as in the case of the Bayard family, or other cities of refuge, as for example for the de Lancey or La Montaigne families. Impatience had driven them to New York through some other more welcoming countries like England. Antoine joins the second wave, increasing the flow coming through the West Indies.

And he is not alone. Calvin's church fills up on Sundays and catechists struggle to make up for time lost by newcomers and their families. Births take place, duly registered, in accordance with the charter of the small town. All of them rediscover the happiness of existing civilly and accept the constraints of the community as the necessary requirements of their rebirth. Therefore, the enthusiasm is, above all, collective and is felt in the effervescence that animates the people. Joy is perceptible and has to be shared in order to decide objectives, where to cut expenses to balance income, each one participating according to his possibilities, each having what is due to him and nothing else. A true religious and agricultural community where the still insignificant differences in resources do not incite the smallest contributors to justify disproportionate claims. The balance is evident, as no one conspicuously outperforms others. The only way to stand out is in the degree of piety that each one of them strives to exercise, as a mark of distinction necessary to establish a hierarchy. In its absence, these communities could not endure. With intrinsic equality being a chimera, Protestants from France, like others, initially resorted to new criteria to avoid re-using imported criteria. In addition, it was necessary to produce, count, care and judge. The distribution of roles could not be answered by drawing the short straw.

Finally, Antoine rediscovers the synods and the official consular organizations of old France within which each occupies the role that best corresponds to his aspirations, skills and morals. But power brings with it resentment of its exercise. In order to return to fundamental equality, it is sometimes necessary to put everyone back on the right track. New Rochelle is no exception. The small town must watch and punish. The practice of the legal profession is very often a passive one, since the founding statutes are a form of prevention. Prevention is still enough. Everything is calm and silent ; the study of jurisprudence has not yet tired the eyes of the jurists who will later practice this art after their working day. True specializations are not yet necessary, each one occupies his place according to the founding acts. Antoine is happy, relieved, calm.

Relations between the two French Protestant communities on the Atlantic coast of the province of New York are good, if sporadic. The two cities are more than twenty-five miles apart and the activity of New Rochelle, created in 1687, is still not enough to maintain a real flow of business with New York. But the ease of navigation that the East River offers will make things simple in future.

People from New Rochelle are not on the edge of the world, and if their New England neighbors still have territorial and political ambitions in the colony and in particular in the outskirts of New York, their natural and spiritual inclination is inland, towards New York.

52

Antoine is curious. He will spend his life here. He knows this very well. He has become a resident of the province even before obtaining naturalization letters for it. He talks, questions, listens and he is always learning. He discovers in particular the monopoly on entry and exit of goods through the only small port. He doesn't have an opinion on this. He just takes it into account ; this, probably, partly explains why the Calvinist city leans toward New York.

The events of his existence to come will be the result of the first months of his residence. Antoine shows a spirit of evaluation, better still, a spirit of synthesis.

"At least there are no soldiers here", said Antoine, starting the discussion.

"Why are you talking about soldiers ?" asked his friend.

"Because I saw a lot of them in New York Harbor."

"Ah, but New York is not New Rochelle !"

"Yes, but why so many soldiers, it seemed like a parade !"

"It was not a parade, but rather a security squad".

"Security squad ! What's going on here that requires such a show of force ?"

"Fights, that's why the Red coats are here."

"Red coats !"

"That's what they call them, the English soldiers. The colony has been English since 1664, but things are not so simple."

"Nothing is simple," added Antoine, "but all this does not tell me what happened."

"It all started in England. When Charles II died, his brother, the Duke of York, became King of England under the name of James II. Until then, there was no problem with the succession, except that the king was Catholic. His brother had allowed him to acquire the province of New York in 1664. The king, who was then still only the Duke of York, had been quick to take prominent families into vassalage by giving them huge estates."

"Like at home," added Antoine.

"Exactly. Except the people here hadn't seen such arbitrary actions in the days of the Dutch Company. They then began to object. Especially since the colony now belonged to the royal domain because the duke had become the king."

"As in Saint-Christophe," added Antoine.

"Perhaps", replied his friend. "In any case, the people here knew that the Catholic King was on good terms with the King of France to the point of sharing his view on the modern conduct of a kingdom and on the fate of the Protestants of France after the Revocation of the Edict of Nantes. They didn't like this."

His friend paused for a moment to try, perhaps, to explain.

"To tell the truth, they were afraid that someone would come and tell them what to do or not to do, because some of them had never known the monarchy since the founding of New York, more than sixty years ago."

"We can understand them", added Antoine.

"Yes, but not all of them were of the same opinion. No more than in London, where part of Parliament did not accept a Catholic ruler either."

"We can understand that too."

"Yes, but disapproving is not enough for things to progress, you have to do something. The events occurred first in England, where they ended up expelling the king."

"I know it ; we suffered the consequences in Saint-Christophe."

"Perhaps", added his friend. "In any case, William of Orange, the Dutch husband of the daughter of King James, was put on the throne. In this way, business remained in the family, and England had found a Protestant king, in William of Orange."

"Well observed," added Antoine.

"Perhaps, except that here the governor was not sure of the transaction and not wanting to make a mistake, he was slow to recognize the new sovereign, especially because his administration tended to be Catholic. He was celebrating mass at Fort James in New York, some even called it Fort Saint Jacques, and they had brought in a lot of Jesuits who were not compatible with the simplicity of the people of New York. In fact, no one complained, but no one approved of it either. But since, sadly, the city was partly turned towards ungodliness, what bothered the people the most was having to report to these bewigged outsiders. Others, Protestants at heart, had never accepted this Catholic king, especially the Quakers who do not like being held accountable to anyone for anything, and even less so to a Catholic."

"But what about the Huguenots in all this ?" asked Antoine.

"We have been numerous here in the New York area for more than 50 years. The Huguenots were not pleased with the events taking place in England because they feared that the King of France would occupy New York from Canada and they would suffer the same atrocities that they had previously experienced. Furthermore, as their integration was successful, they did not want an authority that would paralyze their businesses."

"So, what did they do ?" asked Antoine.

"I'll get to that, but first it's about understanding what happened after the return of a Protestant king to England. Rumors invaded New York" …

"Rumors !"

"Yes, things are never simple. Both the former governor and his administration remained loyal to the Stuarts, that is, to the family of James II, even though not all were Catholics. James had been forcibly toppled, admittedly."

"That's true", agreed Antoine.

"And no one was sure of the long-term consequences of this way of overthrowing a monarch, even today we continue to ask ourselves the question ! On the other hand, the English residents of the colony now had as their sovereign a Dutchman whose title corresponded to the ephemeral New Orange that had superseded New York for a short time in 1673. In short, no one was really satisfied."

"As always", added Antoine.

"Then rumors arose from all sides", continued his friend, "that the French from New France might come to New York and invade the colony, supported by Irish Catholics expelled from Ireland in 1649 or even in the time of Cromwell and why not also James II's Iroquois, while the French were supposed to have the support of the Hurons."

"At lot of people !" Antoine murmured again.

"Too many", added his friend. "Riots broke out, leading in particular to the English residents from Long Island marching on to New York in an unsuccessful attempt to overthrow Nicholson and his city council. But a man emerged from the group of insurgents, and taking things in hand more calmly, he decided to refuse to pay taxes on the grounds that since the treasurer was a Catholic, there was no guarantee that the funds would not end up being diverted to uses for which they were not destined."

"All that is fine", Antoine added, "but what was their aim since the English Protestants of New York had found a king of their own religion again ?"

"This is where things get complicated," his friend insisted. "New York was founded recently. The little port, as you sometimes call it, has its own character. You may have seen soldiers on your way, but you may not have noticed the dilapidated state of the military structures !"

"No", answered Antoine.

"And yet," continued his friend, "they are in better shape than I have ever known them. The little port has always been about business. This is not a military port, there is no arsenal here, no barracks, but it is the only major port between Boston and the West Indies. The small port has no military ambitions. It would like to be left alone and thus continue its development."

"Like a Company !"

"A little more, because today there are three thousand inhabitants in New York, including more than two hundred Huguenot families, all this cannot be managed as a commercial company. In addition, Peter Stuyvesant laid the foundations of an organization for the city, which is why the inhabitants value the freedom of their community and their consular institutions."

"One can understand them. We also value that in France and do our best to reaffirm them in court from time-to-time if necessary."

"Except that things are different here because what happens in Parliament in England has repercussions here."

"What do you mean ?" asked Antoine.

His friend continued talking. Long Island Sound, vast as a giant estuary, etched like the *Cornwall* shoreline, reflected the dense and majestic forests that lined it in the calm waters of the East River. The setting sun crossed the depths of the inlets like a caress at the end of the day, a tender good night whispered to one's child, a last candlelight before the evening prayer.

Antoine loved this landscape, powerful without extravagance, strong but without harshness, invigorating but without coldness. He had not yet savored the winter that could bring its weight of wet snow and its blanket of pure ice despite the proximity of the ocean, perhaps the memory of the great glaciers that had crossed this side of the world in ancient times. The continent had been scratched, beaten under the terrifying thickness of icy water that flowed from Canada up to the shores of the Atlantic, leaving in its wake the Brooklyn moraine as the last vestige of that monstrous struggle.

Towards the end of the Ice Age, the rivers that ran through the province had undoubtedly taken the place of the glacier after its slow work of erosion, recovering their natural slope towards the salty waters. Before reaching the sea, the rivers had enriched the vast expanses that they crossed, shaping the banks, depositing their silt and reviving an entire vegetation ready to reseed the land.

Thousands of autumns had helped cover the ground, sanded by the friction of the sharp ice, with a thick black humus that would eventually feed an entire continent and even part of Europe.

Antoine felt safe in this landscape. He wasn't the only one to have this feeling. In a time when the earth made the people, it was more pleasant to live here than in the *Cévennes*. The soil was beginning to stick to his shoes. He liked the smells, which changed according to the hours of the day. Nature, warmed by the sun, revealed aromas that marked the hours like a scented sundial. Antoine was imbued with this strange world ; he longed for nothing but Louisa and his family.

"You are not listening to me anymore", his friend cried out.

"Yes, yes ... no ; you're right, I was daydreaming."

"Well, we'll talk about that some other time, it's getting late", replied his friend.

"Wait, I'll come with you."

The two men crossed the deserted alleys. It was well into the summer and the settlers had to go to work very early in the morning. Silence reigned everywhere. The houses of the French were arranged in the manner of the provinces of their kingdom, in the middle of a field surrounded by stone walls that these peasants, inventing America, fed with their obstinate and regular collection of the stony remains of the great Canadian glacier. Antoine felt at home now. The parcels of land thus delimited testified to uses borrowed from French tradition and to a job well done. The young geometric plantations of apple trees that dotted certain enclosures, recalled the small town's inhabitants' attachment to the land. The province's flag, already flying near a public building under construction, loudly proclaimed New Rochelle's links with New York. All were already asleep, after evening prayers, like Americans who would continue to speak French for a long time.

Antoine returned to the accommodation that the consistory had managed to make available for him. A small, simple rectangular room, built with good-sized, jagged stones. Its modest size suited a single man, which did not displease Antoine, like a peasant's house and the starting point of a long road ahead in which he himself would set the pace. A simple, straight fireplace gave some relief to an enclosed cell-shaped space intended to house a reclining giant. Its shape and its disproportionate but clearly visible human dimensions gave the whole a utilitarian aspect that must have guided the hands of the builder. Other buildings of the same type were scattered around the small town ; annexes to larger buildings, garden cabins intended for a penniless but voluntary workforce, farmworkers, as a foreseeable and almost programmed evolution of the new settlement.

Antoine fell asleep, satisfied once more with the day that was ending. He sent his final thoughts to the absent ones, whose silence made the air vibrate like the cry of bats that circled incessantly in front of the skylight of his refuge there on the edge of America.

53

The following weeks added to his chain of discoveries, new sensations and encounters. The consistory stood at the heart of the reformed community, calling meetings, establishing rules, and sometimes calling for order. Antoine rediscovered the moments that he had known in Saint-Roman, consisting of exchanges, words given and then retracted, advice and admonitions, a lively and animated community, far from the apparent understanding that sometimes hides indifference.

The group had been formed recently. Therefore, they all knew the basic concepts, which undoubtedly explained the general adherence to the principles and the self-regulation that each intended to implement. The jurisprudence applied to the interpretation of their statutes had not yet taken them away from the spirit that united them. Nobody quibbled to escape customary law, which they considered as a flag, a banner that united and also protected them.

The elders discreetly sought out to see if their rules made the community appear welcoming to Antoine, a question of image without a doubt, and therefore of the future. Antoine quickly integrated himself. He loved these people and the people reciprocated his sentiments.

Everything seemed easy to him in a group of individuals striving towards the same destiny, towards the same objectives. There was not yet any confrontation, any disagreement, in other words politics. New Rochelle was grounded in its founding charters as individuals may be attached to their principles. The personalities that made it up were often strong and convinced of their choices ; the fearful had stayed in Europe.

The page was turned. The decisions were irrevocable because they had been thought out for a long time. The discussions had taken place before and not during their execution. The members of the small town thus saved time, investing all their energy in the implementation of their resolutions. These men kept their feet on the ground and gave a favorable opinion only to what was possible, which made them austere in the eyes of some. They tried to be honest simply by including the future in the constraints of their reasoning only as a last resort or when there was no alternative but to trust in God. Betting on the future was not part of their daily routine ; they only envisaged what they already saw on the horizon, which made them dull. But they were advancing and would advance for a long time. The results were visible and that was the only thing that mattered to them. Their successes reinforced their convictions and their failures were only messages sent by God himself to make them think and to keep them on the right path. These communities did not have major problems, each remained in his place fulfilling the role assigned to him ; an avant-garde collectivism that included private property.

Antoine felt comfortable in his role and he was not the only one. The recalcitrant had no choice but to leave, since their integration into the community only happened after the acceptance of its rules. Techniques changed little in the 17th century and ambitions were often limited to food self-sufficiency. Therefore, there was little reason to change the rules, as in monastic orders. You could always abandon the robe. That was all.

Antoine discovered how New Rochelle worked and this was in line with his hopes, with the city of God that he had always glimpsed during his voyage, founded on moral and religious principles shared by the community. These were the cement that united them. They were building their individual lives on the basis of written and well-known rules, few in number but strict : individual successes could only be achieved by submission to the rules that constituted order. Others could always look elsewhere, simply because there was plenty of room in other places where they could exercise their visionary talents. These men of character were not deprived of it. Dissidents were constantly creating new communities with innovative rules that others could join if they wished, or simply go their own way.

Antoine was there, sitting in the middle of fenced, fragmented and divided parcels of land, and yet he knew that the plots, far from separating individuals, on the contrary, united them. Released from the tutelage of a Lord, the new men could conduct their affairs in their own interests, which would correspond to the general interest as decided by all members. Happy times, he thought, when the challenge to the rule could be resolved by changing the community, thus avoiding endless discussions leading to no results. Happy times in which prohibitions were enacted simply as limits to be respected in order to be able to coexist serenely.

Antoine was far from the overcrowded valleys of the *Cévennes*, in the midst of an ungenerous nature, in a kingdom with the largest demographics in Europe. Antoine felt good ; he felt free.

America had the power to pacify, by favoring only contacts chosen voluntarily and eliminating those that had been imposed. Perhaps this is what prompted thousands of people to move west. It remains one of the characteristics of today's American. Antoine was changing.

Antoine met with his friend that day, at the end of Sunday school.

"We're fine here," he said suddenly.

"We're not badly off", confirmed his friend in return, smiling. "We couldn't be better anywhere else !"

"What about New York ?"

"New York ! But that has nothing in common with New Rochelle !"

"What is the difference ?" Antoine asked him.

"There people want to live together, here they have in addition a common goal, that of building a moral and religious community."

"Don't they do that in New York ?" asked Antoine.

"They did it at one point, during the time of Peter Stuyvesant, but it didn't last long. They regained their autonomy through the Charter of Privileges and Freedoms."

"What is the difference ?" asked Antoine.

"No binding target for New Yorkers, they just set rules for everyone's enrichment based on each own's abilities, whereas in New Rochelle the foundations are laid for the moral improvement of all."

"But they still have churches !" exclaimed Antoine.

"Yes, but none of them sets the tone, or rather they all do."

"What do you mean ?" Antoine insisted.

"That they each relate their vision of the world, differentiating from each other in details. They have a choice and they exercise it according to whatever is convenient for them ; all of this doesn't follow any logic, at least any common logic based on which something solid and durable can be built."

"Maybe one day they will find unity ?"

"It is not a certainty," continued his friend, "because each newcomer brings his own interpretation of the Bible, his rereading of the Gospels, in short, his originality and that is what pleases all. They say it is effervescent and that's the way it should be."

"And how to avoid this ?"

"We cannot avoid this, they are all dissidents, first from the Catholic Church and now from the Anglican or the Reformed Church. Some chapels gather at most a handful of people ; already, dissidents of God."

"They lack a leader," added Antoine.

"Yes, but since they got rid of the Pope like we did, I can't imagine them looking for a new leader. Perhaps as time goes by, they will regroup, or the big ones will swallow the little ones or just pick up their leftovers."

"Here, you risk nothing ?" asked Antoine.

"No", replied his friend, "as long as the Reformed Church governs the community, there is no problem."

"A privilege", added Antoine.

"In any case, certainly a monopoly."

"All this can last a long time."

"Yes, we have just led our community to the baptismal font and the anchor bolts are solid since our founding two years ago. But, if one day we open ourselves to other religions, it will surely create competition that will please and satisfy everyone's expectations".

"That is to be avoided", added Antoine.

"I'm sure of that. That is the way to ungodliness. When you have failed in one Church, you enter another, in a way you become a turncoat or worse still, you absolve yourself, without even the help of a priest as in the Catholic religion during confession."

"That's easy", Antoine murmured.

"And it does not lead to anything", added his friend, "since it does not teach anything."

The two men stood face to face, looking each other in the eye, two men free to speak, express themselves, criticize and understand. Antoine liked this. He had been deprived of that for a long time. He took pleasure in analysis and his friend saw that too.

"You should take on responsibilities in the consistory."

"It tempts me but I cannot take the place of those who are already there. Besides, I don't even know the main stages of the founding of New Rochelle."

The two men found it difficult to separate. His friend wanted to keep talking, happy to have found in Antoine a man he could trust, who had his feet on the ground, someone to whom much could be said, even about the past. However, they separated all the same. Antoine said goodbye and promised to see him again soon.

Antoine had been summoned to an informal meeting with the members of the council. He was worried about the future and he wanted to know the options opened to him in New Rochelle. He walked towards the church. The interior was deserted and the Bible open to the last page of the day's reading. There was a hushed silence, as if muffled by the wood panels that cladded the walls. The quality of silence in Protestant churches resembles that of a living room, a waiting room, even a hall ; we are waiting for a familiar character who will eventually enter, enlivening the tranquility of the place with his simple and friendly presence. The unpleasant rubbing of a chair on cold stone does not hurt the ear, like in a Gothic cathedral. Sounds are muffled like in a house. They are not amplified in magnificent lofty vaults where, no longer finding their way, they eventually traverse the organ pipes, sending out disquieting echoes.

Antoine sat down to appreciate the moment. Everything was clean and new. The comfortable benches did not break the backs of those attending the service. There were no chairs for the rich. Apparently, they cared for the comfort of all the guests. There was also no smell except perhaps that left by drying plaster. Daylight came through the regularly spaced openings placed at the top of the walls, illuminating with a soft and white light the lightly embroidered cloth on which was posed a large Bible, and throwing slight shadows on the colors of a thick woolen rug. Two chandeliers around the choir gave elevation to a place otherwise domestic in nature.

The voices from the meeting room reminded Antoine that he was expected. He knocked on the door that had been left ajar to signal his arrival.

"Antoine, we weren't expecting you through that door !" the pastor said.

"I wanted to go through the church", answered Antoine.

"That's good", concluded the pastor. "Please sit down, we need to talk."

Antoine accepted the offer. He let the pastor speak ; apparently, he was used to directing proceedings in the hall where the session met. The table was long and narrow, simple and straight, a table made for debates and decision.

"You wanted to meet with us so that we could discuss together the possibilities of welcoming you fully into our community. When I say fully, I mean your desire to build your future here with us. After some thought, the presbytery members have agreed to welcome you. However, there is no immediate possibility that you will become a landowner and be able to carry out your own agricultural activity. You will have to depend on people who are already members of the community and who need workers to help them with their task. Be patient, that's all we have to offer you for now. You have given everyone complete satisfaction with your work. We recognize in you a man of value. You should know that your departure would make us all sad, but we prefer to be honest with you. However, we will understand your position and you will always be welcome among us."

"Thank you all for your frankness, but you already knew my intentions : I must move in that direction."

"Meanwhile, I repeat, you are welcome."

The meeting had been short, but Antoine was not disappointed. They parted ways the same way they had met, without a second thought.

Surprisingly, Antoine walked out of the interview liberated. In his mind, his candidacy hadn't been a good idea after all.

He viewed New York as a rocky outcrop against which he would crash or perhaps it would also be a lifeline for the fragile ship he had been maneuvering for years.

The information he had was reliable. He had had the opportunity on several occasions to see New York sailors loading produce from New Rochelle and their flexibility and attitude appealed to him. Antoine knew that the small port would grow larger and that it was possible to carve a place in it. Meanwhile, paradoxically, he needed land : only land establishes lasting foundations. After all, it couldn't be that difficult to become a landowner in a province that was rich and many times larger than Languedoc. You just had to be daring. There was no need to stay here any longer.

Antoine left New Rochelle at the end of the harvest, in the summer of 1691. He had earned enough to last a while. The consistory had entrusted him with messages intended for Huguenot refugees in New York who did business with them. Antoine had earned the trust of the community and had been able to create bonds that would last for several generations of Pintards.

54

When Antoine entered Peter Delanoy's office, he admired at first glance its comfort, the upholstery of the armchairs and the brocades that covered their backrests. The place was larger than one would have imagined from the outside, no doubt due to the facades, all of the same proportion, that placed side-by-side, gave a deceptive scale to the entire neighborhood. The staff were black slaves whose presence was not strange to Antoine. He treated them with familiarity, having lived quite close to them, and having sweated as much as they did on the Saint-Christophe plantations. A servant, dressed as a lord in comparison with Antoine's poor attire, greeted him with a dismissive air. Antoine was not offended and tolerated the attitude without forgetting his mission, which he knew was important. It was a matter of getting Monsieur Delanoy to accept payment and make the corresponding deposit with another Huguenot merchant with whom he dealt in New Rochelle. He had, so to speak, the role of a banker.

The wait was long but pleasant. The place was beautiful, at least in Antoine's eyes, since he was not used to such refinement. It lacked the elegance of the Montpellier hotel that he had known during his trip to La Rochelle, but it seemed obvious that good business had been carried out in this house. The small port was no longer just home to hunters or sailors. The merchants of New York could already compete with those of France. Antoine was silently surprised.

After the wait, Monsieur Delanoy finally appeared : a middle-aged man, well-dressed, without ostentation but without sartorial austerity either. His handshake was frank and quick, the comments short and to the point, the instructions on what to do next clear and practical. Knowledgeable about social interaction, Delanoy wasted no time in formulas, which are often used just to assess the speaker anyway. He had already largely taken on the attitudes of Dutch and English merchants who evaluate men according to their ability to fulfill their commitments. Such a judgment was enough for business. Delanoy seemed to be at the center of a singular struggle, as if he suffered some illness that partially crippled his ability to act or react. He did not seem as comfortable as the environment in which he moved, which seemed to correspond to a previous life, certainly not so distant but nevertheless finished or at least temporarily suspended.

"Please pass on my best thoughts to my friends in New Rochelle !"

"I don't think I'll see them any time soon," said Antoine.

"And why on earth is that ? Are you not intending to join the community ?"

"No", answered Antoine, "not immediately."

"Do you have other plans ?" Delanoy continued.

"Actually, I'm considering moving to New York temporarily."

"Why is that ?"

"I want to acquire farmland and I think that here it will be easier for me to realize my plans."

"It is almost impossible in Manhattan and the surrounding islands. You should have stayed in New Rochelle", Delanoy said.

"There are no more opportunities in New Rochelle, at least not for now, and at my age, I can't wait any longer."

"You are still young !"

"Yes, but it's now or never."

"That is great determination, sir !" Delanoy exclaimed.

"Driven by need !"

"The one that brings us all here !" Delanoy continued, "but beware of mirages, here they are as numerous as temptations."

"I do not know the city, but I am willing to receive advice and warnings, especially when they come from a person of quality."

"You express yourself like you were still in France, it's amusing !"

Antoine, a bit confused, was about to reply, but Delanoy stopped him.

"Don't get me wrong sir, I know what I'm talking about, I was, not long ago the mayor of this city and men of quality, as you say, do not have a life expectancy here that is higher than that of our counterparts in France, quite the opposite. Careers are made and unmade in the blink of an eye, fortunes too, and governors in the same way. New York has just gone through a very turbulent period in its young history. I am a witness to all of it."

Antoine looked carefully at Delanoy, who immediately noticed it. He then explained in great detail the events of the last two years and the terrible incidents that led to the death of Jacob Leisler who was sentenced to dismemberment after his execution for treason.

"Who was this man ?" asked Antoine.

"He had taken power after the confusion caused by the exile of the Catholic King James II from England. Because the loyalist Governor Nicholson refused to recognize the Prince of Orange as ruler without receiving proper official documents from the capital, Jacob Leisler sped up the process by sending Nicholson back to his residence in London. He was also a good man as I have said before and many of us followed him, especially because we all foresaw at the time an easing of the restrictions that weighed on our province. Each one then wrote down what he had in mind to the point that there were as many complaints as there were followers of Jacob Leisler. The expectations of all could never be realized. In any case, Leisler was unable to unite and mobilize this crowd behind common goals. I was the mayor of New York at the time and saw the situation deteriorate because nothing constructive was happening. Meanwhile, the King of England had sent a new governor to the province, Governor Sloughter, who was accompanied by a military man, Richard Ingoldsby. Upon his arrival, Leisler was arrested and later tried. He was sentenced to be hanged, drawn and quartered."

"What should we remember that is positive about him ?" asked Antoine.

"Doubtless the good that he did for the Huguenots in exchange for the support of the French Calvinist community here in New York. He is at the origin of the founding of New Rochelle."

"How did he do it ?" asked Antoine.

"Simply by purchasing part of Pelham Manor from the Pell family.
(73) Members of the French Calvinists bought everything, lot after lot."

"Is that why there are no more opportunities to buy land ?"

"Yes, because there are almost certainly no more plots available."

"Where should I go then ?"

"Maybe to New Jersey."

---

(73) In 1654, Thomas Pell, an aristocrat, bought the area from the Siwanoy Indians and named it Pelham Manor in honor of his tutor Pelham Burton.

"But that's far !" Antoine interrupted.

"The Atlantic coast is not that far from Staten Island, but as far as I know, the situation is not very clear as to the actual owners of the lands in the area. Go and speak, mentioning my name, with the Lord of Lorières, Poncet Stelle, he is a Huguenot from Poitou. [74] He will be familiar with the situation. You will find him in the southeast of Staten Island. Give him my best regards."

Antoine warmly thanked Peter Delanoy for his good advice. The afternoon was beginning to descend on New York ; the city bustle was calming down. He went over it all in his thoughts.

Monsieur Delanoy had told him, while accompanying him to the stairs of his house, that Poncet Stelle had a project to create a settlement, moral and religious, and that he would know how to surround himself with "people of quality", he had added with a smile. Antoine liked the idea and was eager to meet Mr. Stelle.

Walking through the streets of the port, he discovered a nightlife similar to that of La Rochelle, made up sometimes of excesses and nervousness. This torrent contrasted with the calm waters of the Hudson and East rivers that joined in front of him in a majestic embrace that dated back to the dawn of time.

A man came up to him without brusqueness but also without modesty. He spoke in French and was well dressed.

"I've been looking at you, Sir, for a long time, and you seem interested in the spectacle in front of us."

"Indeed, answered Antoine, this mingling of waters is amazing, because one is not aware that here are two great rivers that meet."

"Two great rivers ?" the man retorted.

"Are the Hudson and the East River not really rivers ?"

"No. Monsieur ?"

"Pintard", answered Antoine.

"No Monsieur Pintard, the East River is not a river" . . .

"Is it an estuary then ?" hazarded Antoine.

"Nor that. It is really the sea."

"You amaze me !"

"I do not doubt it ! But in fact, it is an arm of the sea, so to speak."

The man was about to start explaining to him, but Antoine interrupted, wanting to know who he was talking to.

---

(74) Poitou is an old province of France whose main city was Poitiers.

"I'm Nicholas Bayard. You will hear about me in this city for better or for worse."

He explained to Antoine that the East River separated the mainland from the island that the English call Long Island, but that it was indeed the sea because this passage was open to the Atlantic both on the north and the south sides of Manhattan.

"But nobody talks about it here."

"Also, the name is confusing", Antoine added.

"I grant you, Monsieur Pintard, that nobody talks about it because everyone repeats it without trying to understand. It must be said that the coast is very rugged with all these capes, bays, beaches and innumerable inlets, especially further north. Maps do not simplify the task, as they very often do not depict the coastline beyond New Rochelle. But there you have it, this is a fact, the East River is salty and in case of difficulty you can escape by navigating north of New York. You never know, but it can be useful", added Monsieur Bayard, smiling.

"I hope it will be of no use to me", answered Antoine.

"I wish you that too. Even if everything remains to be done in this city, there will still be many places to go to ; but things are not stable here yet and the mistrust of people towards each other will last for a long time. If you have ambitions, it is better to know that the East River is an arm of the sea ; otherwise, to consider it as a river is to deprive yourself of a possible exit through the north !"

"I have some ambitions", Antoine said "but I'm not considering running away, when I haven't even yet started"

"You're right, but don't waste much time either, things are going well around here !"

"I will not forget that".

The two men took leave of each other, each resuming his way in the direction he had come from. Nicholas Bayard retraced his steps a few seconds later.

"Come see me tomorrow at Broad Street. Everyone knows me, you just need to ask".

Antoine bid farewell to Monsieur Bayard, who resumed his journey to the center of town. He later learned that the Bayards were allied with the Stuyvesants since the marriage of Peter who lay in his final dwelling place on the road to New Rochelle.

The setting sun crept over the facades, mingling the reds and greens of the roofs into a dazzling orange that also set the Dutch church on fire. The small port undoubtedly mixed the different communities more easily than other cities, but the inhabitants had already had their problems. The fire was still burning.

Antoine returned to his inn. It was located in the port a few steps from the docks. He opened the door and sat down at a table. The place was clean and dry. A man who was already seated at a table greeted him with a "Monsieur", in French. Antoine responded in kind. The men were silent for a long time. Antoine was eager to eat. He had risen early and had walked a long way back to New York. He was in a hurry to go to bed after his meal. The man was the first to break the silence.

"Do you know the man you were talking to ?"

"I just met him, but sir, with whom do I have the honor ?"

"Excuse me ! I am Isaac Quintard."

"My name is Anthony Pintard", replied Antoine, who was not yet used to mentioning his first name in English.

"His name is Nicholas Bayard ; he is a Huguenot like us but he is very rich. He was in trouble at the time of Leisler's revolt against Governor Nicholson. As a member of the council, he had remained loyal to James II while awaiting instructions from England and had not followed the example of the rebels. Events proved him right. Leisler's arrest allowed him to return to New York from where he had had to flee. It is said that he was the one who advised Governor Sloughter to sentence Leisler to death, probably to set an example, because the other leaders were spared in order to prevent riots breaking out in New York as they had in the Huguenot community of Staten Island."

"Was Leisler popular ?" asked Antoine.

"He had his defenders, especially among us."

"And what is the situation now ?" Antoine continued.

"Nothing is resolved, the city harbors two opposing camps and it will take time to repair the damage."

"The English are not offended by the positions taken by the French Reformed as it was Governor Sloughter who authorized me to stay."

"Why would they, if they were supporting a defender of the new king ?"

"Yes, but Leisler had taken power without receiving orders !"

"Oh ! They could have ignored that detail as it was a sign of submission to the new sovereign, but it was the sequence of events that bothered them. You see, Leisler was talking of freedom that wasn't to everyone's liking, even though it did not make sense sometimes. In any case, part of the population adhered to his ideas. The English preferred to cut off the question, so to speak, and get it over with, once and for all. It was a takeover of the colony by the metropolis. Louis XIV would have done no less. Everyone is needed, Bayard, you and the others."

"And you, how long have you been here ?" asked Antoine.

"From the beginning. I came from Bristol, in England, where I took refuge during the Revocation. I got married there and now I live in Connecticut."

"But you know the affairs of this province well."

"Norwalk is not far from New York by the Sound and New York is so small that everyone ends up being known by everyone else !"

"It's amazing !" Antoine said.

"Everything is new for us but something is being born here, I still don't know what it is but I think it we will have to get used to it. Anyway, the King of England seems to finally accept it, so we can go ahead !"

The two men finished their meal and were satisfied with their meeting and their exchange.

Antoine headed back to the docks of the little harbor. Now everything was peaceful. King William's soldiers had returned to their barracks.

Some passers-by also gave the impression they were enjoying the beautiful evening.

The home of the only Anglican pastor in town was still lit up. He was probably having guests and speaking of something else than of Jacob Leisler, who lay two steps away next to his son-in-law Milborne, who had supported him to the end.

After he had been beheaded, his head was sewn back with a large needle that pierced his neck and shoulders, the thread had gone in and out as if they were closing a sack or putting on the head of a scarecrow. Jacob Leisler was cleared in 1695 by an Act of Parliament and his estate restored to his heirs.

55

The next day, Antoine walked to Broad Street. He didn't know anyone in New York and was open to hearing any suggestions. He walked the few hundred meters that separated him from Nicholas Bayard's house, attentive to the carriages that were invading the streets in a more or less orderly, more or less prudent manner.

The speed limits imposed by Peter Stuyvesant during his time were not always respected. The English had other things to do and the Dutch carters, whipping the rump of their mules, also used all possible adjectives in their language, to impose themselves in the middle of the flow of goods to and from the port. The streets were dry and joyful.

The wagons driven by blond giants hurtled in all directions, their bundles arranged in every way necessary for their transportation. The thud of the spikes attached to the wheels matched the scraping sound that came from the barrels being rolled, interspersed at times with the distant cries of the animals in the hands of the butchers, reminding all with their shrill howls that New York had more and more bellies to feed.

The British takeover had taken place at all levels and immigrants from England regularly entered the colony as it developed.

The Dutch, attached to their certainties and their liberalism, struggled to maintain the character of the small port. The changes that were taking place were striking enough to admit that New Amsterdam would soon pass into oblivion, even among the people that had been at the origin of its founding.

Newcomers kept pouring in from all destinations.

The disputes appeared to be resolved. But the mishaps of the past were the germs of a confrontation that could not disappear or be controlled by the metropolis which was too far away and too alien to the discussions that would animate the life of the city for a long time, to the point perhaps of generating new debates, which could hardly be classified as civic or democratic.

However, New Yorkers had to stop arguing on petty issues and to enter the more peaceful terrain of politics. Jacob Leisler's late acquittal had at least provided the basis for that.

Antoine had arrived in front of Nicholas Bayard's house, which a passerby, very likely a Leislerian, had refused identify and had spat on the ground ; nevertheless, he pushed the door open.

The meeting was cordial but of little use. Nicholas Bayard, who was then recovering his power in the city, had no other mission than to identify "people of quality" so that through a first contact a bond would be established that he hoped would be lasting, as a tribute of loyalty. Antoine understood these encounters well, which basically still resembled ancient France and all the feudal societies that still reigned in Europe. The form was just cruder. He listened politely to Monsieur Bayard, but refused the knighthood, at least in secret. The latter, in turn, evoked in detail past events. Antoine already knew all this almost by heart. This attitude responded to the emerging debate that no one yet saw clearly. Nicholas Bayard was already fully in charge. Antoine discreetly turned a deaf ear.

The two men politely parted, each pursuing the goals he had in mind, wanting to include the other in his concerns by all means. In this game, of course, Monsieur Bayard was stronger because his family had been there for a long time.

But Antoine knew how to navigate the meanders of the great deltas, and in any case, he liked to point out that he had the ability to let the other person speak, to listen patiently and never close a door. He learned that opportunities existed to become a free tenant of the big landowners. However, he kept in mind his desire to buy land and thus enjoy full and total property rights like those of the allodial lands which had from time immemorial dotted the *Cévennes*. In the absence of the tenurial rights of the feudal lord, they were subject only to the tax due to the king. Such was his goal.

Antoine returned to the center of the city. He walked up and down the harbor looking for a passage to Staten Island. This new project corresponded more to his expectations, and his involvement within a community that wanted to build the city of God responded to the values and aspirations most dear to him. This had been his desire since he had left Saint-Roman.

The discussions that animated the city were new to Antoine. He had never been faced with the option to choose one side or the other in the kingdom of France. The king was not opposed by anyone and even if one did not agree with him, as was the case with the entire Reformed community, his legitimacy was never questioned. In New York, things were different. The separation of the city into two camps could not help but affect his own goals. Antoine preferred, at least for the moment, to live in a remote region obeying the rules of coexistence, instead of exhausting himself in fights that had arisen at a time when he was still a stranger in the city. Though the temptations were great here, for Antoine the priority was to stay true to his commitments and not succumb to the opportunities that presented themselves every day. In New York, the ease of meeting people appealed to him, but he still didn't have the tools to have control over them. Antoine believed that it was easier to get lost here than anywhere else. And he didn't want to stay in this town forever.

Since everyone needed everyone else, more and more connections were woven, like in a spider's web where one can hang in the middle of the silk threads waiting to catch a fly !

56

Antoine left New York the next day for Staten Island. The distance was not great, but the capricious winds forced the boat to change directions many times, which made the journey long and uncomfortable. Antoine was happy to be back on dry land when he reached the island. Seagulls invaded the place that seemed sparsely inhabited and exuded an uninviting coldness. The ground was soft, almost spongy. The whole gave the impression of being miles from the sea, since the graciousness of New York seemed so far away. The island looked like a large, cold, flat pebble thrown there by the great Canadian glacier. The dwellings weren't spruce like the Dutch houses in the little New York harbor. Everything was marked by a suspicious tranquility, linked to a lack of activity, a desire to do nothing, not as it is customary during Sunday rest but simply due to lack of initiative.

It should be noted that a large part of the island had been granted to Thomas Dongan, an Irish Catholic appointed Governor of the Province in 1682 by James Stuart, the future James II, when it was bankrupt and in an insurrectionary state. Dongan had the king's full confidence. He participated in the establishment of the Charter of Freedoms and Privileges of the Province of New York, which later largely inspired the US Constitution. This fundamental law organized the administration and established the local authorities, the council and the assembly. It set up a political body on par with the British Parliament, from which it was completely independent. The provinces alone had the privilege of raising taxes and organizing elections.

Freedom of worship for Christians was introduced in the province. Dongan took the opportunity to express his militant Catholicism on a par with Quakers and other Anabaptists. He just forgot that since Catholics were a minority, his action ran the risk of being seen as a provocation by the majority. It was a lost cause for Dongan, who was replaced by Edmund Andros at the time of the creation of the Dominion of New York and New England and the dissolution of the New York Assembly in 1687 by William, the new king. However, he assigned most of the lands to a minority, without forgetting himself in the process, just as he did not forget to grant New York communal franchises and consular freedoms that, unfortunately, never got the royal seal. Later, when allowed once again to reside in the province, he refused to perform other duties and retired to his lands on Staten Island : 25 000 acres known today as Dongan Hills. The legislative work carried out by this lonely man, gazing at the horizon towards Sandy Hook behind the windows of Castleton manor house, would serve as the basis for all the political games that would animate the province until the American Revolution.

Antoine was anxious to get to the southeast of the island where he hoped he would meet Poncet Stelle. The captain of the boat that had brought him there, who knew him, had told him that he was not in New York at that time. Access to Monsieur Stelle's house was via a small wooden bridge that crossed a stream. Antoine hurried across it without heeding the dogs coming to meet him. His demeanor took them by surprise and their barks soon turned into unpleasant growls that their owner quickly silenced. The house was modest and well cared for. It looked more like a hunter's cabin than a farm. The austere-looking owner gave a kind greeting to Antoine who walked resolutely towards him. Stelle must have been a few years older than Antoine. The two men stopped a meter apart, looking directly into each other's eyes. About fifty meters behind them, a young woman was standing on the steps.

"We were not expecting you so soon", said the owner of the place.

Antoine, surprised, took a few seconds to react.

"I'm sorry Sir, but to tell the truth I didn't announce myself !"

"But are you not..."

"Excuse me, . . . Antoine Pintard, I wanted to meet you !"

"Oh, I wasn't expecting you, I'm Poncet Stelle. But come and refresh yourself inside". Antoine and his host walked to the steps where the young woman was waiting for them.

"My sister Catherine", explained Poncet.

"Ma'am, I'm Antoine Pintard, I" ...

"Come in and sit down !" Poncet interrupted him.

The interior was rustic but well decorated. The windows were modest for reasons of economy, no doubt, and to ward off the harsh winters.

The furniture was made of boards roughly but solidly fixed together. The dogs sat at the entrance to the main room and were scrutinizing Antoine with policemen's eyes. The extinguished fireplace gave off a sooty odor, the smell of gases emanating from the ashes. Fireplaces are only beautiful in winter, Antoine thought. The dogs had risen to their feet and were now licking his hands.

"Go out ! Dogs out !" Catherine exclaimed.

The surprised dogs returned to the door, where they turned back, barking at Antoine.

"Stop that !" cried Catherine who, matching her words, pointed sternly to the outside.

The dogs crossed the threshold, agile but disorderly, ending the episode by cheerfully biting each other on the neck. One of them let out a high-pitched bark followed by a long, painful moan. He must have been hurt. Silence returned. All three were smiling.

"Here ! Drink !" Antoine held out his hand in the direction of the glass that Poncet offered him.

"What can I do you for ?" Poncet asked.

Antoine launched into a fairly comprehensive presentation, retracing his journey from the *Cévennes*. The two men already appreciated each other for obvious reasons.

"Antoine, Monsieur Delanoy has given you a lot of information. I have to go to Shrewsbury in the next few days. Meanwhile, we welcome you under our roof, my sister and I. I hope you accept our hospitality."

"It would be my pleasure but . . ."

Poncet's brow furrowed in question.

". . . I don't know if the dogs will agree", he added with a smile.

The three of them laughed, but this did not bring back the dogs that were now frolicking, reassured about the fate of their masters.

Antoine spent two days with the Stelles, making sure not to be a burden. The dogs now followed him everywhere.

Catherine had a beautiful smile that she freely displayed to her guest, who was not exactly indifferent to it. Poncet seemed pleased with Antoine's presence and didn't ask any questions about the person he was waiting for the day he arrived. Antoine said nothing about it, no doubt very happy to be at the heart of the Stelle family's concerns.

"We're leaving tomorrow", Poncet told him during the breakfast they shared. Antoine nodded, satisfied. Catherine gave him a furtive glance, which Antoine caught immediately. Catherine, surprised, lowered her gaze.

The day was spent in preparations for the trip. Catherine would not travel, but she participated willingly in the preparations. The dogs trotted from one to the other side, sensing that something was happening. Sometimes they would calm down and come and sit next to Poncet, backs straight, noses up, clearly visible so he wouldn't forget them.

They left early the next day for the small cove located half a league from the house. Antoine dared to wave his hand toward Catherine, who was watching them leave. The dogs frolicked around the two men, happy to enjoy the outing.

The crossing was short. The two men found another world upon arrival, one covered by a deep, dark forest, silent and austere. Excited by the multiple smells emanating from the undergrowth, the dogs ran in all directions. They took refuge against the legs of the walkers at the slightest suspicious creak brought by the wind.

The men were proceeding at a brisk pace, wanting to reach the community as soon as possible. Large ferns littered the edges of ancient Indian trails that were still used as paths of discovery. They meandered through the trees without there necessarily being a connection between the curves that they formed and the current landscape ; perhaps these incomprehensible traces were the outlines of a former glacial landscape, now extinct.

Antoine did not feel alone in the forest. Apart from the presence of God clearly visible in everything, he felt as if innumerable and unknown eyes cast their ancient looks on him through the tangle of trees as did at dusk the standing stones of the *Cévennes*. Here, the gloom of the undergrowth added a mystery to the forest that confused the traveler in broad daylight. But Poncet knew where he was going ; Antoine trusted him and, to a lesser extent, the dogs. The two men walked silently along paths and through the bushes. Poncet seemed to go astray from time to time, but quickly found his way once again, leading Antoine behind him. The dogs sniffed the ground with new confidence in their master who had momentarily plunged them into almost human doubt. Men and animals shared the same uncertainties, both drawing on their primordial instincts.

"Here we are", Poncet suddenly exclaimed as he came out of the forest.

They had walked for several hours. The dogs and Antoine regained their confidence like travelers lost in the night when they finally see the sunrise. The great trees became scarce. A vast plain lay before their eyes, filled with the promises of a society of opulence that one could only guess at through the meandering river that flowed below, where some huts with smoking and welcoming chimneys were already clustered.

"Is it here ?" asked Antoine.

"Yes", answered Poncet who, attentive to the intonation of Antoine's voice, thought he detected some disappointment.

"Yes, here we are", said Poncet again.

Antoine breathed out for a moment, looking at the landscape.

"It all seems very pleasant", added Antoine.

"Yes, it is indeed very pleasant", continued Poncet, happy to hear an expression of enthusiasm in Antoine's words that the crossing of the immense forest had hidden at first. "I'm glad you like it. Let's move on then !"

The dogs were starting to push each other again and nibble on each other's ears to express their satisfaction.

The welcome was warm, the first settlers were always eager for encounters, especially with new faces, full of hope and expectation. The introductions took place in a formal manner, each aware that the presumed arrival of a new member to the community could not be reduced to a simple, even fraternal greeting. And yet a brotherhood existed throughout the little community that was establishing itself so far away from New York City. Antoine already detected a hierarchy that had undoubtedly influenced the early achievements of the group. These small colonies always responded to an objective of welfare, to a desire to do good and think better. Suffice it to say that, as always, fraternity could only lead to the exclusion of some members, who did not share the same aspirations or the same struggles.

Antoine had a good feeling during the following days, from the questions and comments that came from all sides. Here, there were no doubts, because the objectives had to be met and obedience to the rules was the main condition that everyone had to submit to. Fraternity imposes discipline, self-abnegation, which is the opposite of freedom.

The members had to identify totally with the initial designs of the community. Positive values, of course, could only lead to everyone's moral improvement. Entering or staying within this community was a personal choice. A world of fraternity is a closed world where everything has been thought out beforehand. It is based on respect for rules and the hierarchy. Feudalism developed its roots in this way. These communities had the same aspirations.

All of this did not surprise Antoine. In part, it all resembled the civil society he had left behind in the *Cévennes*. Therefore, nothing could displease him. He preferred to submit to the community rather than to the Lord of the manor ; that was all.

His individualism was limited to his desire to own land.

Men have not taken millennia to break free. They gained in liberty each time an obligation to another no longer had a justification for existing, even if that meant challenging this obligation by force.

Freedom made them apprehensive, as did the vastness and mystery of America that Antoine had just passed through. Men of the seventeenth century needed protection in the absence of health care services or life insurance. The fraternal communities took their place. They would not have understood, even if they knew them, those French devils who already roamed the continent, trappers and libertarians who were not afraid of dying of cold or hunger or of being slaughtered by malicious hands coming out from behind the trees.

Antoine was happy to be here, and that was evident.

He traveled through the region the following days, orienting himself. He breathed, he ran, he gasped like the dogs that never left him now.

According to Poncet, transactions concerning the property rights of the newcomers had been settled. The long-standing confusing legal situation, as Delanoy had pointed out to Antoine, had been finally resolved. So far from New York, Shrewsbury had been the subject of a notorious entanglement, linked to the Duke of York's separation of the provinces of New Jersey and New York. He had given these lands to Sir George Carteret, who in turn had given them to pioneers who were very happy to settle even under a feudal concession. Meanwhile, the first governor of the province, Richard Nicolls, misinformed, had distributed the same lands to others. They were now in the hands of two owners : a free holder and a tenant of the Duke of York who was the direct owner of the land.

All this had been one of the first mistakes of the administration of the province. Poncet wanted to be reassuring about the impact of this mistake. Everything, it seemed, according to him, had returned to normal.

Antoine trusted Poncet's words and submitted his candidature, so to speak, in the event that lands became vacant in the next few months. He was assured that every effort would be made to accommodate him and that, until land was made available, he was welcome to help the community in their daily works. Thus, Antoine lived in the middle of the community, useful and available, learning English and a little Dutch.

Poncet left several times to visit his sister and resolve community issues that required his intervention. He returned on one of his visits accompanied by Catherine. He came more laden than usual and rode a mule. Antoine understood that Catherine was going to settle permanently in Shrewsbury and secretly rejoiced. Confirmation was not long in coming ; the little colony gained a soul that had the features of Catherine Stelle.

The dogs barked, happy to see their owner again. They quickly gathered close to Antoine, lifting their noses at him after circling Catherine and sniffing her calves. Catherine laughed.

"They've switched sides", Antoine dared to remark.

"I'm afraid so", Catherine joked.

"They'll get used to you again", Antoine continued.

"I'm not so sure, Catherine insisted.

"In time, Catherine !"

"In time, Antoine."

Winter passed dark and cold in anticipation of spring. From time to time, the community was visited by Piscataway families who were destitute but friendly. Under demographic pressure, Shrewsbury was carefully managed by its settlers. Sometimes they provided hospitality to needy natives who collected the crumbs falling from the table, of this development pole here in the great American desert.

57

"Good day Antoine !
"Good day Catherine !"
"Where are you going in such a hurry ?"
"To work", answered Antoine, smiling.
"So late ! Oh, excuse me !" Catherine corrected herself immediately.
"You're right, it's late but I've already done part of my day, in fact I was going back to my work."
"Excuse me again, that's none of my business, I don't know what happened to me."
"Maybe you just want to talk."

Catherine did not respond. She looked down. Antoine held her gaze, not trying to escape the reflection of Catherine's green eyes as she raised her head. Sensing her confusion, he came to her aid.

"It would be nice to take a walk, don't you think ?"
"But I can't go out for a walk, I have to visit a lady who is ill."
"Till, the weather is fine and it would be nice to take a walk, but don't tell anyone."

Catherine looked down again. Antoine kept talking. Catherine was embarrassed. Antoine realized this and apologized for keeping her for so long.

They parted, happy to have met.

The river's usually peaceful waters were in motion that day, with a movement which seemed to come from the bottom of its bed, giving rhythm to the slow, steady flow that churned the surface and to the cadence of sounds escaping from it.

They both continued on their way without daring to look at each other. Suddenly, Antoine risked doing so. Catherine had already turned around and was looking at him with a tender smile.

She had not yet reached thirty years of age and moved with grace and dignity.

Antoine was new to the community and he was penniless, so could not display the results of his previous experiences. Anyway, he hadn't accomplished anything yet and he was thirty-three. He said goodbye to her with a wave of his hand, which Catherine did not forget, tracing in the vibrant afternoon air a sign of union that would bring them closer and closer.

Antoine married Catherine Stelle du Laurier on May 4, 1692.

58

From this date, events will accelerate. Antoine has no intention of wasting any time. He has built everything with common sense, trusting as little as possible in Providence, knowing that if too much is asked of it, it will end up abandoning you one day. He still has no land, so he will have to start in business soon. New York, having regained its monopoly of entry and exit of goods to the colony that had been contested by Leisler, will become a city dedicated to commerce. Antoine will use all the means at his disposal to transport goods produced in Shrewsbury to the small port. Surpluses will often go to the Antilles, which do not produce much more than sugar, and where the increasingly numerous labor force on the islands needs to be fed. Antoine knows the market, so to speak, so he dedicates himself fully to it and begins to establish himself. New York is not that far after all, Delanoy had been right. He will develop contacts and become a partner in the operation of a ship, like most merchants in the province. He thus will set up an address book and will maintain relationships with many intermediaries, inserting himself perfectly among all nationalities. In short, a cosmopolitan whose Shrewsbury residence serves as insurance for those who deal with him. They realize that he is not an adventurer. His moral and religious foundation is solid, and his membership of the French Reformed community is a good passport into nascent New York.

A penny saved is a penny earned, Antoine is worthy and prospers. He wanted a family ; Catherine will give him nine children. His own name and those of his brothers and sisters will all be borne by his descendants, including Florinda, the name of his sister who died in infancy. He wanted land : he will acquire parcels one after another.

In a first transaction, on November 23, 1693, with Sarah Reape, a widow, and her son William, he purchases 10 acres for 8 pounds, in a place with the unpronounceable name of Norawaticonck ; definitely a good investment since he will buy more land from a man named Nicholas Brown in 1695. Antoine moves quickly. There was never any question in his life of his being defeated by adversity. He has found in the province of New York the means to refute destiny and his own fate.

Nothing is final, he thinks one day, a little stunned by his success. He is aggressive in his affairs, his transactions, and perhaps his greed. He is just a man. He will always find, thanks to his religious principles, the means not to get lost. He knows that what he has he also owes in part to others, to their slowness or their indecision. He thus fights for them. The money he earns is not taken from his neighbors who do not value the fruit of their land ; rather, he helps them by placing his time and skills at their service. He will become a member of the consistory.

Antoine learns about laws. The English, when they took over the colony, imposed their custom in law, relegating the essentially Romanist Dutch law to oblivion. The latter are displeased because the treatment reserved for wives and especially widows mark a regression compared to what is prevalent in countries with a written Law. Antoine applies this law with resignation ; it is not what he would have wished, as it is not his custom, but he will go along with it. Several centuries of jurisprudence cannot be dismissed. He will become Justice of the Peace[75] with all due honors, as is the custom in England for judges in all jurisdictions. Perhaps by staying close to the litigants, they have allowed themselves to stay away from the politicians. Therefore, they have preserved their independence and the recognition of the majority of the people. Antoine understands this and does everything possible to keep it this way.

For that it is also necessary to give his time. He gives it for the good of the community in accordance with his legal and financial abilities. He will become a member of the County Court in 1700. He is then 42 years old. For that, he also has to share the knowledge that allowed him to reach the place he occupies today.

---

(75) JPs exercised both judicial and administrative powers in colonial counties. JPs were the most important public offices in colonial America. Colonial justices had wide civil jurisdiction and sat as a court of records in criminal cases. The office was reserved for planters of means and standing. George Washington himself was a justice of the peace and so were his father and grandfather. Thomas Jefferson and his father served also as justices of the peace.

It is with that in mind that he enters the home of William Bradford, a printer and bookseller on Dock Street in New York, in the spring of 1696. The man is barely thirty years old. He is originally from Philadelphia, where he had started a printing shop. The English wanted to develop this activity to contribute to the Anglicization of the city. This is again a move to take control. The objective is to publish books on good conduct as in Europe. Since few can read, they are principally intended for the elite whose libertine behavior, especially in New York, is no longer in line with the moral principles that the English monarchy wishes to see flourish in its realm.

Antoine is recovering from a painful illness. It is perhaps the fever or another tropical infection, originally brought in by ships, that has plagued the province for a long time. They may put in place quarantines, but trade does not allow total shutdown. New York is a city open to the world with all the advantages but also the shortcomings of taking part in an overseas activity. These are the counterparts of the economic boom that the city experiences with its exotic connections. While this is not a question of quarantining sedentary residents, many are also leaning toward establishing a moral hygiene control in a city that is devoid of it. Governor Fletcher is one of those who are in favor of this, regretting, since his assumption of office in 1692, the moral decadence of the inhabitants, the free fornication prevalent among all classes of the population and the reluctance of his fellow citizens to marry until their tired and overweight bodies demand the care of a wife with the qualities of a nurse. Antoine wants to contribute to moral recovery in his own way.

In June 1696, the work that he had contracted with the Bradford press is completed.

"I have written a few words as a preamble", the printer announces, "which I hope you will like, in any case they clarify our relationship, in accordance with your requests."

"Can I read them ?" asked Antoine.

"Please do, the book is yours".

"Not really," Antoine replies, "although reading it has shaped my life, in part."

Antoine takes the new copy that Bradford hands him and he feels like an author discovering his work in print for the first time.

"You didn't write it, but it's yours."

"I did not expect to react in this way", adds Antoine.

"This shows that man is a strange little animal !"

"You are right," Antoine concludes for the moment.

He carefully reads Bradford's dedication in which he expresses the difficulties he has encountered transcribing and formatting a 150-year-old copy, when he only has an imperfect command of the French language, and the significant efforts he has made to adapt it to contemporary tases and to local customs. All this is marked by sincere gratitude and an understanding of the reasons that have led Antoine to want to reissue a modern version of the book that had always accompanied him throughout his long journey. Antoine feels the message deeply and says so to the printer.

"Thank you, Monsieur Pintard, thank you !"

"You did very good work" ! Antoine adds. The two men parts ways, promising to meet again regularly. Antoine Pintard has just published one of the first books printed in New York and surely the first book printed in French, perhaps the only one in that city.

Antoine is happy. He now belongs a little more to this city. He walks the streets of New York for a long time, stopping sometimes to appreciate the pleasure of being there, alive, in a city he loved, clutching closely his old and new versions of the Treasure of Consolations, not daring to look at them and reserving this pleasure for himself when he would be alone, sitting in the inn or elsewhere, under a roof. He can feel the two copies in his hands, one rough and brittle, the other smooth and new. He is in no rush to go through them. Their mere presence at the bottom of his pockets links him to his past as well as to the present. His hands, hidden from view, encircle the Ancient Treasure and the Modern Treasure in an affectionate embrace. Antoine is not alone that day, his family is out on the streets of New York. Yet something is lacking in his happiness. Antoine takes out the old copy and sniffs its pages smoked by more than a century of chestnut wood fire, the one that his mother lit at the end of the afternoon and that was watched over by his father just before bedtime. He stands there, motionless for a moment ; the poker rings against the ash-covered stone. Golden embers crackle in the stove. Antoine looks at the open book. The pages are all the same blackish color, the color of the passage of time, death and oblivion. He buries the old manuscript with his left hand in his pocket deep as a grave and resumes his way down Dock Street. He walks briskly forward, his right arm swinging as it should, holding at his fingertips *The Treasure of Human and Divine*

Consolations or a Treatise in which the Christian can Learn to Overcome the Afflictions of this Life.

At the bottom of the cover, it reads "In New York, at the house of William Bradford under the banner of the Bible 1696".

An issue of this book still exists at the Lewis and Clark Law School in Portland, Oregon, or at the New York Historical Society, on line or at many academic libraries in the US.

59

The city took a little more pride every day in its achievements, in its beautiful facades that emerged from the ground, in its now numerous churches, its warehouses and its docks. The exercise of Catholic worship was prohibited. The Jews did the best they could. England had supplanted Holland. There were the French Protestants, united but integrated. Though they had created a community in New Rochelle, which they led, though they participated in Shrewsbury, and elsewhere in Connecticut, in the creation and development of religious communities, they never did so in a spirit of withdrawal among themselves, as if they were alone against everyone else.

From the beginning, these people had the intelligence to realize that their future lay there, at the mouth of the Hudson, in Protestant lands, as was Governor Fletcher's goal. Of course, there was no question of making alliances with Quebec in la Nouvelle France, with a king who no longer wanted to know anything about them, but they could have been tempted to create a singular entity, which they did not, either, very likely for lack of means, but above all because the idea never occurred to them. Their membership of the Reformed community surpassed all other divisions, all aspirations that could have originated in the old continent but did not exist here.

That made them New Yorkers.

The Dutch, merchants and sailors, contributed to the uniqueness of the city through their liberalism, always preferring mediation to trial, highlighting their openness to the world, as a fundamental necessity when a great people came from such a small territory. The English imported their lords with their arrogance, enlightened by their judicial system and their ability to make it evolve to new heights. They introduced parliamentary debate whose confrontations in the metropolis had not remained without echo in the province through the pro and anti-Leislers. The Protestants from France carried their morality, more intellectualized than militant, and their blue blood, to the point of giving the city an aristocratic, cultured and elegant air, which made it so *chic* and attractive to most of the peoples of the old continent. New York is still today the last European city before entering America.

Antoine, that day, crosses New York and goes to the King's Arms coffee house. This is where New York's business elite meet, regardless of their activity. The butcher who has become an entrepreneur meets the sailor who has become a shipowner. They all seek success and autonomy from the old orders that constitute European society, thereby already beginning to configure the traits of individualism. The only thing they have in common is their interest in the development of the city, in which they participate claiming their personal enrichment as the necessary counterpart for their investment. "What is good for me is good for the city as a whole" is their creed. The city is run by entrepreneurs who, joining forces, compete in originality, creativity and ambition. Although the will to succeed drives them all, they favor all kinds of business associations. As in Amsterdam, Venice, Genoa or in other cities in the Mediterranean basin,[76] they fill out their orders and accounting books, which they close at the end of each trip or business and await with eager pleasure the fruits of their transactions. The appetites are great and the wooden spoons, sometimes too large, denote greed and induce some to fall into temptations. Therefore, it is necessary to convene the New York business protagonists to friendly meetings where the interested parties get to know each other and learn to respect each other.

Established in 1696, the King's Arms is one of those places. Antoine quickly makes it his quarters when he's in New York. It is a place of meeting and trade, a place of free speech where people discover in themselves the powers of dialogue and commitment : the beginnings of politics. These men are aware that they can create mercantile emulation, just as they realize that they could also thus stimulate other activities, even unwanted ones. In short, they are all aware that each freedom acquired in communication has its corollary of drawbacks. But with the collective advantages outweighing the disadvantages, the

---

(76) The world oldest Chamber of Commerce was founded in Marseilles in 1599. The translation of its name Chambre de Commerce has been used worldwide since.

New York authorities support and promote this approach, as is already the case in England.

Antoine is now well known in the small port. The reprint of the *Treasury of Consolations* has simply added an additional line to his resumé. When he enters the King's Arms, his group of friends are already there and greet him warmly as they should. Nicholas Bayard is there too, whose eulogy to *Fletcher Freeing New York from Jacob Leisler* was the first book to come off the Bradford press. Author's solidarity or not, in any case, the two men meet and greet each other.

Antoine's attraction to New York is total. He often goes there for business and also for political reasons.

In fact, in 1701 Antoine became a member of the Council of the Eastern Province of New Jersey when an agreement resolved, at least in part, the longstanding dispute over land ownership and jurisdictional control. As for his property, Antoine is a beneficiary : Poncet Stelle, through ignorance, had anticipated the resolution of the conflict. So much the better, thinks Antoine, for had he been correctly informed, he might not have acquired the lands.

The King of England convinced that the development of vast territories can only be achieved through the private initiative of many settlers, resolves the dispute. Justice will return to the Crown while the small owners will be definitively confirmed in their rights. The great feudal lords have lost much with the final ruling.

New Jersey, which was subordinate to Sir Berkeley and Sir Carteret, who had ratified in 1676 the division of the province into two blocks, the East and the West, in 1702 becomes a single royal province reunified by Queen Anne, at the request of their owners. Some of them had bet a lot of money on land speculation in the Jerseys. Antoine was probably also involved in those transactions. In fact, the possibility of a seat in the Provincial Council, created that same year, is reserved to owners of a thousand acres, or about 400 hectares. Most likely, the rule was already in effect in Eastern New Jersey in 1701, so Antoine was already in control of a beautiful and extensive domain.

However large these plots may appear, these areas must be compared to the area of Eastern New Jersey that had been given to Carteret, which was equivalent to more than eight percent of the total area of England !

Antoine must also take the pulse of what is happening in the province of New York. It ranks higher than the province of New Jersey in the relationship they all have with the metropolis. In fact, New Jersey will not have its own Governor until 1738 and must be satisfied to be under the Governorship of New York - the result of the Duke of York's enfeoffment.

Antoine, in turn, has become Anglicized and his attendance at the King's Arms cafe is a good proof of this. This is to be compared with the absence of Berkeley and Carteret in New Jersey, where people now want their total eviction, under the new land grants by Governor Nicolls. Suffice it to say that with this dispute resolved, the inhabitants now want everything immediately. The protest will hamper the province's economic progress for a long time, to the point of causing frequent disturbances and, at times, a situation of almost anarchy, with the desire of some to fully recover properties that others now own. Two worlds collide, the new and the old, but on thousands of acres, on an American scale. As no one sees beyond his own interests, efficiency inclines some towards modernity while others take refuge in tradition. In any case, a nail has been driven into the feudal system. It seems that the vigor with which it was planted there, gives rise to ideas that are debated by the regulars at the King's Arms.

In less than ten years, Antoine has become one of the richest men in East Jersey, as the provincial council comments at the time of his appointment. It is in the King's Arms that politicians meet, agree, or air their disagreements. As a wealthy businessman, but also as a politician, Antoine is a stakeholder at these meetings. Colonial America often brought the two together, shaping the contours of a tradition that still lives on today. Antoine feels comfortable in a debate that seals the challenge to the established order. In any case, his duties as a Monmouth County Judge, a position which he will hold until 1704, keep him away from the violence of the protesters against feudal rule in the province.

He flourishes. His life is spent in discussions, in legal proceedings, in commercial transactions that give him a different goal every day that passes : the satisfaction of a good deal and a job well done. A new man is being born, made of personal enrichment but also eager to consolidate his success through service to an organized community.

However, while passing through New York, Antoine witnesses clashes in which Leisler, perhaps unjustly, still serves as a demarcation line. Fletcher, the previous Governor of New York, wonders what has prompted the British Army to bring in this educated and controversial mercenary from Frankfurt. In love with order and wishing to inculcate the English way of thinking in his community, Fletcher finds nothing better than to impose the Protestant tithe on all residents, in order to provide for the livelihood of Anglican pastors, in fact of the only Anglican pastor, that of the military garrison. This means that the majority of the inhabitants are restricted in the exercise of their worship, like the Catholics have been for some time now, with priests being asked to leave the city definitively, and huge fines being imposed on those who hide them. In fact, European conflicts have been brought to New York, whether they concern papists according to an old tradition or dissidents of the Anglican Church, which is not surprising in itself ; the states have reached a development threshold that requires the establishment of new organizations. The importance of religion cannot be underestimated in the new constructions.

The Catholic king or his Protestant counterpart have the same constraints and therefore have implemented the same solutions. Centralization erases differences : all must merge into the same community to fulfill the objective set by the monarch in the interests of the majority. Antoine is happy in New Jersey, where the Anglican monopoly has not yet questioned the exercise of his Reformed faith and where dissenters and especially Quakers are thriving.

In New York, the Reformed Dutch are struggling and do not want to pay the price for the English decree. So, they negotiate with the Governor, imposing the weight of their community, and escape the Anglican tithe. Fletcher finds allies for his project. They are quick to ratify it to the detriment of others, inventing lobbying in the process. New York advances. Anglicanism has almost become the state religion and Fletcher is an absolutist governor, but without troops to crush his opponents. Suffice it to say that the man in the street does not care, preferring to have fun on Sundays or every day of the week rather than adhere to collective goals. The result is disastrous for Fletcher. Irreligion advances as well as individualism and materialism. New York becomes tolerant or indifferent, weaving in the process a liberal net whose meshes are large. Everyone, in turn, can pass his grasping hand through the net and help himself easily in the surrounding land of plenty and, why not, reach out across the whole world.

Governor Fletcher, steadfast in his powerless absolutism, continues to seek allies. He continues to promote an Anglo-Dutch bourgeoisie, no doubt taking advantage of the absence of other New Yorkers too busy having fun. He organizes the province of New York and distributes huge estates in feudal tenure, other smaller estates in full ownership, creating thus a group of people beholden to him, always the source of misappropriation and corruption.

The great merchants, the great families help themselves generously to all these advantages. Fletcher needs them as they need him. Each one getting others in a corner, together they will build a society unlike anything known. New York is not a monarchy ; it is a province far removed from the King of England whose bond with the metropolis is as fragile as the corroded feudal bond. It is not surrounded by enemies, apart from the French who have settled in the far north, and the economic opportunities are great. The best option is to get into action, and the sooner the better. All means are acceptable. Once the lands are distributed and the oaths of allegiance have been taken by the American lords present in their dominions, unlike in the previous enfeoffments, a hierarchy will be established. All these fine people have to do is help themselves. For this, it is necessary to accelerate things, to jettison the protocol and the etiquette that still reeks of the old and narrow-minded Europe. Here, there is no court that paralyzes the most enterprising. The newcomers will easily ally themselves with their well-to-do neighbors to jointly promote their selfish designs. A single objective drives them, and that is to make money without worrying about what other people say, sporting titles that remind of the old world without worrying about the duties that come with them : besides, nobody ever asked them for anything. There is only profit in the transactions of which they are part. It is just a question of having strong allies, without paying too much attention to the quality of the ones chosen or their long-term loyalty. The mere fact of being an outspoken and powerful anti-Leislerian achieves political recognition.

Under these conditions, you don't need to promise much. One authorization and they will gladly take care of the rest. The Augsburg League war is not over between the King of England and Louis XIV. Fletcher takes the opportunity to license pirates that call in at New York harbor, for a fee of course. This adds an additional service activity to the small, specialized port. Therefore, the black skull and crossbones flags are temporarily stored in the wheelhouses of ships that come to refuel at the southern Manhattan docks, a stone's throw away from the longhouse where Peter Stuyvesant once worked. The Bayards, Nicolls, Van Cortlands, Schuylers and others buy shares in these private companies, thus supplementing their landed wealth marked by royal stamps, obtained through favor, with cash acquired by letters of marque[77] which only wants to be reinvested.

New York is getting rich while doing harm to others. However, the sums raised are insufficient to the point that the owners of these unique vessels sometimes turn a blind eye when pirate captains also attack British or American ships. It is necessary to live well. Besides, the rascals who land on the docks have their own needs. The city benefits from all the economic gains that this lucrative traffic inevitably brings and no matter if the streets are less safe than before or if prostitutes have invaded the alleys at night. Here again, what is good for a few is good for the many, especially since the merchants who have been retrained in piracy have settled in Manhattan. They don't transfer their earnings to exotic tax havens.

New York already has all these facilities. So, they build, they beautify, and they develop. All are witnesses to a boom that has come so far from the coast, that it drowns out the cries of fear of the crews burned after having their throats cut. Only the result counts, is the prevailing thought along the docks. New York grows for a time at a double-digit rate that delights all involved.

But good things are coming to an end, and events in London continue to influence Fletcher's career. The Tories have eventually annoyed the king. Things are not going as well as he would like and the war against the King of France has depleted the royal coffers. It is time to put the house in order in England, while the King of France is given new rights in 1697. He will recover Alsace and Saint Domingue thanks to the Treaty of Ryswick. William calls back the Whigs who legislate and limit the ultra-liberalism of the Tories represented in New York by Nicholas Bayard and his gang, who had outsourced to the New York pirates what they could not achieve directly in full view of the world. Fletcher is accused of corruption and returns to England with a heart less heavy than his wallet. The Leislerians are called upon to take over. Peter Delanoy, the Huguenot, is now mayor of New York again. Antoine is undoubtedly satisfied, the pirates much less so, since they must pay the price of the new legislation.

Captain Kidd of New York, a repentant and later recidivist pirate of the high seas, who undoubtedly participated in the eviction of the

---

(77) Letters of marque were issued by the king to authorize buccaneers to attack and loot the ships of foreign enemies.

French from Saint-Christophe, is hanged in London in May 1701. His corpse, smeared with tar, will be locked in a cage on the Thames for days, so that all can be informed of the new ban on piracy, even if they cannot read.

Leisler received a dignified burial in New York Cemetery.

The wheel of fortune had turned.

60

The Anglo-Dutch oligarchy of Stuyvesant and the Duke of York is now defeated, at least for the moment. Powerful for a time, it has finally bowed to the demands of the people of New York and to royal desires. Queen Anne wants to turn the page. The Leislerians are back. The Queen regains control of New York oligarchs who, too used to Fletcher's generosity, might one day stand up to her and do not respect the feudal obligations. The land distributions undertaken by the former governor are stopped, freeing up virgin spaces and fostering the thirst for territory. New York now discovers fluidity and transforms land into a commodity. And as demand exceeds supply, naturally prices go up.

New Yorkers living on the borders of America still don't actually manufacture anything. Agricultural products are their only production. In the absence of religious convictions, they have become merchants at heart.

That is why they welcome the end of the distribution of thousands of acres with much satisfaction. Redistributing the land makes it possible to re-shuffle the cards because it is the land that makes a man. Opportunities must be seized by the most visionary, the most enterprising, the luckiest or the cleverest. There is now a shift from an aristocracy with little commitment to the duties of its order, to a bourgeoisie not willing to be fooled.

Thus, the early monopolization by a limited number of American aristocrats has been followed by speculation by the majority. It could be said that this was the price to pay and that Queen Anne's economic experts did not see it coming.

Some New Yorkers were not wrong, because they were closer to the market than to God or the London castles. They incorporated other parameters into their simulation. Of course, each hiding their financial equation from the other, there were winners and losers as it should be. As the art of speculation is nothing more than a representation of the future, it must be admitted that talents in this area, as in others, are unevenly distributed. New York was the demonstration. Among all the new entrants to the market with more or less the same distant origins and the same means, some succeeded while others lost, giving value to competence as the sole criterion of differentiation between individuals.

Antoine consolidated his assets. How ? Nobody knows exactly. Perhaps he took advantage of the land sales made by the municipality to finance his municipal investments. The fact remains that his will, dated February 24, 1729, mentions a piece of land, located in New York City near the New Dutch Church, that he bequeaths to his daughters Marguerite, Florinda, and Françoise, as well as his house in New York where he will end his days.

His eldest son, Antoine Junior, has already received a considerable share. This could correspond, in terms of real estate, to the New Rochelle property in which Antoine is believed to have invested and where the family lived after their Shrewsbury home caught fire around 1701. His son Samuel probably receives the lands and docks of Shrewsbury since his descendant Glencross Pintard is proprietor in Shrewsbury where he bears the surname Glencross, that of Samuel's wife.

The French Church receives a donation of thirty pounds to pay its pastors. Louis Roux, pastor of the French Church, receives ten pounds directly.

Membership of the French Church is in line with the new division between the mercantile interests of merchants, ocean going ship owners, and the interests of the large landowners who are grouped around the Presbyterian Church. The Anglican Church, whose supremacy is once again desired by the government, still represents only the new governor. Opposition among members of New York's economic elite has replaced the former opposition which was based on whether or not one followed Leisler's ideas. Suffice it to say that the old dispute is now definitely buried.

As the situation evolves in Europe and the war of the succession in Spain reignites the conflicts between the King of France and Queen Anne, tensions between the communities are reactivated. The mercantile group to which Antoine belongs prefers to circulate its goods without the customs barriers that the war in Europe will create once again. The mercantile world prefers peace above all else and wants to continue trading with the French in Canada and especially with the French West Indies. The future is thought to be in the Caribbean, as long as ships can sail freely there. It is very likely that since the accession of Queen Anne to the English throne in 1702 Antoine has worked for the development of Antillean trade at the behest of the De Lancey family,[78] which contributed greatly to the construction of the second French church in New York, built on King Street in 1704.

The circle has been closed. Antoine is a widower when he dictates his will. His wife Catherine has already died. His witnesses are Daniel Bontecou and Peter Quintard. The latter, a renowned jeweler, is the son of Isaac, whom he had met when he landed in New York in 1691.

Daniel Bontecou also belongs to the Protestant French diaspora whose importance and influence in the founding of the city is underlined by the archives of the French church through their names : Pintard, Prévot, Quintard, Tétard, Iselin, Lorillard who introduced the tobacco industry in Manhattan, Le Conte, Vincent, Maynard, De Lancey, De Peyster, Faneuil, Gallaudet, Bayard, Jay, Desbrosses, Carré, Beaudouin, Boudinot and many others. The two witnesses to his will are members of the French Church founded in 1628, proof of the antiquity of the Huguenot presence in the city, when religious services were still held in French in the Dutch Church. Antoine is the patriarch of a large family : his nine children are alive. All of them are married (except for Samuel and Florinda) but not necessarily in the Huguenot community.

Therefore, the integration is now complete. Antoine has made a fortune. He possesses assets both in New Rochelle, the city of the Reformed of France, and in Shrewsbury in East Jersey, which had welcomed him. Finally in New York, the small port which he could not resist but in whose heart he has built his Church, the French Church of New York, better known as the Church of the French Refugees in New York or the Church of the Holy Spirit.

---

(78) Etienne de Lancy (1663-1741), a Huguenot, was born in Caen (France). He obtained an act of denization in 1683 in England from King James II. He emigrated to New York in 1683 and became Stephan De Lancey. He was a major figure in the life of colonial New York as did his family until the American Revolution. His house still stands today 54 Pearl Street in New York City and is known as Fraunces Tavern. It was George Washington's headquarter in New York and the actual owner, *The Sons of the Revolution*, claims it is the oldest surviving building in New York. The De Lancey family stayed loyal to Great Britain during the American Revolution and finally left the colony.

Loyalty to the city will never be abandoned by Antoine's descendants, who will continue to thrive there and participate, in great numbers, in its flourishing future as one of the world's cities to be reckoned with.

When leaving Saint-Roman in 1687 through the upper La Baume valley, between the Col de l'Exil and the Col Saint-Pierre,[79] where today the *Corniche des Cévennes* winds its way, Antoine dreamed of a City of the Eternal. Publisher Bradford shows him the first printed map of New York City in 1731, a few months before he passes away. He did not know, when he disembarked with his suitcases onto the docks of America that spring day in 1691, that he would contribute to the construction of what would one day be New York. Nor could he have known that one of his grandchildren, who would one day bear the strange name of Rip Van Dam, would have a grandfather who would become the Governor of the Province of New York. Antoine had dreamed so much that his dreams had turned into incredible realities, shaping the art of being American.

But without naivety : it is thus that on July 31, 1731, Antoine, seventy-three years old, amends his will with a codicil stating that Rip Van Dam, the father-in-law of his daughter Isabelle, is not yet up to date with the payment of a dowry initially set at a thousand pounds, which should be entered in the accounts on the day of his death. The fact that Rip Van Dam has assumed the governorship of New York on the death of Governor John Montgomery does not alter that. Antoine keeps accounts, and even elderly and disabled, he is in a position to recall their obligation to merchants like Rip Van Dam, whose prosperous businesses can not exempt them from honoring their commitments.

Antoine dies in the spring of 1732.

The funeral procession travels through southern Manhattan to reach the French Church Cemetery.

La Cabanarié is deserted that day just it has been deserted for a long time. Silence reigns all around. There are no more memories as there is no one left to have them.

Jean has left the family farm. He lives, remarried, with Claire Marsial, in the farmhouse of La Fabrègues near Sainte-Croix-Vallée-Française which he received as a dowry from Marguerite de Thonas, his first wife, who died after giving birth to his daughter, Marguerite, also deceased.

---

(79) Robert Louis Stevenson walked this pass and the Vallée-Française the 12th day of his *Travel with a Donkey in the Cévennes* (1879)

Françoise had married on February 12, 1709, Monsieur de Payen, counselor and auditor of the king at the Court of Accounts, Aid and Finance of the city of Montpellier, in the church of Notre-Dame-des-Tables, after twenty years of concubinage so as not to have to appear before a priest ! Her son was present at the ceremony, opening up perspectives for new generations.

Suzanne and Isabeau have passed away. Very likely denounced, they had to flee to Lausanne where we find them on October 9, 1691, according to the records of the French Refugee Company. They ended their days in Hameln, in Lower Saxony, near Hanover where they took refuge. Isabeau Pintard died on October 12, 1693, at the age of twenty-five. Suzanne, in turn, passed away on July 10, 1696. She was about to turn thirty-three. His aunt from Peyrolles, Madeleine Pintard, a refugee in Franconia, died the same year near Nuremberg.

As for Samuel, the assembly records show that he was captured at Moissac on November 5, 1689 and sentenced to serve in the galleys at Marseilles by de Broglie on January 20, 1690. He remained 10 years in forced work. He appears in La Grande, a galley, in 1695 alongside Jean Baptiste Bancilhon, bearing shackle number 11858.

Antoine probably never got news of these events, just as the news of his death never reached his hometown. Baptismal records have not been updated to record the passage of time. The birth of Antoine as it appears in the Moissac record has never been accompanied by the date of his death. However, a life is not concluded without death.

The wind of oblivion enters more easily through this wide-open door.

Antoine had long since disappeared from the memory of the place. This spring day, he unties the ribbon that still binds him to the land of his parents for one last goodbye.

Nobody knows ; no one is aware of this.

The cool April air whistles sadly through the beech trees still covered in their winter coats, as in an eternally motionless procession, feet sunk in the last patches of old snow.

Antoine's coffin sinks gently into the Manhattan soil, marked by the death knell ringing at the Church of the Holy Spirit that echoes down King Street, as the earth accumulates and settles over it forever, in darkness, silence, and oblivion.

The map of New York City printed by William Bradford in 1731.

61

New York is no longer a small port, but a city of eight thousand inhabitants. Many immigrants have invaded the city, more or less well-accepted, more or less respectful of the natives, free or indentured workers, conscious or not of their obligations as immigrants, Scots, Germans, Irish, and others. The great Anglo-Dutch and Huguenot families dominate the city, the fruit of their efforts, their will, and their audacity. Their power is equal to that of the bourgeoisie of the cities of metropolitan Europe. This is America already. The triangular trade is being grafted onto the Antillean trade. New York has grown, shipowners and merchants have become rich, the docks are more crowded with ships than ever, and the taste for beauty has entered the city as if it was a capital.

But the economic crisis is in the making ; it is surely the result of a growing number of operators entering the market for sugar and basic agricultural products. Following their larger competitors, they push for lower prices and lower incomes. New York is an island in a huge English colony (if the Antilles are included), it is like globalization ahead of its time.

The twenty years that have followed Queen Anne's war after the Glorious Revolution have been years of growth. When Antoine falls asleep to dream his last dream, financial difficulties are already beginning to accumulate. He, who should have left this world as a Christian, is obliged during his last moments to impart recommendations to his children about the course they should follow and the mistakes they should avoid.

The crisis is violent and the city will pay the price since it has partly built its fortune on its successes in trade and capital gains. New York is not producing anything yet. It makes a living from international commerce. Therefore, it is subject to the laws of the market. In the event of a crisis linked to overproduction, or a slump in sales, New Yorkers are in the front line and then tempers flare up. Ongoing institutional reforms will do nothing, at least not immediately, to calm things down, especially as slaves, imported in large numbers to adjust the costs to decreasing incomes, compete with less-skilled freemen. Leaders appear, satirists appear, prophets appear and political parties appear, ideas arise, as also do insults and recrimination.

New York is rediscovering its first demons, as the non-renewal in 1695 of the censorship law (which had led to the birth of publisher Bradford) also makes possible the printing of nonsense. Someday it will be necessary to re-organize all that.

Meanwhile, each Christian, as it is written in the *Treasure of Consolations*, keeps in mind the total of his assets that worries him in his last moments. This is a new man who is on his death bed, one of the first *homo economicus* concerned with the salvation of his soul as well as his inheritance. America will produce others, the world too. May they rest in peace.

Antoine's descendants will not be satisfied with the map of New York hidden like a relic in a desk drawer or placed on their nautical chart tables. Their talents will be combined with their father's connections that he did not include in his will, but in the memories he left behind.

John Lewis Pintard, his son, will become alderman of the Wharf ward, that is, councilman for the city of New York, for ten years starting in 1738. He is now about forty-two years old. He still speaks French, but as a second language, English now being the first. He is now a ship owner since he went in partnership with Captain John Searle, to manage a rope walk,[80] and later as owner with him of several vessels. Captain Searle later had married his sister Catherine.

Governor John Montgomery had delivered a new City Charter to the mayor of New York on February 11, 1731, bearing the royal seal that had been sorely lacking in the Stuyvesant and Dongan letters.

New York is finally adorned with the recognition it deserves. Sufficiently endowed with pre-existing public buildings and facilities and with land, particularly on the waterfront and in the wastelands of Manhattan, the Free City at last had the means to realize its dreams

---

(80) A rope walk is a place where rope is made, a rope factory. A long straight narrow covered pathway where long strands of material were twisted into rope. The Searle – Pintard rope walk was located along Broadway.

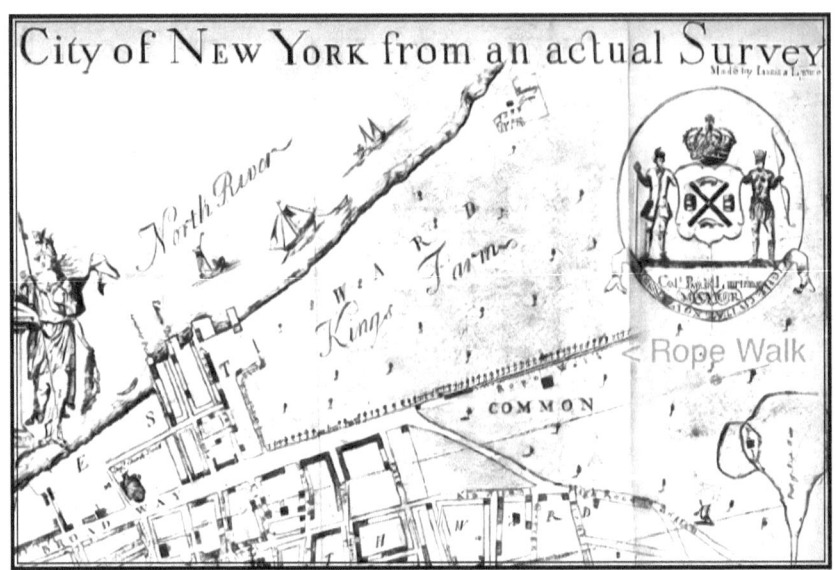

The Searle-Pintard Rope Walk on Broadway near Ground Zero.

and ambitions with all the real prerogatives, personal and legal. The mayor, however, is not elected but is appointed by the governor.

This was not the case for the municipal councilors of the seven districts, who represent free men according to the prevailing feudal terminology, that is, two-thirds of the men of the city. New York had taken a leap, at least on paper, because in reality the voters without assets were not interested in office or in elections, very likely due to lack of education but also due to lack of confidentiality, since the vote was not secret and free men had to openly express their preferences.

All of this has been useful because all advances are good but the crisis of the 1730s has devastated everything. The men no longer speak to each other. They look askance at each other. The difficulties of some are associated with the behavior of others. The edges of the piers at low tide are gray and sharp like oyster shells, sometimes open like the hulls of wrecked ships, empty, swayed by an incessant swell.

New York is doing badly, the city is scared, people say anything they want. Some are hungry. It is time for things to change. Change in calm suddenly becomes the new motto. Ten years of famine is a long time and ten years of desperate political turmoil, even longer. New Yorkers are called to the polls in 1738. John Lewis Pintard runs for elected office and wins. He will remain a New York City Councilor until 1747, representing the Docks.

New Yorkers have understood that they could no longer be indifferent to public affairs. That is why they participate, opening up opportunities to people with limited resources, carters, bakers, butchers who discover the gilded splendor of the City Hall for the first time. They are not greatly impressed.

New York is not Paris nor London, although it has fine-looking buildings. The merchants comfortably settled in life accompany them in a profound reorganization of the political spectrum. John Lewis is one of them. He is satisfied.

He walks the docks on election night, aware that it is time to put the house in order but above all convinced that the town will not overcome its difficulties by relying on others. Sugar has made the city's fortune in recent years, but white gold is too easily earned. All of this, in the end, cannot last forever. It is time to create prosperity with something else. John Lewis supports the theories that prevailed in the last elections. The city will have to become partially independent of world trade without overtaking or competing too much with the production of the metropolis.

New York must work, manufacture and reflect. All of this will not happen in an instant. It will take years, but it is time to start. New York already knows how to build ships. It remains for them to manufacture pots to be embossed and so many other utensils ; the task seems important. All this may be boring, but the future of the community depends on it.

England has started its first industrial revolution, fifty years before France. All that's left for New York is to follow her lead. Furnaces, foundries, minerals and technical know-how will be needed ; it is necessary to get going and the sooner the better, although the change in production conditions will not have the magnitude or the force of the wind of modernity that will blow first in England.

The 1730s and 1740s will see this mechanism set in motion. It will not stop soon. However, the Pintards will not take the plunge. They remain attached to their lands, patiently acquired by Antoine. And this heritage will leave its mark on the unconscious for a long time, the urgent need to have one's feet firmly anchored to the ground, as a last refuge when everything goes wrong. This earthly connection will never paralyze them, but it will not help to propel the family into the industrial revolution. They are now part of the New York bourgeoisie which acquires land as they do in Europe. The model of the merchant landlord fits them perfectly. This model has been put to the test, but they won't stop there. Such is the case with the sons of John Lewis.

It is the death of John Lewis Pintard that apparently puts an end to his mandate, printing Pintard's name for the first time in the city archives. It must have been in the year 1748. Business was flourishing once again.

His successors will not let this stop them, sitting comfortably in their homes in New York.

62

John Lewis Pintard has four children. One of them, John, has sea legs and aims to take over his father's business and make it prosper. He will become the owner as well as the captain and purser of his own vessels. He will set sail for the Antilles where he will be shipwrecked and will disappear at sea in 1760, while on his way to Port-au-Prince. His wife, heiress to John Cannon, also a Huguenot, and one of the great fortunes of New York, had died a year earlier, a few days after giving birth to their son John, who comes into the world under the double patronage of wealth and Uncle Lewis who takes in the orphan. Both will have an impact on his life.

Lewis Pintard, as eager as his late brother to persevere in the maritime trade, will create his own shipping house, Lewis Pintard & C° and will bring up his unfortunate nephew, taking over his father's trading business between London, Madeira and the Indies, at the age of sixteen.

Lewis also enters into a good marriage, wedding Suzanne Stockton of Princeton, New Jersey, whose family mansion in Morven, built by her brother Richard, was from 1945 to 1981 the official residence of the state Governor. Lewis is interested in politics and undoubtedly derives this passion from his father, the New York alderman. He feels at ease in a milieu whose business opinions coincide with his.

England slows down trade and tries to prevent merchants from organizing themselves as they wish, without having to depend on the metropolis.[81] Each vacant ministry must await the good will of the

---

(81) Finding no other provision for the supervision of colonial religion, Henry Compton adapted the commissary system applied in the English diocese to the American colonies. As of 1689, he appointed representatives called commissaries to provide some leadership to the Anglican Church in America. By the 1740's the commissaries were supervising the Anglican clergy in nine colonies. The Irish Robert Jenney was the husband of Catherine

Anglican Bishop of London for the appointment of a new pastor. The American gentry begins to get irritated with the delays involved in the procedures. And, if England had limited the sovereign's powers in its 1689 Bill of Rights, it was to serve a purpose, and not just a remonstrance addressed to the king. Suffice it to say that discontent begins to simmer in New Jersey mansions and in New York houses, where they have become used to living as in London, and where they have adopted the bad habit of philosophizing in the French way. Conversations flow freely and if the elegance does not quite reach the heights of Paris, the depth of views do, especially on issues such as customs tariffs. But England pretends to turn a deaf ear and on his return from London, Richard Stockton, Lewis's brother-in-law, confirms verbally that the metropolis will not give in unless forced.

Lewis is at the heart of the historical breakthroughs that are emerging at Morven Manor, out of conviction certainly, but also thanks to Richard's moderate and considered positions. The latter is not weak, but he has traveled through Britain as a representative of the colony and, as such, knows that any substantial change requires strong endorsement and support. He also knows that heated words will not resolve anything, unless minds are prepared for a brutal break with the metropolis. It turns out that a significant part of the population remains loyal to the king and is certainly not prepared to kill Redcoats. Political loyalty exists and should not be ignored.

In addition, during his trip to England, Richard represents the College of New Jersey, which would later become Princeton College, and as a scholar and professor of law, he gives the keynote speech in the ceremonies in which he participates. He doesn't lose his cool or go into a rage. These individuals try to reach an agreement before embarking on a conflict that can only be long and dramatic. These educated men will not hesitate to go to war and offer their lives, but first they will do their best to resolve differences peacefully, technically and politically. They know more than the hotheads who might laugh at their supposed cowardice and who would be the first to quit if things go wrong, and to collaborate with the enemy or at least proclaim loud and clear that their leaders should never have embarked on such an adventure. They distrust public opinion that, if still unsure which

---

Pintard, widow of Captain John Searle. He was appointed commissary of Pennsylvania (mainly dissident) and Delaware (mainly Catholic) in order to mission these colonies from 1742 until he died in 1762.

way to go, is volatile and ungrateful. If they win, the overwhelming majority will say, peremptorily, "we won." That is why the intellectuals and the economic elite think and procrastinate, especially since the metropolis is powerful. England is in the process of displacing France on all continents, not only in North America but also in the East Indies, where French ambitions are being cut to a minimum.

England does not have a universalist discourse, but the political advances of the previous century have created conditions for the implementation of conquering and mercantile national objectives : and it must be admitted that this works. The English are becoming more and more proud of being English as they ease the French out of their former possessions, and that pride is formidable. Because the English are not wrong. They know that France reigned over Europe throughout the seventeenth century and her hegemony greatly enraged the English monarchs who adorned themselves with the title of Kings of France. Their victory is not an accident of history, but a sign of the superiority that this Anglo-Norman nobility still openly displays (taking care, however, to do so with subtlety, so as not to offend their Celtic or Saxon subjects).

To do this, the kings of England have accepted Parliament and its increasingly democratic evolution, making sure to add to their ambitious feudal projects, a wealthy bourgeoisie that can continue to enrich itself and adorn itself with exotic and unlikely titles of nobility. But, in any case it works and its clout is formidable. The Americans know it well. That is why they will hesitate a long time before taking the plunge. They also count on France, which could make George III lose his largest farm, he who, like Marie Antoinette of France had acquired the habit of playing farmer.

Lewis is in this position, eager to curb the powers of the metropolis, but aware, as a wise and educated merchant, that the game is far from won and that he has everything to lose if he participates in the conflict. As much as he associates himself with the nascent American political elite, he will not place his signature on the parchment of the June 1776 Declaration of Independence, ten years after Richard's return from his sixteen-month trip to Britain. Richard Stockton, his brother-in-law, will be one of the signatories. Lewis comes close to making history alongside Lewis Morris, the grandson of that other Lewis Morris, the Monmouth Chief Justice who sat next to his grandfather Antoine at court. The latter, surprisingly, had responded to his cousin, who was worried about the consequences of signing : "I don't care about the consequences, just hand me the pen !"

His brother, Samuel Pintard, a colonel in the British Army who had also married a Stockton, Abigail, will refuse, when the time comes, either fight his king or to turn his weapons against Americans, maintaining a total neutrality.

Lewis will become the representative of the Commissioner for Prisoners Elias Boudinot, also a Huguenot and also another of his brothers-in-law.[82] He will take full office when Elias becomes the second President of the Confederation Congress, the executive branch of the insurgents : in other words, the President of the yet unborn United States.

Meanwhile, John Pintard, his nephew (the orphan), has already grown up ; he is seventeen years old at the time of the Declaration of Independence. He does not intend to remain an outsider and does not waste time on pointless questions ; no doubt this is due to his young age. He is eager to get into action and is biding his time at Princeton College, where he is studying law.

The example of Richard Stockton, the signatory, is not without influence on his choice. John has been raised with an independent mindset and has reached the maturity to understand all the challenges and consequences of a war for freedom. He enlists when the first British troops arrive in New York, because the metropolis has not heard the voice of America asking Britannia to stop strangling the colony, to stop raising taxes without their consent, to stop obstructing the trade with the Antilles with a prohibitive customs duty, and to allow them judicial and fiduciary autonomy, in short, the colony asks to be left alone.

The merchants and the economic elites have come to this point.

The wars with France are now over and the possibilities of easy profits from piracy have ended with the fall of Quebec, once again exposing the colony's structural flaws. All of this has long been the work of the ruling families, the ones with the upper hand, while on the streets, King George's birthdays were just an occasion for demobilized buccaneers to get drunk, victims of the history's ups and downs, competing with the growing number of newcomers seeking land and a future.

---

(82) Elias's older sister Annis (1736-1801) had married Richard Stockton. Known as "The Duchess of Morven" she was one of the first women writer to be published in British America. These families belonged to the New Jersey elite and the Mid-Atlantic circle.

Nothing seems to link the population with its king anymore. They have relegated the divine right of monarchy to a bygone superstition, and England to ancient times. The possibilities are immense and New Yorkers are once again eager to help themselves.

So are also the newcomers, to whom America has been promised, and who on arrival discover the crisis, linked in particular to the embargo on imports from England. They have not yet been taught that economics is based on managing scarcity, and if they had been, they would not have believed it, surrounded as they are by abundance, at least in the form of promises of a brighter tomorrow. Under these conditions, who cares about unjust restrictions and regulations ! You have to turn everything upside down and finally figure it out for yourself. The newcomers are quickly won over by the insurgents, who have only one desire, to grab all they can. It is the triple revolution founded on freedom, property and the abolition of customs duties demanded by the Sons of Liberty since 1765 or the Bill of Rights of 1766. It is no longer about general ideas or philosophical concepts.

All this is very concrete and the discussion, technical if ever there was one, should have been successful because it is easier to negotiate than a "Liberty, Equality and Fraternity" whose contents are broader, at least in appearance. But the King of England does not understand any better the content of the settlement that was proposed to him than his cousin in France a few years later, until it is too late.

New Yorkers want to free themselves from their dependence on British manufactured goods, simply by making them themselves. But the experts have already decided otherwise, reserving the industry for the mother country and the potatoes and rye for the American colonies, even if it means tolerating certain deviations in the behavior of "these damned Americans", when the diplomatic and warlike adventures of the sovereign require a touch of piracy. But the Americans have got tired of the irregular influxes of money, despite the fact that, on a moral level, the monarchical anointing of divine right technically guaranteed them entry into the afterlife. In the meantime, they no longer want to return to George III what they stole from the French or from others. They want to keep everything to themselves and this is understandable. They are ready to be slapped on the wrists for it and if that's the case, they have warned, in all fairness, that they will return the favor.

Given that the patriots make up about forty percent of the population, King George should have become suspicious. The situation becomes even more explosive as staunch loyalists are but a minority. Misinformed or incredulous of his administration, the king and his parliament send ruffians or alcoholics to restore order, men like the Scotsman John Murray, whose "old-fashioned manners" would quickly lead to his replacement.

Another problem is that the colony is now educated. Yale, Harvard, Princeton (The College of New Jersey) have already been founded. New Yorkers are rich and sometimes impulsive ; there are about twenty-five thousand. They have an enlightened sanguine disposition, self-made men capable of both the best and the worst ; they are capable of saying no to their king. But they are slow to do so, especially those who meet in the Chamber of Commerce, of which Lewis Pintard was one of the founders in 1770. They still trust the common sense of the mother country.

The craftsmen, who call themselves the "Mechanics", no longer expect anything and let it be known to the representatives of New England, passing through New York, who are heading for Philadelphia to decide on a plan of action. A new division arises in the heart of the city, between the great families of English culture who want to avoid trampling the robe of the Anglican bishop, and the Mechanics who dream of offering a dress to their wives who do not have the right to sew at home. Anglicans will eventually join the majority to retain their power once matters with England are settled, even if the republic is not to their liking at first.

Aware that London is going too far, they too embark on the adventure because the owners of the country should rule it, as affirms John Jay, another Huguenot who gradually joins the revolution. Power must remain in the hands of the owners, particularly since the insurrectional situation provides the occasion for popular outbreaks, condemned by the revolutionary committees. And while the Public Security Commissions condemn them, public opinion asks for more, because stripping some Red Coats or stealing stockpiles is fun for the mob.

John Pintard does not necessarily share these comments with his fellow students at the university, nor does he see all this as a collective letting off of steam. However, young people tend to be more spontaneous than their elders because they do not think ahead, which always simplifies the resolving of equations. But for them events have meaning, as Thomas Paine writes when he describes Britain as a "royal beast." The monarchy is being questioned and this will lead Paine to participate in the debates of the Convention of 1793 held in the Tuileries Palace in Paris, as Victor Hugo will report later, qualifying him however as American and temperate. The Continental Congress and the Provincial Assemblies are constituted. Subcommittees begin to work. The political branch works : it remains for the armed wing to do the same. The youth volunteer, and the journey of Washington through New York heading for New England sparks general enthusiasm among them.

But private initiatives have made the city unsafe, especially as the Royal Navy occasionally lets off steam by bombing New York when abuses become intolerable in their eyes. By 1775, there are only five thousand inhabitants left ; twenty thousand have taken refuge in the countryside where tensions inevitably arise. New York is the weak link in the American revolution on the move. The city still has loyalists to the king, and some old families from the old Anglo-Dutch oligarchy praise the Patriots while holding their pretty handkerchiefs to their noses.

Benjamin Franklin's son, similarly suffering from a cold, joins the royal troops. Spies are everywhere, and the rebel troops setting up their barracks and latrines in the expensive districts attract not an outburst of sympathy but buckets of cold water thrown on the backs of the Patriots. New York is having trouble staying comfortable. It must be said that beauty is fragile and the city is difficult to defend. It would require a fleet of ships and New York does not have one. It would require order and the Mechanics are behaving like precursors of the *Sans-Culottes*,[83] sowing terror, stoking resentment, especially among the Tories, the monarchists in Parliament. They may have dressed for a while in the clothes of success, many of their fellow citizens know that the Mechanics have eaten with their mouths open for a long time ; crises exacerbate differences, jealousy and bitterness.

It remains obvious that there is no leader anymore and the city is doomed to end in ashes.

On June 29, 1776, more than a hundred warships pass Sandy Hook again and cross the passes to take up position off New York City. The city named after the Catholic king, the Duke of York, looks gorgeous

---

(83) The Sans-Culottes did not wear short trousers as the nobles did. They wore trousers. They were staunch republicans during the French revolution and did not hesitate to use weapons to fight for a direct democracy.

adorned in this way.[84] The wind from the bay unfurls the banners to greet those who are about to die.

On July 2, 1776, Congress approves the Declaration of Independence, which is ratified on July 9 by the New York Provincial Assembly. Hundreds of Tories now strive to join the British troops landing on Staten Island. On July 12, an additional 150 ships anchor in New York Bay and 15,000 troops land. The army is considerable, worthy of England : the largest concentration of troops ever deployed by the metropolis. The Americans are stunned, four hundred ships, more than thirty thousand soldiers, thirteen thousand sailors, hundreds of guns. The numbers are impressive, commensurate with what is at stake. The Americans did not know or had already forgotten, by looking only at their immediate interests that they belonged to a great nation. They discover this and are dumbfounded. They understand then that the war will be long. The mother country is powerful.

John is a boy. That day he understands that all this is not a game, as do his comrades as well. The English are attacking and have no intention of making a deal : young and old will be pierced by their bayonets or nailed to the Long Island trees where the battle has begun. The Brooklyn Heights will be covered in corpses. More than 1,500 Americans will die on the moraine of the great Canadian glacier off the Atlantic break. Death is everywhere, and it takes all the cunning of a Washington to flee this hell of blood, tears and mud while trying to avoid a rout. It rains forty-eight hours without stopping. The young die, still revising for their end-of-year exams, with their fingers stained with ink, in one of the most beautiful bays in the world, before having had a chance to live, with their foreheads girded with their tricolor cockade in front of the impeccable lions of the royal flag of the Duke of Normandy. Some of them were to be crowned with laurels at Princeton or elsewhere ; they will know the *Paths of Glory* in Brooklyn. England, never invaded since William's conquest in 1066, is determined to preserve this historical record and not be stripped of her overseas dominions. The empire is on the march and its troops are ready for battle. It cannot fall without the cunning or help of a foreign power.

John knows this well, he who speaks French. He will cross the East River on the night of August 29, 1776, during the total silence

---

(84) James II was a Church Papist until he openly converted to Roman Catholicism in 1669 i.e. he previously kept his Catholic faith a secret.

imposed by Washington in order to return to Manhattan to escape the hell of the Red Coats and turn the British parade into an urban guerrilla warfare that the American General has incorporated in his strategy. Nine thousand men will cross the Long Island Sound under the noses of his Majesty's commandos. The American army is saved.

Johnny, Bill and Pat will remain impaled for days and days in the trees of Long Island, holding, like children in their soft, white, plump hands, the little flutes that still played the happy Yankee Doodle a few hours earlier. Their adolescent eyes, immobile, will gaze for a long time on the masts of the great warships, open like a sheet of music without notes, scattered across New York Bay. The biggest battle of the War of Independence has just taken place. Battle Hill. Americans don't know that. The dead will never know. Their mothers will not forget.

The following days, the British, confident of themselves, want to negotiate. Two-thirds of Washington's troops have already defected. The Mechanics speak less loudly and flee in turn. It's a rout. Washington realizes that New York could become his grave and decides to leave Manhattan, although he rejects John Jay's idea of setting the city on fire. But on September 21, New York is on fire. "Providence or a helping hand," says Washington, who watches the beauty burn in the distance from the banks of the Hudson. "We would never have had the courage to do it ourselves" he adds.

The English recover the site as a field of ruins. All the fire pumps were neutralized or destroyed ; New York is a pile of ashes.

John returns to Princeton where he takes his exams at the last minute and with success. He will remember his whole life the summer of 1776. John Pintard is one of seven hundred New York Patriots who have answered the call.

Washington retires and crosses to New Jersey where he knows he will find support, especially in Princeton. The English who are not fooled go to Morven and set fire to parts of the Stockton mansion whose occupants only have time to flee, having burned all the files containing the names and agendas of the patriots around them, John Jay, Elias Boudinot, Lewis Pintard . . .

Richard Stockton, a signatory of the Declaration of Independence, is arrested in Monmouth, his native county, where his family had fled. During his trial in 1777, he gives his word of honor to remain inactive until the end of the conflicts in exchange for his freedom. He is diagnosed with cancer in 1778 and will dies three years later in 1781.

Cornwallis' troops have established their headquarters at Morven in 1777, when they have also destroyed the furniture and the library. The Stockton family remains dignified in the face of adversity and the echoes of these abuses resonate in John Pintard's head, like the tales of the abuses by dragoons in France still related by his uncle Lewis who heard them from his father John Lewis, the son of Antoine.

John understands that there are no bad or good people, just circumstances which sometimes make kings intractable. This will be remembered by him throughout his life, when he feels the urge to classify men, to oppose ideas with violence. That is surely why, just like Antoine, he has never rejected France, nor will he reject England.

From that point on, his life turns to militant philanthropy. He understands that he will be more useful to the American Revolution if he follows in the footsteps of his uncle instead of fighting up hill and down dale.

63

"John, the nation needs you !" exclaimed his uncle.

Lewis didn't give him time to reply.

"I understand your scruples but you will be more useful to our cause by replacing me in my role than by joining the troops in battle. Congress also needs a contingent, and discussions with the British about the fate of the prisoners are as important as the laurels earned on the battlefield. You participated in this fight and you did it by disobeying your teachers and myself. I remind you that when you enlisted, you were only seventeen years old and you haven't stopped fighting since. Today we are in 1777, you are eighteen and you are free to do whatever you want because you have shown that you are a man capable of making your own decisions. Your teachers have also already forgiven your disobedience."

"Some of my comrades have not returned from Brooklyn and the Battle of New York and I must be faithful to my commitment. The war is not over. It will be long, according to the military."

"Indeed, the war is not over and neither is its parade of tragedies. The task before you may not be glorious, but it is useful. The British are making the patriots who they call rebels pay a high price, and the conditions of their captivity are dire. I myself have been appointed deputy to Elias Boudinot, my brother-in-law, in this task. He has just been called to the General Commission of the United States Army, which is a great honor for him, his family, and also for the Huguenot community as a whole. I'm therefore taking his place. When your great-grandfather Antoine arrived here in New York, he had no idea that one day we would be honored so much for such a delicate mission. It is not easy. The English have nothing but contempt for what we represent, we are shopkeepers, that is all we are to them, and when we take up arms, we become savages. They forget one thing : we are brave and also educated. However, it is not just about bravery. All these events occurred in a context of legitimate demands. We could no longer tolerate seeing them plunder the product of our efforts, of our ingenuity, of our endeavors, forever submitting to the unique will of London. Our territories need to live and develop, and we have to prosper. It is a long and difficult struggle that we started in France, over there in the Languedoc. We did not come here just to satisfy our personal ambitions. Besides, what's the point now that our ships have been burned in New York Harbor ? We have come here to build a new world, free from all the vices of the old. We have won our religious freedom and even here that has not been without difficulties. We still have to complete our mission. For that, we need people like you who know how to keep themselves in the background in the public interest and take on tasks that, at first glance, are administrative tasks."

"That's what it's about too," John ventured to suggest.

"And even so, the world that we intend to build will not consider these functions contemptible, as French nobles do. The society we want to build must be administered and for that we need all kinds of talents. We have to invent and create a nation from scratch. We have depended on the metropolis for far too long, vociferating and complaining without really taking the reins. It is now up to us to prove who we are and to drive out those who do not know more than to speak without knowing what they are talking about. The war will end and at that moment we will have to be prepared if we do not want the rest of the world to laugh at us. Only a nation can give strength to all its peoples. That will be our glory !"

John understood that his uncle was right. His uncle was almost fifty years old. He had just lost a good part of his fortune and yet he still had faith in the future. Under these circumstances, it was not possible to put things off any longer.

John passed through New Rochelle where he had taken refuge after the Battle of New York. The French Huguenots, now numerous, were not abandoning the great task of working the lands of America. The tools stored at the edge of the barns, were taking a well-deserved rest as did the men ; the silhouettes of their forged teeth against the setting sun testified to certainty and stubbornness, like haughty battlements signaling to the English that they would not surrender.

John loved New Rochelle, the bastion of the French Reformed. The Calvinists there did not always have the means to pay their pastor, and the Huguenot community in New York favored them with their donations. These peasants at heart maintained a small France a few leagues from the great city, which delighted the French Protestants of the great port who, for their part, had not renounced their taste for beauty and a sense of their greatness. They now reserved these qualities for the young American nation that had just been born.

The United States of America ! It was the first time that John pronounced the name of his country, at least the first time that he understood its meaning and scope and the commitments it represented. John was happy. He understood that day that he had entered his life as a man in front of a well-defined field, fragrant and colored like the new covering of spring after the last snow had melted.

The Plowman of America had been born. He will stubbornly hold the handles of the plow, like a peasant in the *Cévennes* mountains, never despairing, building low walls, plowing the land, diverting streams, building canals, digging, planning New York itself. He knew how to fly the flag of Calvinism while remaining faithful to the French Church of New York, the Church of the Holy Spirit. All that was in him that day.

A nation ! he thought, reflecting dreamily.

64

Meanwhile, the Quaker Church on Pearl Street had become Provost Prison. Erected in 1775, it preserved in its new warm-colored bricks the fragile rays of the December 1777 sun, and warmed the exhausted bodies that were piled up, stretched out on the icy floor-tiles of its crowded cells. The interior had lost the smooth, shiny surfaces of its young and sober architecture. Half-naked American prisoners shuddered in this hell that the English had set aside for the rebels.

On that winter's day, the jailers themselves, disgusted by so much accumulated garbage, had decided to put an end to it by opening the prison doors, so that men and filth would flow into the street like a sewer. The men, dripping with fluids and vermin, had difficulty in walking. Their legs, thin and brittle like dead tree branches, no longer supported them, after months in this place of agony. The blows could not do more. The English themselves could no longer bear living in that hell.

But the much-desired runoff could not take place, so much the beings that were dragged by their arms and feet clung to their guardians' hands. The brutality of the soldiers, in a hurry to finish with all this, exposed body muscles. The corpses mingled with the dying who vomited their last bile, their eyes bulging in the daylight. The surroundings of the prison were beginning to look like the interior of the church. By opening the doors of the Provost, the English had accomplished only one thing : spreading the poison further. The much-desired runoff had not occurred. The men could not walk and their legs carried them only towards their death. The streets began to get covered with corpses. The few New Yorkers who had remained in the city witnessed the return of the living dead that the walls of

Provost had hidden from their eyes for so long. Attempts at comfort were fruitless. It was too late. Nausea seized the city, as well as fear of epidemics, the condition of the prisoners being so bad that they were in a state of decomposition. Shapeless masses lay in their last throes of life. The city was shocked when it discovered what was happening behind the gates of the previous place of worship, transformed into antechambers of death.

As night fell, silence settled over Pearl Street, Franklin Square, and Oak Street. Provost Hospital, as the English called it, was empty. The bravest tried to flee to the Jerseys for the next few days. The English did not dissuade them, preferring to entrust to the palliative care of Quakers these people at the end of their lives, who only inspired terror.

The sugar house on Liberty Street contained the same viscous, swollen and bloated matter from which sometimes eyes could be seen popping out.

John Pintard had been appointed deputy commissioner for prisoners by his uncle Lewis. The latter had been elevated to this position by General Washington himself, who knew that unacceptable things were happening in his Majesty's prisons. John Pintard took up the issue, while his uncle rushed to raise funds from the Patriots to bring relief to the inmates.

Each manifestation of generosity was the object of a receipt that would be validated against the nation's treasury once the war was over. The young republic began in the most complete destitution and the war effort could only be resolved in the future, with a large loan, or in any case with a vast balancing of accounts, the writing of which had yet to be invented.

Meanwhile, the burgeoning patriotic fervor largely covered the risk-taking of the early funders of the young democracy, and Lewis Pintard was recording ever larger sums of money. The American Revolution may have been the first or the only one driven in part by accountants and bookkeepers. Lewis Pintard was one of them, as evidenced by his files which he signed in his capacity as auditor. When the war ended, he received congratulations from General Washington, who later became the first president of the United States of America.

John thus traveled for several years to the English prisons set up in the Reformed Churches of New York, while England preserved the Protestant cult in the Anglican Churches, the guardians of Orthodoxy according to the government. He also visited the holds of the prison ships that the British Navy had anchored in New York Bay. Prisoners rarely escaped from those wooden Alcatraz that bore singular names of nightclubs such as Scorpion, Good Hope, Falmouth, and even names of hotels, such as The Prince of Wales.

Unfortunately, several thousand corpses left these unstarred establishments. Their occupants, deprived of the beauty of the sky, could not rest at night ; huddled together, they continued to perspire as during the day, even in winter. The unbreathable atmosphere created the conditions for abominable relationships. The only hope was the flight to the afterlife, a journey that some made before going crazy.

The most malicious Englishmen sometimes transferred the most recalcitrant prisoners to the churches of New York ; the punishment was reduced to a confinement on the frozen stones of the alcoves where the dissidents had prayed only a short while before. The transfer from the furnace of the patriots' ship holds to the cold of winter quickly carried the bodies to the afterlife. All that was left was to bury the corpses in the trenches that New Yorkers had prepared to support the siege of the city, unaware they were digging their own graves. The situation was the same in the surrounding islands of the New York archipelago and lasted for several years.

On these barges, John discovered nakedness because the heat was stifling. The British and the Americans had reached an agreement that allowed reciprocal visitation rights for their prisoners. But when one day, visiting one of these prison ships, John commented that the treatment meted out by the Americans to English prisoners seemed more decent to him than that given by the English to American prisoners, the jailer replied that these people were nothing more than rebels.

"The harsher and more painful the treatment, the less these scoundrels will drag after them a whole swarm of deserters and traitors to our king", he asserted.

"Do you think this is how things are ?" John asked him.

"I am sure of it", concluded the jailer, "your prisoners are our soldiers, ours are your traitors. The treatment cannot be identical."

"By acting in this way, you confirm the opinion of some of our officers who remind the soldiers that it is better to die on the battlefield than end up in English prisons."

"They are not wrong ; their point of view is full of common sense."

John realized that the discussion would be long and difficult. In the first place, it was necessary to make the enemy camp admit that the qualification used with respect to the Americans should be the same as for the English soldiers.

John knew from that point on that it would be necessary to revisit the British military authorities regularly until a definition was agreed.

The Battle of New York had been a defeat. Initially, a thousand men had been taken prisoner, followed by another seven hundred with the fall of Fort Washington, to the north of Manhattan.

Since then, the fighting had been reduced to skirmishes, and the British had so far only suffered with a few dozen being taken prisoner. John perfectly evaluated the situation. He understood that the evolution of English common sense would only be determined by a still unknown variable : the number of English prisoners his Majesty would tolerate.

While waiting for the model that the British General Staff would submit for the approval of the generals of the young nation, it was necessary to continue with the visits and alleviate the suffering, thanks to the donations made by the patriots themselves. The American military, on all their missions, had to make sure they did as much damage as possible to their enemy so that they would collaterally agree to review their position on the treatment of prisoners.

John thus steadfastly and unhesitatingly visited prisons, churches, barges and hospitals of the dying until 1781, confronting everyday distress, which can transform or hardens one or plunge one into paralyzing sentimentality. John discovered the horror that no amount of education could have prepared him for. But he also learned about humanity which reveals extraordinary men in extreme situations or discovers only poor souls in beings made only of assertions and postures.

John discovered men as well as his compatriots, those with whom he would build America, and who, at the moment, were rotting in the English ship holds. He understood, during those moments that he spent with them, that the construction of the nation would not be done with bulldozers but with small touches, leading people to their own assertions, sometimes to their own traps.

John Pintard will perfect his strategy in the dungeons of the British Army.

For its part, the English admiralty competed in military ingenuity to negotiate the release of the cohorts of prisoners taken by the rebels in the camps set up for this purpose, especially after the Battle of Trenton.

But the situation was changing. First of all, this costly warfare was becoming less and less popular on the banks of the Thames. The people and Parliament were beginning to protest. After all, perhaps the Americans had good reasons to revolt, they told themselves across England. Washington was not fooled and was even well-informed about British morale. He took advantage of this and rejected all the proposals the representatives of his Majesty presented to him. He reminded them that given the state in which they had put his fellow citizens, there was no question of exchanging the dying for healthy young people.

The negotiations were still dragging on. John discovered that the field of accounting was huge and that at one point or another something would have to be measured. Otherwise, they would end up reinforcing the enemy troops with well-treated freed prisoners, while the Americans filled their hospitals and cemeteries with dead ones.

The English rejected such calculations. The situation continued. The fate of the prisoners was resolved in specific negotiated exchanges and spectacular group escapes, as well as by individual initiatives that led to the attack on prisons, as well as the movement of ships to more distant areas, in particular to the Sound of the East River. The issue was not resolved during the American War of Independence.

Ten to fifteen thousand prisoners died. Many French volunteers, among the American troops or as soldiers of the regular army of the King of France, were taken prisoner and shared these wretched moments with the rebels.

They were quickly informed of the decisive victory at Yorktown.

A month later, the King of France had the parish priest of San Roman de Tousque read, as in all the churches of France, the story of their victory over the King of England.

Rochambeau rejected the sword of Lord Cornwallis, who, pale-faced, refused to give it to that "savage", as he termed Washington.

France entered the history of young America through the front door.

John Pintard was probably happy that day like most Americans.

Forty thousand English-speaking loyalists fled to Quebec. . .

65

The war is finally over. The leading politicians participate in the drafting of the Treaty of Paris. British and American envoys regularly converge on Versailles, where they incessantly discuss measures to be taken or to evaluate the cost of their discussions, reparations, and the future of the two, now equally-sovereign, nations.

Louis XVI is very happy. He does not realize that by leading the American republic to the baptismal font, he has seriously shot himself in the foot. He will perhaps become aware of it in his last moments when he is climbing the scaffold. The history of France does not recall Yorktown, where the French, more numerous, it is said, than the Americans regulars, dealt a decisive blow to the English army. The only thing they remember is the King's flight to Varennes in a carriage in order to escape arrest during the French Revolution. The Americans on the other hand are indeed grateful to him.

The English will not forgive the French, and especially King George III who has ended up losing his largest farm, as London Cockneys mockingly claim.

France has lost nothing this time. The balance of the expansions of Tobago, Senegal and some cities in India is positive. The Bahamas, taken during the war, must be returned to the English for the sake of peace, as must Saint Kitts and Nevis in the Caribbean Sea. The Spanish now control much of Florida. The English have lost a lot and refuse to participate in the last photo.[85] The Treaty is signed in Paris at the Hotel York, another symbol. One of the three signatories[86] is a Huguenot :

---

(85) Great Britain overcame this defeat once she got over her vexation.

(86) The Treaty of Paris was signed on September 3, 1783, by Benjamin Franklin, John Adams, and John Jay. The negotiators were Benjamin Franklin, John Adams, John Jay, Henry Laurens, and William Temple Franklin (Benjamin's grandson). William is buried in Paris where he ended his life.

John Jay, well known to the Pintard family. Henry Laurens, another Huguenot and a Virginian merchant, owner of large estates and a slave trader, is one of the five negotiators with John Jay.

John Pintard, meanwhile, has married Eliza Brasher, daughter of Colonel Abraham Brasher, the patriotic hero of Paramus in New Jersey, thereby unconsciously forming a blue, white, and red aristocracy.

The United States, prevented from trading with the East Indies since 1685, has acquired the freedom to trade with whomever it pleases. Lewis Pintard is contacted by a group of Boston businessmen, merchants and ship owners, still under the spell of the travel accounts of Captain James Cook, who had died in Hawaii in 1779.

Adventure and trade with China tempt them, especially since the echoes of the journey of the Empress of China, a three-masted brig that reached Canton and had returned to New York in 1785, have eventually reached their ears. They also need sponsors. The Lewis Pintard & Co. house is known as far as New England, and independence now erases resentments against New Yorkers. These Protestant freethinkers do not drown in religious orthodoxy, any more than they would do in the Pacific. The road to the West through Cape Horn is opened, while the American continent remains largely in the hands of the Indians, the French trappers, the Spanish and English kingdoms. The latter retained freedom of movement on the Mississippi when the Treaty of Paris was signed. But, right now, that is not the point. Repeated readings of the hapless Captain Cook's diary have whetted their appetite, as the fantasy of China keeps them on edge. The return on investment has been superficially calculated, without the help of financial mathematics.

For now, one has to believe in it. In other words, integrating the future not as a variable evaluated according to previous experiences, but according to the resources that are collected for the enterprise. These must be optimal and Lewis' Pintard & Co. is summoned to the adventure.

These men come together because they belong to the *"crème de la crème"* of the Atlantic coast shipowners. This is their only patent and, in those old days, it is the only way to tilt the odds in one's favor.

John Marsden Pintard, son of Lewis, will play an active role in building the Boston fleet.

We are in the year 1787. He is only twenty-seven years old. The fifty thousand dollars in funds needed for the project have resulted in the need to issue fourteen shares. Two ships are purchased, the Columbia

Rediviva[87] and the Lady Washington. Symbols. The children of the young republic fear nothing. The ships are armed with cannons and *The Lady Washington* is commanded by John Kendrick, a former privateer. Independence was only the first step. "The Pacific is ours !" they must be thinking when the two officially accredited ships leave Boston on September 30, 1787.

Cook's voyages had been for exploration. The purpose here is clearly commercial, although before departure a commemorative medal is struck figuring all the participants in the enterprise and the captains, as if to give a solemn character to the first trip between America and China. They have also hired, certainly within the framework of patronage, an astronomer, to bring the academic world closer to the business world, as well as an artist, Robert Haswell.

America invents a lot and quickly. John Marsden Pintard, John's cousin, and with whom he grew up, is one of these innovators, he is the great-grandson of Antoine who one day in 1687 crossed the *Corniche des Cévennes* to immerse himself, amazed by his own audacity, in the valley of *La Baume*, in the middle of the benches admirably suspended over the *Gardon de Saint-Jean* river. Like father, like son, even a hundred years later, almost to the day.

The trip to the Far East will last three years. The gains are not what were expected and Lewis Pintard & Co. withdraw from the venture. Before that, the captains of the fleet have renamed, for use by American sailors, the Queen Charlotte Strait between Vancouver Island and the Queen Charlotte Islands, calling it the Pintard Strait, as recorded in the American Gazetteer of 1804, the national geographic directory published in Boston. The Pacific for us ! The Columbia returns to port on August 10, 1790, sailing round Cape of Good Hope. Being the first American ship to have circled the world, it gave its name, Columbia Rediviva, to the first Space Shuttle Columbia[88]. As soon as the imported porcelain and skins have been unloaded, she sails again for China on September 28, 1790. Along the way, the men of the Columbia will discover the mouth of the river Columbia that today bears her name and will take possession of the surrounding land on May 11, 1792, in the name of the United States of America, thus entering into several decades of negotiations with England !

---

(87) Saint Columba (521-597) is an Irish abbot and missionary credited with spreading Christianity in Scotland. He is venerated in the Church of Scotland, the Anglican Church and the Catholic Church.

(88) https://www.nasa.gov/centers/kennedy/shuttleoperations/orbiters/columbia_info.html

John Marsden does not stop there. China is not the jackpot, so onward to Louisiana ! He establishes a cotton plantation in 1796, Laurel Hill, along the Thomson Creek in the parish of Feliciana, north of New Orleans and south of the border of Mississippi, which is still just a territory. He operates a general store and exploits slaves. Incidentally, his ships are sunk in the Mississippi, which the English would like to keep just for themselves. Too bad, let's go on ! His son, John Manuel, will also be the beneficiary of a United States Supreme Court ruling on the sale of farmland in Arkansas, which is just beginning to open up to colonization.

The Pintards are everywhere, even in the English court where John Marsden's sister, Martha Bayard, who had entered one of New York's most distinguished families, delights the English aristocracy with her diary. So much so that in the future, the former occupants will be wary of disrespecting New Yorkers. Martha Pintard Bayard, the niece of Richard Stockton, one of the signatories of the Declaration of Independence, will bring to England a touch of originality from Broadway when she becomes a regular visitor to the royal family.

If the English generally regard the Founding Fathers as Pilgrims and the Puritans as fanatics, it is very different when it comes to New Yorkers, to whom they attribute Venetian talents. They would like to do business with them, except that the two nations are not done with fighting, since now the stakes are elsewhere. England has understood that the only ambition of the young America is to drive it completely off the continent.

Meanwhile, in 1789 John Pintard has entered politics, and is in turn elected Alderman in the East Ward, next to the Dock Ward which his grandfather John Lewis had ruled for ten years during colonial times. He enters politics as one enters a religion. He is not the only one to do so.

A whole generation of Americans supports the civic virtues that Jefferson represents. John Pintard is one of them. Elected Member of Parliament in 1790, he is a member of the New York State Legislature. He, in turn, has become a ship owner and is trading with China thanks to his two ships, the *Belgiosa* and the *Jay*, as in John Jay. John, who has become financially independent, will be part of the Chinese challenge from New York and follows the adventure with great enthusiasm. They do not intend to arrive in China with empty holds to bring back shipments of porcelain. New Yorkers have also read Cook's stories and are familiar with the great Chinese taste for ginseng. All the better if it is in short supply in China, because this root grows wild in the Mississippi Valley. Tons will be loaded on board ships bound for China. Hopefully the English will cooperate in the great river, otherwise the Americans won't wait for the matter to be settled. John increases his wealth in this trade with the Far East as much as a John Broome or a Robert Lenox. His office is located in the Ward at 12 Wall Street. Moreover, he is the translator for the American government of the Treaty of Friendship drawn up in French between France and the United States, signed before the Declaration of Independence behind the backs of the English who, involved since 1760 in real estate in Quebec, were unwisely admiring the Saint-Laurent.

John is active and does not intend to remain on the sidelines of the great experiment that is unfolding here, democracy.

His businesses prosper. He is now at the head of the immense fortune that his late Cannon grandfather has passed on to him. He believes in the American nation. He also lives on Wall Street, where he regularly crosses paths with Alexander Hamilton, the elegant and brilliant young man in his thirties nominated aide-de-camp by General Washington, who owns a home just a stone's throw away. He is the lead author of The Federalist papers where he explains in more than eighty articles the intricacies of the American Constitution in order to rally the states to the federalist thesis. Hamilton is also the Secretary of the Treasury of the United States. He lives at 57 Wall Street.

New York is the capital of the United States of America and its population of approximately 30,000 will soon surpass that of Philadelphia. While the city has not fully embraced the pro-independence cause, it appears that it has started to play the game, since the Federal Administration has established its offices at 26 Wall Street and is investing £ 100,000 in annual public spending in the town. New Yorkers keep their accounts well. Either way, John is on the right side. He is now part of New York, on the even side of Wall Street. The odd side is not to be outdone, and as in a game of roulette, it only takes a little good luck to win or bad luck to lose it all.

This street will become the center of new ideas, often disruptive, being born with the reorganization of nascent America, whose deviations are already mocked by England. Preserving the monopoly on the imposition of customs duties, it refuses to allow states to practice the dumping of customs duties at their convenience. Customs policy will be applied uniformly at the outer borders of the states and serve as a protective barrier against the rest of the world, as a first line of defense for the nation. This is the great preventive measure that the United States intends to take to protect itself.

France benefits from the most-favored-nation clause. Everyone agrees that trade must continue with Europe but also with the Antilles and, why not, with China.

66

Financial credit granted to a young nation must be recognized by the rest of the world, which is not yet the case with US. The local currencies of Boston and New York were supplemented in revolutionary times with the issue of the Continentals, which ultimately meet the same terrible fate as the *Assignats* [89] in France. It soon becomes necessary to know how to deal with a currency that has lost a large part of its value before it becomes a collector's item, especially since the States also have outstanding debts from the revolution clinging to their balance sheet, like ticks on the back of a dog. Therefore, their currencies also depreciate ; and inflation threatens the great financial equilibrium.

This is the dilemma that Wall Street is going through, both the odd and even sides of the street. The United States is over-indebted both at home and abroad. The revolution had a cost that will have to be paid, sooner or later. For that, it is necessary to achieve growth. The first condition to meet the intended goal is to win the people's trust in the currency in circulation and in the federal government's ability to pay : without trust, there will be no investment.

Hamilton, the treasurer, has a plan. The Dollar will replace the local currencies and the Continentals must disappear from the liability's column of the republic's balance sheet. The exchange of the latter will be done at parity. One against one.

---

[89] N of T : The *Assignat* was a fiat currency established during the French Revolution. After the John Law system, the *Assignat* was the second fiat money experiment in France in the 18th century : both ended in resounding failures. Originally, it was a debt issued by the Treasury in 1789, the value of which was secured in national property by assignment. *Assignats* became a currency of circulation and exchange in 1791, and the revolutionary assemblies multiplied emissions, leading to runaway inflation. The legal tender of *Assignats* was abolished in 1797.

The new currency will be guaranteed by public and private deposits. This plan is unknown to the general public, but Hamilton knows that this vast exchange cannot take place without the help of a national bank, a Bank of the United States, which the constitution has not provided for.

To carry out this plan, it is necessary to say as little as possible, if only to gauge the support of the entrepreneurs, who will be the guarantors of the operation. Hamilton might not say anything much, but in Wall Street friendly meetings and dinners were inevitably the subject of scrutiny and evaluation.

They all know each other. Those who eat at one's home are delighted to have coffee at another's, who in turn tries to interpret the words they hear. Certainly no one has spoken, but what political and financial interest would there be in the matter if it were only a question of converting three Continentals[90] for one Dollar. Why should rich people be willing to lose large sums of money or Patriots be mistreated ? Hamilton lets things take their course. He thinks that, failing to get the support of pure souls, the role of the authorities is to make sure things don't get out of hand. Everyone is free to sell or not to sell their Continentals, including the Patriots. The formalization of the exchange confronts both parties with their autonomy that they have newly acquired thanks to democracy and the Constitution. Citizens thereby have to come to terms with their responsibilities. No one can complain. It is written. To do this, it is necessary to rely on an elite of entrepreneurs, who can thereby also be controlled, given their small number. They also evidently facilitate the setting up of operations whose technicality and complexity are self-evident. The United States has just been born and it has no experience in these matters. Everything has to be invented and worked out, perhaps, relying on existing friendships.

From now on, a game of poker will be played in which businessmen and some politicians will take turns in inviting each other to join in. Each will buy back Continentals at a low price, traveling the countryside on foot, on horseback or by carriage, and rooting out of the farms of rural America bonds as famous those of the Panama Canal or the Russian Loan, a century later. American patriots can't wait any longer and are selling to roving financial advisers their debt securities issued by the United States Treasury, the States of New York or Connecticut.

---

(90) Continentals were a fiat currency established during the American Revolution to finance the war against Great Britain.

Elias Boudinot, Huguenot and brother-in-law of Lewis Pintard, former President of the Confederation Congress after the Declaration of Independence, is one of the largest buyers of depreciated securities : 50 million Dollars in New Jersey. Perhaps, he did it on behalf of the US Treasury.[91] The people may well be aware that they are being cheated, but they prefer three pounds six shillings to nothing at all. Credit securitization has found its market on both sides of Wall Street. A financial euphoria follows in which many will sink. It reinforces the thesis of Virginians Madison and Jefferson who, from the beginning, had opposed Hamilton in the institutional conflict, whether federal or not, the organization, federal or otherwise, of the institutions of the young nation. Perhaps through a domino effect, they reject his plan for the financial rebuilding of the republic, as not moral enough. The other solution would have been to establish an exceptional tax, whose revenue would have been used to pay the debts and the Continentals. Hamilton is convinced of his views, but he needs everyone, even the Virginians who, unlike others, have paid their war debt and do not see why they should pay for someone else's debts as well.

Meanwhile, *Wall Streeters* go to the National Bank tellers and deposit their Continentals there. In return, they receive their equivalent in newly minted Dollars, which they immediately lend to the Bank of the United States to finance the reactivation of the economy. All of this is effective and conforms to Hamilton's original plan. However, he is aware that collusion between politicians, the federal government and Wall Street brokers does not look very good. He negotiates the Virginians' support for his plan in exchange for the commitment to transfer the capital to the banks of the Potomac.

A few months later, the government of the United States of America moves to Philadelphia awaiting the construction of Washington DC, a measure that is undoubtedly aimed at remedying the too close proximity of the business community to politics in New York City, and thus attempts to wipe out this scandalous inbreeding. The gossips

(91) According to Albert F. Koehler, author of *The Huguenots or The Early French in New Jersey* (Clearfield 1955), Alexander Hamilton was born on the island of Nevis. He left the island of Saint Kitts at the age of 15 and found his way to Elizabethtown where he was received at the home of Elias Boudinot and started his schooling there. His mother, Rachel Fawcett Lavien, died when he was young. She was a Huguenot and Hamilton spoke French. Boudinot's mother, Mary Catherine Williams was born in the British West Indies (Parham, Antigua). Boudinot's daughter, Suzan, married William Bradford, Attorney General under George Washington. Bradford was the son of William Bradford who had published Antoine Pintard's *Treasury of Consolations* in 1696. Small world !

say that Jefferson was the owner of the land on which, ten years later, the capital city of the United States would be built.

Meanwhile, Hamilton fights back. He creates the Bank of New York to facilitate the operation and divert speculators from the remote countryside where they shortchange poor patriots. He offers them a great nut to crack and the status of semi-public company, since the federal state will be associated on equal terms with private investors. This should reassure everyone. Private shareholders are free to sell their securities to whomever they see fit ; and this stock market will quickly emerge. The Bank of New York also issues marketable debt instruments, in order to continue to trade the Continentals, whose profitability has been the subject of intense debate.

Once the payment is made, the lenders come out of the woodwork and pounce on the Treasuries Bonds. Faced with the success of the Bank of New York, a group of New York entrepreneurs decides in turn to create the Million Dollar Bank, as it is called in its founding bylaws, to compete with the Bank of New York. The goal is to keep the price of the shares of the Bank of New York low in case investors are tempted by the Million Dollar Bank. Thus, they could make a profit later during the resale of the Bank of New York shares, when the artificial downward pressure on the securities' price had ceased. John Pintard is part of the group as well, and has, in December 1791, participated in the informal club of stock price manipulators in New York. It was a daring thing to do.

The money men come from America, but also from France, England and Amsterdam. These securities quickly turn into gold. They can also be exchanged very quickly, on the street, generating a comfortable added value.

Speculators are getting involved, including William Duer, who is the founder of the Million Dollar Bank. He lives at 12 Partition Street, near Wall Street. He was Hamilton's assistant at the United States Treasury. He has just resigned from his civil service post, explaining that he had better things to do. The Bank of New York price falls as expected. This man buys but also takes out various loans to buy the Bank of New York shares, expecting to repay once the capital gains are in his pocket. He engages and involves John Pintard in this venture giving him his power of attorney. The two men take out large loans at monthly rates of up to four percent. The ants turn into grasshoppers.[92]

---

(92) As in La Fontaine's fable *The ant and the grasshopper*.

Men in the street are getting involved, convinced that this is how the world of tomorrow will be made. Their meager savings accumulated with difficulty come out of the woolen stockings and are loaned to Duer. The value of work takes a back seat. It's the big night!

John Pintard, decidedly very active, opens the first stock exchange in the great hall of the Merchants Coffee House located on Wall Street. Someone should have thought of that, so he did. People sitting comfortably can learn about their investments six days a week, buy and sell, consult share prices. The first New York Stock Exchange is born.

In short, New York is reconnecting with its old demons of easy money and speculation. From beaver hides to stock market speculation, including West Indies sugar speculation and real estate speculation, this city has always focused its immense talent for profit-making on trading ventures that pose a risk similar to that of gambling in casino halls. The business works but not for long. Other astute people follow in the footsteps of the Million Dollar Bank and start new banking operations until everything stops due to lack of cash flow, as rumors begin to reveal the excesses of this financial turmoil.

Hamilton moves his pawns. He tightens up the credit and the discount rate granted by the Bank of New York, thus drastically reducing the currency in circulation. In a few days the streams dry up and Duer finds himself alone with his debts and the thousands of ordinary New Yorkers that he has dragged along in his path, and who now want to dismember him like they did Jacob Leisler.

In those days, a bankrupt could avoid jail as long as he remained under house arrest, with authorized outings on Sundays. Duer knows he is risking his life taking this path, and quickly rings the bell of the New York jail, thereby inventing voluntary incarceration.

John Pintard is ruined, because he recklessly endorsed a credit note issued by Duer. His loss is one million dollars. John Pintard created the first New York Stock Exchange at 22 Wall Street and a little later was one of the main contributors to the first stock market crash of the American financial center, today the most famous in the world, to such an extent that some economists and historians recall Pintard's name when they talk about this first financial scandal. Duer then becomes Duer - Pintard. The latter is not very proud of this, however, and not wishing to have Sunday as his only authorized outing, he flees to New Jersey. There, he will remain eight years as in a land of refuge. He will fill his diary with horticultural information, having used the first two years of his exile to cultivate his garden while waiting for a comprehensive law for bankrupt merchants, undoubtedly inaugurating thereby a long tradition.[93] He will return to New York after being incarcerated for fourteen months in Newark prison.

Antoine, his great-grandfather, would have turned in his grave. John, an honest man at heart, will nevertheless try to redeem his soul by seeking, in the study of ancient authors, the necessary means for introspection, which he would like to see shared by as many of his fellow citizens as possible, also inaugurating a tradition among the repentant on Wall Street.

Those in the New York business community are especially eager to turn the page. They have lost political power that shifted to Philadelphia on August 30, 1790. They are convinced that the elected representatives will become bored on the banks of the Potomac River or in Philadelphia. George Washington does not care ; he didn't love New York. New Yorkers comfort the other politicians by telling them to come back and see them from time to time or use the United States Post Office to deliver their news. The city remains the financial capital of America : the city of capital, rather than the Capital City. The business community has a lot of money. The richest merchants decide to reactivate Pintard's office which, they admit, was not such a bad idea in the first place. But it is no longer possible for so many players to operate in the market. A financial aristocracy must be created, or rather an elite that will act as a filter, since it is well known that too many players in the market make stocks too volatile.

For this, statutes are needed in which the signatories commit to respect a code of ethics and rules, in short, private norms that probably were already called "standards". This says it all. Those New York devils invent Wall Street, thus leaving out the federal state that has moved South. They also exclude private operators, let us say individuals, who deal on their own account and who, multiplying thereby the number of players, accelerate the realization of capital gains, of financial bubbles.

The Buttonwood Accord, which instituted the New York Stock Exchange, was signed on May 17, 1792, on Wall Street, as legend has it, under a sycamore tree, the American plane tree, in the old-fashioned way. Only the grasshoppers are missing. New Yorkers really don't do anything like anyone else.

---

(93) The first US Bankruptcy law was enacted on April 4, 1800. Highly controversial, society came to view the financial collapse of businessmen as a normal part of risk-taking rather than moral degeneracy : Bruce H. Mann, Republic of debtors, Bankruptcy in the Age of the American Independence, Harvard University Press, 2002.

The notion of elite or aristocracy not being to everyone's taste, they create a monopoly of stock agents who are supposed to regulate themselves, starting by not admitting new participants beyond the twenty-four founders, and agreeing on the commissions they will charge for their mediation.

Of course, all of this is not appreciated by those who would like to benefit from the talents of New York financiers without risking being misled. But the financiers have vowed, sworn and promised that they will not be caught doing that again if their work is recognized at its fair value ! Already !

Those who disagree can simply create their own Stockbrokers Guild. Independent trading will ultimately be unsuccessful and investors will be satisfied with Wall Street, which, despite what they say, ultimately reassures them. The great families and the business community have won. The federal government leaves them alone because its members have other things to worry about. Wall Street is located on the floor of the Tontine Coffee House on the corner of Wall Street and Water Street. Four of the signatories of the letter are actively responsible for the first financial scandal that started on this street in March 1792, including Léonard Bleecker, John Pintard's short-lived partner in 1790. The pragmatic world of finance believes that it is undoubtedly preferable to see them incorporated in the institution rather than letting them be seated outside.

The original idea of John Pintard is, however, the beginning of remarkable institutions and the economic strength of the nation, although he and others did not always distinguish between the public interest and their own.

The neighborhood Antoine passed through on his way to New Rochelle in 1691 has hardly changed since the times of the Dutch West India Company, New Yorkers think. Because the wall, the Wall, originally designed as a palisade of uncut tree trunks, intended to prevent Indians from entering New York or pigs from leaving, still retains some of these functions. Gluttonous or not, the financiers will long do wonders in a city that still finds it so difficult to start its Industrial Revolution. On the other hand, the banking and financial structures are in place and the echoes of their successes will drown out all the previous complaints of their detractors. The brokers will not make a difference when trading or issuing industrial securities, the main thing for them will be the opening of the market every morning to the sound of the bell, perhaps reminding them, as a warning, of the protection requested in his time by William Duer.

In Newark, late at night, John looks out over New York. The magnificent view of the city, at sunset, saddens him. But he has no choice, he has to go to the skylight to look at the little piece of New York that he can see over the rooftops. New York is his city. He was born there. It wields the same fascination that it undoubtedly wielded on his great-grandfather, Antoine the *Cévenol*, for different reasons as New York today has 75,000 residents. And yet, he knows that when the bankruptcy bill passes in the House, he will have to leave. His life would be impossible in New York, where he thinks he is no longer welcome. In any case, he has no money, he has lost everything. He will have to try his luck elsewhere. He is approaching forty and can still build a future for himself. His cousin John Marsden Pintard, who he grew up with, tells him about Louisiana. Why not ? he suddenly thinks, at least Louisiana is a pretty name.

The houses lined along the Hudson River glow pink like the facades of Toulouse that his uncle Lewis, who guarded the fragments of his father's Languedoc memories, told him about. Lewis also encountered difficulties in his maritime trade. His Irish transport agent returned a bill of exchange due to lack of funds. The wheel is turning, John thinks. Perhaps it is time to act.

The sound of the bells of Trinity Church comes to New Jersey tonight ; the Atlantic swell must be strong, he thinks, attentive and dreamy at the same time.

Similarly strong were the capital gains on the real estate of the entire district above Wall Street, acquired at one time by the Huguenots Abraham De Peyster and Nicholas Bayard, and sold almost a century earlier by Governor Dongan, who had previously helped himself generously and covertly. The buyers had the intelligence to donate a lot to New Yorkers to build their City Hall and helped finance the construction of the first Trinity Church, thus enhancing, in the process, the value of all the other lots with the establishment of emblematic buildings. History repeats itself.

67

John will not witness the massive influx in New York of the French expelled by the Terror in Paris. Robespierre has decided that all the enemies of the Revolution must be exterminated. This solution attracts neither moderate Republicans nor ultra-Royalists who prefer to escape.

All this little world has gathered in New York, which is no longer the capital but has kept its flavor and manners. French immigrants will contribute their know-how and make it known, undertaking a thousand-and-one small jobs, literary, artistic or social. Life must go on. They will create their *Gazette Française* characterized by the good taste that America still finds in French productions and thus promoting the Francophilia necessary for a rapid integration of all these aristocrats, all these bewigged intellectuals : Chateaubriand, Talleyrand, the economist Pierre Samuel du Pont de Nemours, the philanthropist de La Rochefoucauld-Liancourt or even the future king Louis Philippe.

The contrast is great with the sailors of revolutionary France who disembark on the docks of New York, bringing their patriotic ardor and their internationalist revolutionary discourse. Poor New Yorkers love it. The well-off a little less, who see in this cacophony a questioning of their shaky power and who sometimes indulge in whistling the notes of God Save The King. Some admire the Paris fashions, others the sartorial excesses s of the French revolutionaries. In short, there is something for everyone anyway because New Yorkers have invented liberalism.

New York will thus continue to live for a few years in the French fashion, which will be reinforced with all the tropical excesses of the thousands of magnificent French landowners, accompanied by their slaves, who will disembark a few years later, expelled from *Saint*

Domingue, all dressed in white, in feathers and gold, on the arms of their beautiful mulattos. After us the deluge. [94] The great carnival continues and New Yorkers love it. As always, prices go up, plots are subdivided and buildings are sold, apartment by apartment. New York is once again full of the great excitement that has always animated it : reselling at a high price what it has acquired without a sweat.

John Pintard, once again seduced by the stock market, is now dedicated to journalism. He will not stay long at the Daily Advertiser, the publication which his uncle has entrusted to him and in which he has taken a financial interest.

"I appreciate everything you've done for me, uncle, since I got back from that unfortunate adventure in Newark, but I have to create something which I can be proud of".

"John, I understand your feelings and approve of your approach, even though you were a great help to me in the newspaper."

"I need to forget the past and all its disappointments. I have to leave and try my luck in another place, where I am unknown, although the people here have understood that I was as much a victim as I was guilty in this whole venture."

"Let's not talk about that anymore, dear nephew, it's time to turn the page. This continent is huge. Go to Louisiana. I wish you good luck in your ventures."

John arrives in New Orleans in 1802. The city is already largely Creole. The black population is free in large part as a result of the mingling of races, through free unions and marriage. He discovers a French population that he did not expect, sporting beautiful Louis XIII mustaches, their hair thick, brown and black, like the nobles in Spain, or in curls, as in the Court of Versailles.

Their clothing is of soft leather, the buckles are often silver, and sometimes swords hang from their belts. This is all strange. People speak readily to each other, in a barely comprehensible French, their manners are courteous, and sometimes even attractive because of their great amiability. John is on his guard. The ebony women have a haunting almond-eyed look.

John Pintard feels uncomfortable in this land of lagoons and swamps that he does not know. The colorful food is spread profusely

---

(94) Louis XV of France foresaw during his long reign (1715-1774) the decline and the criticism of the monarchy in France. He declared : *Après moi le déluge* ! (*After me the deluge* !). This expression was well known in France, and it is still used sometimes nowadays.

in the full sun amid carnivorous insects that feast on meat but also on fish and sometimes vibrate on a bare shoulder. The architecture is equally amazing. The luxurious houses are adorned with irons in pastel colors, similar to that of the mother-of-pearl of the shells that line and protect from the sun the covered walkways plunged in shade. The surroundings are permeated with sweet smells that seep through the muslin mosquito nets and evaporate into the alleys. Even the noises are strange, the voices of the women and the stares of the children make him uncomfortable. Creole France is terribly beautiful. Without a doubt, life in these places requires a long apprenticeship, he thinks. The silk and lace of the Old Regime have covered the generous finery of African women, transforming the girls of Dahomey into queens of Port-au-Prince, who arrive here in great numbers, driven out by the men of Toussaint Louverture, the leader of the Haitian Revolution. John understands that it will be difficult for him to acclimatize, especially since the heat and humidity are excruciating. He thinks of his father, whom he had never met and who travelled extensively in the Caribbean. He knows that he died in this sea, he had never been so close to him or so far from New York.

However, he will spend several months there, taking advantage of his trips through the delta to discover this region which neighbors the United States. There are possibilities. Another white gold is about to settle in the Mississippi lowlands : cotton. John is interested. His cousin John Marsden Pintard has also been interested in it for a few years now. The settlements in the Natchez region founded by the French, such as *Fort Rosalie au Pays des Natchez*, appear to be successful. A "world" thinks John Pintard as he navigates the river. The lands upstream must be vast to collect so much water.

The Mississippi must have traveled hundreds of miles to reach the shores of the Gulf of Mexico in such width. You need powerful tributaries to carry away so much dirt and silt in an incredible advance full of force and majestic overflows. John is impressed. The banks are crossed by the slight shudder of the reeds that border them, meeting the immense and serene sky in an astonishing silence, so close to the millions of cubic meters that flow downstream. The blue of the cloud-washed sky rubs against the dry yellow of the tall grasses that line the silty streams, surrounded by green grass as short as an almond shell. Pelicans come and go like big crows covered in white plumage. The edge of their wings is bordered with black, like the keys of a piano accompanied by a sonorous bass from the expandable bags placed under their necks. The delta is empty, flat, and quiet.

John walks, rows, and sails, writing everything down in a little notebook that he keeps close to him. These are the notes of a businessman, a merchant, a man in a hurry. He gathers information, talks and asks. After a few weeks, he knows full well that he will never surface again in the countless channels that irrigate the lowlands of this great delta. John is neither a farmer nor a craftsman, much less an industrialist. He has never really sweated, crouching until sunset, leading men, leading a team. John handles concepts.

In a few weeks he collects the essential data for the synthesis that he is already preparing in the secret recesses of his brain. In his own way, he plows, models and assembles. His records are more and more detailed and more and more numerous. Every hour of the day is devoted to the grand design he envisages for this distant French possession, divided into its Old Regime parishes and now listening to the loud echoes coming from France. Perhaps it is time for him to act before these territories become impregnable bastions of a fiery and violent republicanism, like the refrain of the Marseillaise that now attracts the ordinary people of New York. John loves France, but he is American. He doesn't mix things. He has a goal in mind. His last observations will be oriented according to this objective. He hopes that when he returns to New York, to the East finally tamed and to him reassuring, his project will be embraced as a national ambition. John, bankrupt, acts as a patriot with beautiful Louisiana, cheerful and bewitching as a carnival mask.

He quickly returns to New York.

John Pintard writes a report in which he describes all the advantages of acquiring Louisiana and hastens to discuss it with James Monroe, the father of the Monroe Doctrine, who is a relative by marriage.[95] Thomas Jefferson is a great friend of France, but the French presence on the American continent could lead him to change his mind. The political doctrine of the *pré-carré*,[96] much loved by Vauban, which made its

---

(95) James Monroe (1758-1831) one of the Founding Father was the 5th president of the United-States. His wife, Elisabeth Kortright was the first cousin of Elisabeth Brasher, John Pintard's wife. Monroe was Thomas Jefferson's special envoy to negotiate the Louisiana Purchase with France. He was one the signatories of the Treaty of Paris (1803) with Robert Livingstone.

(96) *Pré carré* (square meadow) is a French expression of agrarian origin. It means to avoid having a neighbor in the middle of your property. French engineer Vauban in charge of

way into the mind of Louis XIV in his time, has ended up crossing the Atlantic. Americans are less and less satisfied with the presence, friendly or not, of the European powers in what they consider to be their living space or their area of influence. John Pintard's promising report definitely convinces Jefferson of the merits of the Louisiana Purchase for fifteen million dollars from Napoleon in 1803, who is in dire need of money to finance his war effort.[97] It is a huge amount for the young North American nation, which, however, is satisfied, considering this colossal outlay as an investment. France is happy because selling a fourth of a continent populated by only one hundred thousand people does not mean anything else other than millions of dollars received.

The Americans are happy and one can understand why. So is Napoleon, having finally got rid of that thorn stuck in his side that could have cost him dearly, since Jefferson had warned France not to re-settle in Louisiana, and ends up being very profitable for him. Selling Louisiana was like selling the Moon, they probably thought in Paris ; but the Americans have made their dream come true and that has made them stronger. From then on, nothing can stop them. The American nation does not underestimate the Declaration of Independence but the nineteenth century is more marked by this purchase. Never mind that the constitutionalists challenge the formal deed with the argument that the government of the United States has exceeded its prerogatives, the Americans want more of the same.[98] They are independent, fearless, enterprising. America is not yet rich and has to fight to find her place under the sun. The vast territories that open to the distant horizon will arouse the greed of speculators. The convoys will leave for Saint Louis and from Saint Louis in good mood and without hesitation. Gun in hand or plow under the covered cart, they will cross swords. Everything will culminate in the legend of the West. John Pintard is the author of one of its first chapters.

Louis XIV's policy of defense counseled the king to "negotiate or start a good war" in order to get rid of the neighbors particularly in north-eastern France, which he did. Nowadays, Pré carré means a zone of influence like that implemented by the Monroe doctrine in Latin America.

(97) Barings Bank, astutely, financed the purchase in London even though Great Britain was at war with France. Business as usual.

(98) N of T : The purchase of the territories of Louisiana (more than 2 million square kilometers), implied doubling the surface of the United States, and due to its magnitude placed under stress the powers of the Constitution, which became strengthened when the Doctrine of the Implicit Powers in the Federal Constitution became accepted.

The Arkansas hills are the last frontier. But other stretches of savannah are already looming on the horizon, so vast, and so desolate that parts of the vast Prairie will not meet their last pioneers until 1920, when German minorities from Central Europe, often in search of their own piece of land, will settle in the Dakotas after the First World War.

68

John Pintard opened the heart of America ; not necessarily alone, because you are never the only instigator of momentous events : Jefferson had been thinking about it since he was young. John Pintard in 1803 made his favorable report to Albert Gallatin, the American Secretary of the Treasury who taught French at Harvard. Jefferson made the decision and reached an agreement to purchase Louisiana, the Americans paid for it. What matters most of all is that the republic collects all assets to satisfy the ambitions of its citizens and prevent them from sinking into a fiery republicanism that only creates factions. These, entangled in the search for their great men, establish nomenclatures of great and small republican saints, according to the degree of purity of each one. Exclusion is thereby set in motion, based on the measure of greatness of each individual.

As for solidity, the task becomes titanic and the transparency of the man must reach such a paroxysm that it is no longer possible to hide imperfections, no matter how small. Nobody is recommended anymore because everyone has their dark side.

The republican sky darkens with saints who are no longer so holy and no one believes in anything anymore. As a consequence, debates are only a waste of time, when each one becomes a historian and the citizen turns into a trainee jurist. All statements are subjected to a grammatical analysis as an instruction only for the prosecution. Everything is mixed up and even victims are sometimes transformed into culprits. The Reign of Terror.

In the democratic universe under construction, John prefers for his part to weave ties that unite men together, just as Antoine, his great-grandfather, in his time untied one by one the ribbons that bound him to the Old World.

John is convinced that without a talented surveyor, the segments of America will never constitute a nation. National geography is subjective and the boundaries drawn on world maps represent only systems joined together, in which those who have decided to live there are forced to share the common destiny that the majority has chosen. John wants to shape this destiny. Perhaps he owes it to his motherland, as a way of seeking forgiveness for what he did during the Wall Street crash of 1792.

John will succeed in this challenge by simply redeeming himself. Redemption is a word that suits him best, because he believes that he will only be remembered for his philanthropy. He also understands that America is dedicated to welcoming the rest of the world because it is huge and almost empty. The founders have drawn up the constitution, which establishes the powers of institutions and the relationship that citizens will have with those institutions. Everything else needs to be developed. While a nation cannot limit itself to being a large internal market, it cannot be content with just being a democracy, even the largest or the most modern. It needs signs of belonging, symbols that, when in a distant land, calm and reassure even stateless people. Citizens must see in this protective approach a first bulwark against insecurity. It is necessary to build together with the aim of promoting the betterment of all. John Pintard dedicated the end of his life to this construction.

America is in its infancy. Now is the perfect time to plow and sow, but also to graft and work hard.

Washington Irving is not yet famous when he meets John Pintard. The two men share legal training. Irving is twenty-four years younger than John and neither of them wants America to be left behind culturally.

The English, who have not yet digested their defeat, mock the Americans whom they regard more as feathered savages than men of letters. The two men want that to stop, but they know it won't happen overnight. Solid foundations are needed.

In the short term, it does not make sense to enter into a conflict with the former colonial power for this reason because the game would be lost even before they started. You cannot always win. Irving is afraid to write because he is clearly worried that his work will not reach readers who are attached to daily Bible readings and to the tragedies of William Shakespeare. The competition is tough. He dreams of England but is afraid of being ridiculed.

John has experience of the Tammany Society, a kind of ministry of culture in New York that does not exist in Washington. He created the society's constitution as a "political institution founded on a strong republican basis whose democratic principles will serve in some measure to correct the aristocracy of our city". He reoriented the goals of the Tammany Society of New York in 1791 which was established as a club for "pure Americans" in 1789. He received praise from George Washington and Thomas Jefferson for his work. This patriotic association quickly became a center for research and collections encompassing all aspects of North America life, be it historical, natural or geological : a cabinet of curiosities on a national scale, open to a wide audience marked by a wide and boundless curiosity as if to make up for lost time, in a pleasant disorder and an understandable voracity. All of this was to be merged much later in 1869 in one of the most important museums in New York, the American Museum of Natural History, where everything related to North America was catalogued and scientifically classified. Members of the Tammany Society adorn themselves with coats of arms as in Europe and wear ceremonial clothing whose main quality is that of being made exclusively in the USA, underlining the fundamental importance of English customs policy in the origin of the American revolution. Not a single trouser button or ribbon should be imported.

The first sagamore, who was undoubtedly John Pintard, hated to appear in the spotlight, especially since the statutes forbade it. He gathered his members, dressed as Iroquois warriors, for festivities where folklore and authenticity were shared with the ceremonial clothing of the American Indians. No one felt ridiculous because the birth of a nation prohibits mockery.

Thanks to him and Mooney, the president, America will designate the 4th of July as its national holiday. It will be the same for Columbus Day, Washington Day and so many other national milestones[99] of a huge country with a small population in the throes of the "democratic experiment", as Tocqueville reports. A large structure is needed for such a small population in a country so big.

America has clothes that are too big and if it is necessary to make the population adapt to the size of the country, this cannot be done by scaling down collective ambitions, but on the contrary by making

---

(99) National Museum of American History, Washington, D.C. The Museum is part of the Smithsonian Institution

its fellow citizens get better. Like many men of his generation, he is convinced that this requires a class of civic-minded citizens who have to pioneer it.

John Pintard has partly built the homeland by including Native Americans among its Founding Fathers from the very beginning. The Europeans scoff, widening the gap between the cousins of the two Atlantic coasts. But mocking smiles will not affect their progress.

John the republican goes even further

69

Washington Irving is becoming a master in the art of searching for American authenticity, and if he has not yet written the history of New York, he studies it with great interest, in piecemeal fashion, in the course of his discoveries. The Dutch period cannot be consigned to oblivion. It forms part of the heritage of the city. Some traditions have not completely disappeared and sweets or toys are still distributed to children on Saint Nicholas Day in some neighborhoods that have preserved the Dutch tradition. In some other wards, the approach to New Year's Day is the occasion for abundant drinking, mockeries, even aggression, and sometimes, small disturbances caused by the heathen supporters of the winter solstice. The authorities somehow contain the protesters who, under the influence of alcoholic vapors, violate basic inhibitions.

New Yorkers no longer like to be beaten up at Christmas time and want everything to be resolved with more repression, but to no avail. John Pintard analyzes the problem. He studies the peaceful and domestic way the Dutch celebrate Christmas and tries to find out the best way to share it with the New Yorkers.

Pintard will succeed in 1806 by creating the Banquet of Saint Nicholas. It will be held every year on December 6 at the facilities of the New York Historical Society that he established in 1804 and that still exists today. This dinner will be an opportunity for members to gather around a table and share good food and Madeira wine. The success is immediate and many of his fellow citizens follow this example. The others, the pagans, are not so easily convinced, and will continue to enjoy harassing passing pedestrians. But there are fewer and fewer pedestrians to be harassed this night on the streets of New York and during the day the police watch over the 75,000 inhabitants of the city, who have transformed themselves on the occasion of this holiday into big consumers of *Made in the USA* products and supplies.

All this is not enough for John Pintard even though the results are encouraging. Because the pagan solstice festival usually lasts throughout the month of December and on December 7 the blows rain again. While the people avoid going out, pagans punish each other and it is not uncommon to find someone early in the morning lying in his blood, eyes open in front of a rising sun he will no longer see. De Witt Clinton, Mayor of New York and a friend of John Pintard, wishes this would stop. John ponders the situation.

Washington Irving had once spoken to him about the importance of each season, including the fact that if each can be assigned a color, it may also be possible to dedicate to each an atmosphere more or less suitable for introspection. Winter emerges from the analysis as the most propitious season for self-reflection, to make a great inventory, perhaps for redemption before facing the new year. The message is found, and it only remains to shape the images of those who would carry it. In 1822, the two men turn to the poetic talents of Clement Moore, a professor at New York Theological Seminary, of which John was one of the founders. Seduced by John Pintard's idea, he is present when it comes to sketching the portrait of what will be Santa Claus : the specifications are clear and precise. Everything that is in the Dutch tradition must be preserved, if only to pay a final tribute to the domesticity of these people whose memory the city will never forget.

Santa Claus will be able to enter through the door even though the fireplace is preferred. This will suit Christians as he will be coming from heaven, but also pagans as in the heavens there is also the sun ; they will not see through the stratagem ! The food will relax the more religious while the pagans will find an excuse to sit down to eat, feasting becoming more pleasant than receiving a strong punch on the nose.

But for all this to be credible, Santa Claus must not resemble any known person. There is no question of portraying Saint Nicholas, a Catholic bishop, in a country of Protestant dissidents who a vast majority are now. It is necessary to invent a character that satisfies everyone. The portrait of a genial, plump and familiar man is retained. Where he comes from must be shrouded in mystery. America is still covered with deep forests, furthermore, does not the word forest come from the Latin *foris* which means outside and even that which belongs to none ? All of this is undoubtedly mysterious and should be acceptable to Christians, as an expectation of heaven, and to pagans, as the human reminiscence of a fairy tale. Yes, but the representation of a human is not credible : so why not a dwarf, an elf ?

This is how Santa Claus appeared, under the pen of Moore and under the dictation of Pintard, who had drawn his sources from Irving's knowledge. Later, the illustrator Thomas Nast's red dress would be just right as the coronation color of the king that was being born. The white beard would recall that of patriarchs like Moses or Abraham. The red nose would amuse young and old. The Protestants of New York wanted to make the date of Santa Claus coincide with the feast of the nativity of Jesus. Because the date of the birth of Christ, widely disputed by dissidents, and the Catholic origin of the celebration of Christmas, brought them the immense pleasure of merging the two and thus putting December 25 in the drawer of superstitions of the Church of Rome. Everyone agreed, each for his good reasons, the effect was quick and a quite a few decades later Coca Cola would transform it into a true commercial success, turning this good little fellow into the most famous garden gnome in the world. It was simply a touch of genius. However, the problems that arose from the New Year celebration took many years to disappear.

If this book began under the shade of the chestnut trees of the *Cévennes*, it is pleasant to think that it ends around a bonfire on the bank of the Hudson, with the family reunited and the children discovering the first enigma of their existence : how does Papa Noel come down the chimney fire without burning his buttocks ?

The great and the good will draw whatever conclusions they want about the relationship between the first New York Stock Exchange and Santa's invention, but aren't they both the creations of one man ? I take off my hat to him !

However, John will not stop there !

Tempted, for some time, by real estate speculation in Manhattan, he obliges himself to abandon it and leave it to others, considering that all this drains his generous passions, to which he would consecrate the end of his existence. He is appointed Inspector of the City of New York, the first to hold this position. As such, he will fight for the creation of a civil status office worthy of the big city, perhaps in memory of the prohibition imposed on his ancestors under the reign of Louis XIV. He will also promote the organization of the New York Firefighters who are now famous throughout the world.

After leaving his municipal functions, not without having started a health surveillance service, he will become secretary of the First Mutual and Insurance company, created in New York in 1787, and will remain there for twenty years. He is the "enlightened founder" of the New York Historical Society, whose activity is devoted entirely to the history of the city since its inception. It is precisely there that his portrait is found.

John Pintard gave roots to a city that had none, serving on the board of the New York Library, generously contributing his bibliophile knowledge for acquisitions, and helping to establish its free school.

He is also the drafter of the statutes of the first New York Savings Bank established on November 29, 1816, of which he will become one of the directors together with De Witt Clinton, his faithful friend, the great mayor of New York.

He will resign, as usual, when the institution is launched. However, he is called to its presidency in 1828 and remains there till 1841, the year of his final departure, when he becomes blind. Meanwhile and for unknown reasons, he will reject the position of treasurer of the Bank of Mechanics that is offered to him when it is founded in 1810. The man is everywhere.

John Pintard, the Protestant, will translate into French the Book of Common Prayers of the Episcopal Church, the American equivalent of the Anglican Church, now the Church of the old New Yorkers, that of the patrician families, the Knickerbockers as Washington Irving calls them from now on. These families oppose and resist the wave of Yankees coming from New England who, less liberal in spirit, are nonetheless attracted by the success of New York, even while they criticize it.

He will be one of the founders of the American Bible Society, whose importance in the history of the North American nation is well known, as well as the Theological Seminary.

De Witt Clinton, John Pintard and their successors will found prestigious institutions such as the New York Literary and Philosophical Association in 1814 or the American Academy of Arts in 1816 and the New York Atheneum in 1824 to compete with Boston in these areas, as stressed by François Weil, president of the French School for Advanced Studies in Social Sciences, in his historical and sociological work dedicated to the megalopolis. New Yorkers have a complex with respect to their rivals in New England or Philadelphia. New York must create from scratch a soul and the basis for the development of its own cultural and intellectual activity, whose originality distinguishes it from other large cities on the East Coast of the United States. These men, and in particular John Pintard, will prove to be judicious creators who mix the arts and culture, the history and the genealogy of the Batavians, Huguenots and Englishmen of 1664, the founders of the city, to the extent that we can consider them today as the "inventors of New York" - the word is François Weil's - because they gave the small port its roots without which it is impossible to call oneself a New Yorker. They also played an important role in its development throughout the 19th century, with which future generations will forge their identity. John Pintard is manifestly one of the great representatives of this movement along with De Witt Clinton, the Mayor, with whom he worked all his life.

The millionaires that the city will spawn will never miss the opportunity to construct and beautify buildings, like the ever-changing skyline of Manhattan. Their achievements are the basis for the attraction that New York holds for the rest of the world, just like Paris, London or Rome.

Two achievements are missing from this inventory. John Pintard is the promoter of the reactivation of the project to link the waters of Lake Erie with the waters of the Hudson through the Erie Canal. Suspended during the War against England of 1812, it will give New York a privileged access to the heart of America across the Great Lakes. The New York Savings Bank is a collective idea of the Canal Men (John Pintard, William Bayard and Thomas Eddy), in order to promote the collection of popular savings to finance this huge project in a safe framework, since the institution had to restrict its investments only to securities issued by the State of New York. You never know.

In gratitude for his dedication and commitment, he is appointed secretary of the committee in charge of the inauguration of this immense engineering feat. One cannot help but think that Jefferson's admiration for the engineer Paul Riquet after his development of the *Canal du Midi* [100] may have been part of the story.

The canal was completed in 1825. New York at that time had 160,000 residents. For health reasons, John was unable to participate in the opening ceremony that should have led him to welcome the waters of Lake Erie upriver from New York City on November 4, 1825 !

---

(100)　N of T : The *Canal-du-Midi* (France) connects the Garonne river to the Mediterranean and along with the 193 km (120 mi) long Canal de Garonne forms the Canal des Deux-Mers, joining the Atlantic and the Mediterranean. The canal runs from the city of Toulouse down to the Étang de Thau near the Mediterranean Sea. Jefferson studied it when travelling through the South of France in 1787.

"Happy America, happy New York. We have no rivals as a nation, as a state and as a city" he wrote on Saturday, November 5, 1825, to his daughter when he was invited by Mrs. Clinton, the mayor's wife, to share the moment in the tricolor barge of the City Council specially fitted for the occasion. The analysis is relevant.

John Pintard, the visionary, spared neither his time nor his money to set all these institutions in motion, affirming, furthermore and not without humor, that he would be the executor of his own testament.

By way of a testament, John leaves us what should move us the most. His family, who for decades participated in the updating and remodeling of the Moissac and Saint-Roman tax land registry of the *Ancien Régime* in Languedoc, full of vineyards, olive trees, chestnut trees and the chirping of cicadas, was far from suspecting that one of its descendants would draw in part the plan of New York.

In fact, after removing all references to the monarchy in the names of the streets of the city - half of the island of Manhattan - in his capacity as first Municipal Inspector, after the American Revolution, John Pintard created a committee and named the commissioners to plan the streets and avenues of the other half of Manhattan.

He would be, according to American historians, the author or the great inspirer, the nuance that concerns him is difficult to grasp, of the plan of 1811, the grid, of the northern part of Manhattan, what is today called Upper Manhattan, from Central Park South to the banks of the Haarlem River.

The circle is thus closed.

John realized the dream of the eternal city of all Huguenots in France and of his great-grandfather Antoine who, one day in September 1687, crossed the *Corniche des Cévennes* that had not yet been mapped as a road by Marshal de Villars and, ill at ease, travelled through the valley of the Baume amid the brooms that no longer bore flowers.

His descendants, following in his footsteps, reappear now and forever in the heart of New York through numbered and right-angled streets and avenues, symbols of America :

The fifth Avenue !

There are days like this, when the King of France. . .

John Pintard
(1759 – 1844)
by Samuel Waldo, 1832, oil on wood panel, 36 x 27 1/2 inches, neg. 6343 ;
© *New-York Historical Society.*

Epilogue

John Pintard, whom we left asleep in his chair in Manhattan at the beginning of this story, passed away at his daughter Louise's home in New York on June 21, 1844, at the age of 85.
The small port then had four hundred thousand inhabitants. He was buried in Saint Clement's Church at 108 Amity Street (now West third Street), along with his relatives, according to the custom of the old New York patrician families. He was the last of the Huguenots, for the fidelity with which he had preserved his Calvinist faith, in the Church of Saint Esprit of which he was Vestryman, counselor and sacristan for more than thirty years. But also, for the affection he professed for France, concluding the letters to his daughter with a farewell in French and rejoicing in his grandchildren's mastery of the language.

John Pintard is one of the four hundred personalities of the city who by his actions contributed to its development and international reputation. This list, known as The New York 400, was compiled in 2009 by the Museum of New York to mark the fourth centenary of Captain Hudson's landing in 1609 and commemorates only one hundred persons per century. We find Frank Sinatra, Michael Bloomberg, Franklin D. Roosevelt, Leonard Bernstein, Salomon Guggenheim, Lou Reed, Louis Armstrong, Woody Allen, John Lindsay, De Witt Clinton, Peter Stuyvesant among scholars and doctors, and the list is long . . .

Marcelle Pintard, the last representative of the family in Saint-Roman-de-Tousque, in the department of Lozère (France), died in December 1999 at the age of 102, in this hamlet of one hundred and eighty inhabitants. It is crossed by the *Corniche des Cévennes,* a road drawn to facilitate the fight against the Protestants. Her relative Georges Pintard, president of the local section of the *Cévenol Club,* gave this road in the 1930's, a paradox of history, the well-deserved national and European tourist recognition that it has today.

She died without having been able to clarify the mystery of Antoine's fate and without the news of his successes ever reaching her, not even echoes of it.

She was a descendant of Jean Pintard, Antoine's brother who one day in September 1687...

Her tombstone, located in the family graveyard according to Protestant custom, is at the foot of the hamlet, under a blanket of greenery. It was the object of the attentive care of the family of Michel and Laurette Flayol, when Antoine's American descendants visited it in March 2009, like a new ribbon unfurled 322 years later over the Atlantic.

Saint Roman, as a sign of fidelity.

Ex Libris belonging to John Pintard

On September 11, 2001, two kamikaze planes attacked the World Trade Center towers in New York at 8:48 a.m. local time. The city then had eight million inhabitants. The two towers, devastated for hours by fires, collapsed in the afternoon, killing 2,792 people. The cadastral land register investigation carried out by the New York City Council determined that the parcels of lands on which Ground Zero is located, belonged, among others, to Lewis Pintard, in the 18th century.

New York is sad tonight like Psalm 137, but our modern-day Babel will be proud and will be reborn tomorrow when the exiles, its children, will present the verses of King David to the rhythm of the Jamaican reggae of The Melodians, which the group Boney M performed with success in the 70s :

> *By the rivers of Babylon*
> *There we sat down*
> *And there we wept*
> *When we remembered Zion…*
>
> *Sur les bords des fleuves de Babylone,*
> *Nous étions assis*
> *Et nous pleurions,*
> *En nous souvenant de Sion…*

In memory of my grandmother, Marie-Marthe Pintard

Pintard Genealogy

This genealogy is restricted to those persons that appear in The Plowmen of America or on the photographic documents or where their inclusion is necessary for the good comprehension of the work.

(Archives Départementales Hérault, France, C 4697 allows the partial establishment of the genealogy of the French family)

FRENCH GENEALOGY

1 Jean PINTARD (end of 16th century)
 Married Anne PAREDES in 1609
  2 Louis PINTARD (1625-1672) birth doubtful
    Married Marguerite ROUX in 1654
      3 Jean, born on October 12, 1655, at La Cabanarié, baptized at the Protestant church of Moissac on December 13th, 1656
      3 Florinde, born on May 2nd, 1657, at La Cabanarié, baptized at the Protestant church of Saint Roman de Tousque on May 13th, 1657. She might have died in infancy
      3 Antoine, born December 7th, 1658, at La Cabanarié, baptized December 22nd, 1659
      3 Francoise, born July 19th, 1661, at La Cabanarié, baptized at the Protestant church of Moissac November 1st, 1661
      3 Suzanne, born August 31st, 1663, at Fauguières, baptized at the Protestant church of Moissac December 2nd, 1663. She died in Lower Saxony (nowadays Germany) where she was a refugee
      3 Isabeau, born in 1668, and died in 1693 aged 25 in Lower Saxony (nowadays Germany) where she was a refugee

3   Samuel who was condemned to the galleys La Grande in 1689/90 aged 20. Must have been born 1669/70

This genealogy highlights Antoine's fidelity to his family and to his brothers and sisters since, apart from his own first name transmitted to his eldest child, and that of his wife Catherine transmitted to his seventh child, his other seven children were baptized with the first names of his six siblings including Florinde which is not in widespread use and with the exception of Margaret (Marguerite) which is his mother's first name. Having had nine children, he was forced to tap beyond the first names of his six siblings. Thus, the first name of his fourth child corresponds to that of his aunt Madeleine who represented his other aunt, Anne, his godmother, absent during his baptism. He does not forget his father either by appending Louis or Lewis to his son Jean's first name. Remarkably, these first names have been transmitted over several generations and maintained in the kinship, even during the marriages of the daughters who also had the strength to sometimes impose the preservation of the name Pintard in their descendants, perhaps a sign of their belonging to the Pintard alliance yet to be born.

American Genealogy

1   Antoine or Anthony PINTARD (Dec. 7th 1658 – May 1732)
    Married Catherine STELLE (1673 - 1729 ?) she was alive in 1712
    2   Anthony PINTARD (1694 – 1755)
        Married Abigail HALSTEAD (1696-1756)
    2   Jean Lewis PINTARD (1696-1740)
        Married Lydia BOWNE (1703-1729)
        3   Antony PINTARD (1725 - ?)
            Married Catherine CARRÉ (1698 -1794) She belonged to a well-off Huguenot family in New York (her second marriage)
        3   Lydia PINTARD (1727 - ?)
        3   Louis PINTARD (1732-1818)
            Married Susanna STOCKTON (1742-1772)
            4   Martha PINTARD (1769-1837)

    Married Samuel BAYARD (1767-1840)
  4 John Marsden PINTARD (1760-1810)
  4 Samuel PINTARD (1763- 1833 ?)
 3 Jean PINTARD (1734-1760)
  Married Mary CANNON (? – 1759)
  4 John PINTARD (1759-1844) Founder of the NYHS, inventor of Santa Claus and of the first Stock Exchange in New York City
2 Samuel PINTARD (1697-1756)
 Married Ann GLENCROSS (1713- 1748)
 3 Samuel PINTARD (1735-1783)
  Married Mary BORDEN (1739- ?)
   4 Isaac van Dam PINTARD
    Married Ann BORDEN from whom Bill and Betsy PINTARD are descendants in the US
2 Madeleine PINTARD (1701-1730)
 Married Jacques HUTCHINS (1703-1748)
2 Catherine PINTARD (c.1704-1746)
 Married Captain John SEARLE (1677-1733)
 Married Reverend Doctor Robert JENNEY (1687-1762), rector of Christ Church, Philadelphia. This Church played a major role in the founding of the Protestant Episcopal Church in the United States
2 Margaret PINTARD (1706-1735)
 Married Joseph LEONARD
 Married Pierre LECONTE
2 Isabelle PINTARD (1708- ?)
 Married Isaac VAN DAM
 3 Rip VAN DAM
 3 Isaac VAN DAM (1736-1776)
  Married Sarah YOUNG (1736- ?) from the Caribbean Island of Montserrat
2 Florinda PINTARD (1710- ?)
 Married George SPENCER (1738-1784)
2 Anne Francoise PINTARD (1712 - ?)
 Married Moise GOMBAULT from the Caribbean Island of Martinique

Saint Nicholas and New York

England had banished the saints from her Anglican vulgate or speech except for St. George and a few others who survived. The Reformed Churches of France and Holland had done the same, the latter going to the point of imposing fines on those who kept the memory of Saint Nicholas during the month of December. The Catholic Counter-Reformation adhered to these Protestant practices. A wind of rationalism swept away a thousand years of devotion to this compassionate saint who brought various offerings to those who requested it in different parts of the Christian world.

Protector of the sailors, Saint Nicholas had traveled as figurehead of the first ship of the Dutch West India Company when landing in Manhattan, but the memory had already been lost, to the point that there are no archives that relate to a hunt of the slayers of the forbidden in New Amsterdam. Widely considered by the Church as a miracle worker and a small-time saint in the week of Christmas, it nevertheless remained present in European countries where it had spread from the basilica of Saint-Nicolas-de-Port in Lorraine (France) that preserves, thanks to king Saint Louis, a phalanx of *Nicolas de Myre* (Myra) collected in Bari (Italy) where he was canonized after his transfer in 1098 from Myra (nowadays Turkey). Research carried out in the archives of New Amsterdam and New York does not allow us to attest to the presence of Saint Nicholas before the year 1773. It should be noted that Dutch Calvinists had long classified hagiography - the history of the saints - among the forbidden books. Saint Nicholas could have stowed away on the island of Manhattan. He only circulated in families whose children secretly passed the word . . .

He also served as an emblem for New York patriots, tired of the display of St. George on all occasions by the English. Saint Nicholas pleases dispossessed Americans. He is the standard bearer for New York. He is a proletarian who stands in front of Saint George and provokes him for a short moment. He reappears the following year before disappearing again. He did not reappear until twenty years later before settling permanently in the island's landscape from 1809.

The two revivals will be under the leadership of John Pintard, the patriot. In 1793, first of all, as part of the writing of an almanac for private use, which refers only to Saint Nicholas alongside Christmas, New Year, Easter and Pentecost, while the American almanacs do not mention it. Pintard added to these celebrations the 4th of July, the Feast of Independence, thus confirming that he is the author and that he also intends to give a civic character to the celebration of the Saint. The New York Historical Society of which he is founder will ensure the dissemination of these festivals to the general public before Nicholas becomes, according to his wishes, the Patron of the city, and celebrates it as an institution every year on 6th of December.

Washington Irving, the writer, is a member of the NYHS. He will take the torch and dress Saint Nicholas in his Christmas robes in his *Knickerbocker History of New York*.[101] Associated with John Pintard's poem *Sancta Claus goed heylig man* published in December 1810, the story will still undergo some modifications made by other members of the NYHS. But it is a true fact, that this is how Santa Claus was born to the point of being associated with New York and adopted by thousands of immigrants seeking integration in American society as they passed through the customs gates of the major port of the Atlantic coast. He too will quickly partner with thousands of consumers, which was initially the fundamental rebuke against him made by the Churches.

St. Nicholas of Manhattan has since traveled the world.

Courtesy of the New York Historical Society.

---

(101) The content of this annex is partially extracted from Charles W. Jones *Knickerbocker Santa Claus, The New York Historical Society Quarterly*, October 1954, volume XXXVIII number 4.

Photos credits

- Book cover and inside : Antoine Pintard : identifier : 1975.9 (1658-1732) attributed to Gerardus Duyckinck ; oil on linen ; Overall : 31 x 25 x 1 in. (78.7 x 63.5 x 2.5 cm) ; *New-York Historical Society*.
- John Pintard : identifier : 1928.1 painted by Samuel Waldo, 1832, oil on wood panel 36 x 27 1/2 inches, neg. 6343 ; *New-York Historical Society*.

Contents

Translator's notes 7
Introduction 9
Prologue 11
Book I – Step into Exile 13
Book II – The plantation in Saint-Christophe 127
Book III – Shelter in New York 211
Epilogue 335
Genealogy 339
Saint Nicholas and New York 343
Photographics 345

www.ingramcontent.com/pod-product-compliance
Lightning Source LLC
LaVergne TN
LVHW090035080526
838202LV00043B/3323